WHY SMART WOMEN
BUY THE LIES

Praise for *Why Smart Women Buy the Lies*

Annie's wicked sense of humour and brilliant insight shine brighter than ever in *Why Smart Women Buy the Lies* – great storytelling that is engaging, educational and laugh-out-loud hilarious! Compulsory reading... and not just for women.
Kate Raison, actor

One of the smartest things Annie McCubbin ever did was write this book. She proves that some of the smartest people you know can make the dumbest decisions. So, read this insightful, hilarious book and find out how to avoid buying the lies. Don't be a smart dumb person. I'm reading it twice to make sure I get it right.
Georgie Parker, actor

Annie's writing is an antidote to the sea of disinformation that hits our inboxes every day. Funny, sceptical and compassionate. Read it.
Juanita Phillips, ABC News presenter

Annie has amusingly integrated the art of critical thinking with the everyday experiences of intelligent women. Her conversational tone and priceless scenarios make her book an enlightening read.
Catherine Ebert, clinical psychologist

Every bone in my corporate body told me that my 'gut call' was always the right one and my decisions were watertight. What nonsense that was! *Why Smart Women Buy the Lies* has shown me we are all susceptible to untruths and can lead ourselves astray with our decision-making. I now see that great leadership comes from actually having the discipline to apply critical thinking and take the time to understand our cognitive flaws.
Ann Burns, Senior Executive, CEW Member, Non-Executive Director

Why smart women buy the lies

and how critical thinking reveals the truth

Annie McCubbin

MAJOR STREET

*For David and Odile.
For knowing that macaws are not to be kept
in a flat, and other important facts.*

Also by Annie McCubbin: *Why Smart Women Make Bad Decisions and How Critical Thinking Can Protect Them*

First published in 2023 by Major Street Publishing Pty Ltd.
E: info@majorstreet.com.au W: majorstreet.com.au M | +61 421 707 983

© Annie McCubbin 2023
The moral rights of the author have been asserted.

A catalogue record for this book is available from the National Library of Australia

Printed book ISBN: 978-1-922611-65-9
Ebook ISBN: 978-1-922611-66-6

All rights reserved. Except as permitted under *The Australian Copyright Act 1968* (for example, a fair dealing for the purposes of study, research, criticism or review), no part of this book may be reproduced, stored in a retrieval system, communicated or transmitted in any form or by any means without prior written permission. All inquiries should be made to the publisher.

Cover design by Tess McCabe
Internal design by Production Works
Printed in Australia by Griffin Press.

10 9 8 7 6 5 4 3 2 1

Disclaimer: The material in this publication is in the nature of general comment only, and neither purports nor intends to be advice. Readers should not act on the basis of any matter in this publication without considering (and if appropriate taking) professional advice with due regard to their own particular circumstances. The author and publisher expressly disclaim all and any liability to any person, whether a purchaser of this publication or not, in respect of anything and the consequences of anything done or omitted to be done by any such person in reliance, whether whole or partial, upon the whole or any part of the contents of this publication.

Contents

	Preface	xi
1.	You should have taken the ragdoll	1
	Your internal lie detector	19
2.	Someone is sobbing in the toilet	24
	Spotlight on Lisbeth	35
3.	It's a Dyson Airwrap!	40
	Believing is seeing	51
4.	Lydia is the worst boss	58
	The big lie of empowerment	66
5.	An accident with a wheelie bin	71
	Help, is there a psychic in the house?	84
6.	Spanakopita	87
	What's with all the meetings?	97
7.	Mr Yee's garden	102
	What actually is wellness?	117
8.	How good are margaritas?	121
	Of gnostic gods and corporate values	129
9.	Why aren't you in Morocco?	133
	Snakes and burnt hair	146
10.	Lydia is no longer the worst boss	152
	Weep not for Lydia	166

11. **Kat is sacked**	**170**
I think I'll be a personal trainer	186
12. **How many curses are there?**	**189**
People drink champagne at the airport in the morning	203
13. **The stylish relatives lose it**	**206**
Oh Kat, what were you thinking?	223
14. **The seance**	**226**
Charlotte's web	248
15. **The thermos**	**252**
The garden of happiness	257
Conclusion	**261**
References	**263**
About Annie	**267**
Acknowledgements	**269**

Preface

As I write this book, Australians are losing $1 million a day to scams. In 2022, $570,000 worth of scams were reported to Scamwatch – and it's estimated this represents only 13 per cent of money lost to scams.[1] What happened to the other 87 per cent? Why are victims not reporting these crimes?

It's because we're embarrassed. We're ashamed of our gullibility. We shouldn't be. We are the victims of our brain wiring. We need other humans; we are reliant on them to survive, and our brains are designed to trust them. When we're being scammed we are hard up against our intrinsic nature.

And it is not only financial frauds where our brains betray us. From the slew of untruths we happily tell ourselves every day to the lies told to us by those who profess to love us, our capacity to deceive and be deceived is alarming.

As humans, we have used our huge brains to understand the world better. We have told each other stories over millennia, and through these stories we have learned how the world works and how we can make it better. We've gone from campfire grunting and cave drawings to high-speed internet – so now, our brains are attempting to process millions of stories a day. They're coming at us at breakneck speed from all directions. How are we meant to know which stories are real and which are designed to mislead us?

Humanity's aptitude for deception is as old as time itself but the connectivity enabled by broadcast media, and more recently by the internet, gives clever, cunning, media-savvy people myriad new ways to distract, delude and defraud en masse. Shady characters whose business it is to sell you lies in exchange for your money or your vote abound – from unrefined Nigerian email fraudsters to TikTok influencers peddling unregulated 'wellness products' to the Russians who infiltrated the 2016 US presidential election.

This book is less about why people lie, scam and obfuscate and more about why we are vulnerable. It's about what happens in the mind of the buyer, not the liar. My focus is on the bit you have *most* control over: the way you receive and interpret information. Let's map out the territory so you know what to keep an eye out for.

Lies take many forms

There are the lies we tell ourselves. Our capacity to fool ourselves is outstanding.

There are lies that protect people's feelings: 'white lies'. 'You should cut your own hair more often. It looks great.'

There are strategic lies. 'I have two buyers lined up to buy this house, so you'd better make a decision quickly.'

There are lies that hurt people: lies that influence others to act against their best interests. Such actions may have immediate financial consequences – such as when a person invests their retirement savings in a Ponzi scheme based on a glossy prospectus, or transfers money into an account believing it will help save the life of a romantic partner they recently met online.

Sometimes the lies we tell ourselves result in passivity: the decision to stay in a relationship with a toxic person or organisation, based on the belief that leaving would be worse.

All of us, at some point, are someone's target; deception could strike at any moment. The best news is that you can protect yourself and the people you care about from buying the lies by practising critical thinking.

The following sequence is common to all scenarios in which a person is influenced to take action based on a lie.

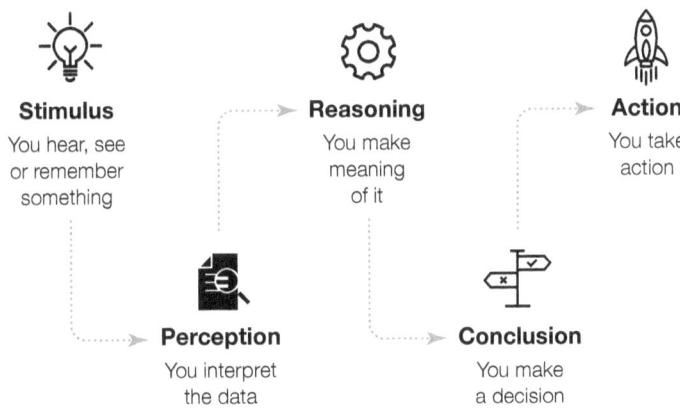

You're never going to stop the stimulus – unless you withdraw entirely from society and take up residence under a rock. Where you *do* have control is in the *perception* and *reasoning* stages. Once you've reached a conclusion and acted, you've bought the lie. The action might be putting a down payment on the purchase of a fictious property or vehicle, or it could be believing the lie a duplicitous partner tells you. When you have been influenced to act, or chosen *not* to act, you have bought the lie.

When there is pressure to move quickly, you will fly through this sequence so fast that you won't notice each step. For example, you quickly stop when you see a red traffic light. That is a very handy intuitive response to stimulus. It's useful that it happens quickly.

But what if the traffic light malfunctions? What if there is a green light when it should be red? In this case, the speed of the intuitive response is potentially harmful.

Imagine you receive an offer that seems too good to be true. You could make the deal of a lifetime. It's also possible you could be duped. This is when thinking about your thinking – a process known as metacognition – could be the best thing you could do.

The first point of the sequence you have control over is *perception*. Do you see the world the way it is, or do you see a version of the world that is specific to you and your experiences?

Perception is riddled with potential for cognitive errors, from confirmation bias to impostor syndrome and the spotlight effect (we'll look at all of these in detail throughout the book). These cognitive errors act like internal smoke and mirrors to distort your evaluation of reality.

Opportunities to depart even further from the truth abound at the reasoning stage, where we're vulnerable to arguments (known as logical fallacies) that seem to make sense but actually don't. Often motivated by unconscious drivers, logical fallacies add weight to flimsy arguments and help convince us to take the bait. This is the case for women especially: so much scammy marketing and pseudo-spiritual nonsense is aimed at women. Many studies suggest that women are still more at risk of becoming victims of online fraud than other genders.[2] An Australian study found that females are 50 per cent more likely than males to report identity theft, and identity theft victims over 65 years of age were almost exclusively female.[3]

So, let's install some failsafe strategies to keep your internal lie detector in top shape.

Become your own lie detector

Lie detection has long had a complicated relationship with the truth.

For millennia, human beings have employed techniques to distinguish truth from lies. One method, understood to have been used in China around 1000 BC, involved filling a suspected fraudster's mouth with rice, having them hold it for a period and then disgorge it. If the rice was dry their guilt was confirmed.

This method is not as random as it first appears. Dry mouth is a common indication of anxiety, which can be attributed to the suspect's fear of being found out. However, dry mouth also appears when people have a blocked nose or are simply dehydrated. Sadly, many dehydrated ancient Chinese prisoners would have been punished for crimes they did not commit.

The European version, practised in the Middle Ages, was to give the suspected liar a lump of hard sheep's cheese. If they could swallow it in one bite, they were innocent. If they struggled, they were guilty.

Other medieval techniques relied on God's judgement. The accused would be subject to a test and, depending on their performance, God's judgement was revealed. One such test involved the person being forced to hold their hand in a cauldron of boiling water. If the hand emerged without blistering, this was a sign that God was on the person's side. A scalded, blistered hand confirmed the liar had been caught red-handed.

The cold-water test was similarly binary in nature. The accused was put in a sack and dropped into deep water. If they bobbed up to the surface too quickly, it was a sign that even the water did not accept them. They were guilty. This practice was used to expose witches in the waters of the Danube in 17th-century Slovakia.

In the late 1700s, German neuroanatomist Franz Joseph Gall pioneered the theory of phrenology, suggesting that dishonest individuals could be identified by the lumps and bumps on their skulls. According to this theory, the brain houses a collection of different entities, each responsible for localised functions. Gall travelled across Europe delivering public lectures featuring lumpy-headed criminals with skulls shaved to point out the significant anomalies. He was enlisted to provide testimony in legal disputes.

The first polygraph was invented by Leonarde Keeler and John Larson in the 1920s. The device recorded breaths per minute, pulse rate, blood pressure and skin conductivity. Sweat increases electrical conductivity across the surface of the skin. The graph paper that scrolled out of these machines was observed and interpreted to determine truth-telling from lies. Polygraphs are still used today as an interrogation tool, even though this method has proven to be no more reliable than taking a mouthful of rice.

By the 1990s, functional magnetic resonance imaging (fMRI) was being used to peer inside our brains, observing the neural activity associated with lying and being lied to. By tracking blood flow, it is possible to see which parts of the brain light up when a subject is telling a lie. However, a recent study showed a large percentage of liars could prevent being detected by fMRI by employing some simple techniques.[4]

Lie detection is clearly not an easy ask, but there are muscles you can turn on and strengthen to help you reveal the truth.

In my first book, *Why Smart Women Make Bad Decisions: And How Critical Thinking Can Protect Them*, I introduced Kat: a 30-something woman who, while in the midst of a fractious breakup, has to deal with the everyday challenges of being a working woman. As the story progresses, Kat begins to understand some of the flaws in her thinking. This book picks up where the last book left off (but you don't have to have read my first book to enjoy this one!). Kat's story provides a canvas upon which to present a range of personal and professional dramas that contain lies of all colours. At the end of each chapter, we will revisit the menu of cognitive flaws that undermine our ability to pick a lie when presented with one.

So if you've ever been lied to – and, let's face it, who hasn't – read on.

1

You should have taken the ragdoll

'Porridge, come on. Come here, Porridge. Come on. Come on, who's a good boy?'

You've been calling for an hour. He is not a good boy. He's a bad boy. A very bad boy.

'He's got a real personality,' said Miriam on the phone. Personality in dogs, as we all know, is code for maniac tendencies. That should have been the first red flag. 'We're sorry to see him go, but Doug's hip's gone. We're just keeping the ragdoll cat.'

You bet they're keeping the ragdoll. You bet the ragdoll comes back when it's called and doesn't chew all available pieces of soft furnishing.

'I have a cat,' you'd said.

'Porridge loves cats.'

'I live in a flat and have elderly neighbours. Is he obedient?'

'Oh yes. We got him in the first place to be an assistance dog. Doug's real sad to see him go.'

Liar. Doug must have clapped his hands when Porridge was loaded into the pet transport van. He must have cracked open a tinny and danced around the vacant spot where Porridge's dog bed had been.

'What did he assist with?' you'd said.

'Oh, you know, this and that.'

'Does he bark much?' you'd said.

'Only if he thinks you're in danger. He's very protective.'

You must always be under extreme threat from unknown assailants because Porridge barks constantly.

'He might need some Xanax,' Penny, the tiny vet with the tiny high voice, had said.

Xanax? What is he, a 30-something advertising exec with a hot social life?

'Are you anxious, Porridge?' Penny had cooed at him.

Porridge had put his sizable paw into Penny's tiny hand and looked at her with large, doleful eyes.

'He's a good boy at the vet, aren't you, Porridge?' she'd said, tipping a liver treat into his mouth. 'Do you use treats when you do behavioural training?'

'Yes,' you'd said. 'I go through about a kilo a day.'

'We have a dog behavioralist,' Penny had said. 'I can refer him.'

'You want Porridge to go to a dog shrink?'

'Well, no, it's your decision, Kat.'

'Okay, I'm good, thanks. I'll take the Xanax.'

'No, you can't take the Xanax.'

'No, I meant I'll take the Xanax for Porridge. Though now you mention it, what would happen if I did take the Xanax?'

Penny's lips had compressed.

'It's okay; I'm just joking. Though, what if the cat's having a rough night?'

Penny had sent you out with the Xanax (after you pledged not to give it to the cat) and the name of the dog shrink, should you change your mind. You'd eyed the Xanax next to you on the seat as you'd driven home.

Back in the park, you stamp your feet pointlessly. 'Porridge, Porridge, come on.'

Owning a recalcitrant groodle was not part of the plan you'd mapped out during the goal-setting Saturday session you'd attended at your gym. The only reason you'd stayed for the session was to collect the free water bottle emblazoned with the words, 'Be that unicorn!'

'If you don't know what you want, how will you know what to go for?' said Tobias, the trainer. 'Write it down, legends. Write it down.'

So, you'd written it down. *1: Stop being indecisive.*

The trainer had looked over your shoulder.

'Maybe rephrase that into a positive.'

'Right,' you'd said. '*Be decisive*, or *start being decisive*?'

'You decide,' he'd said.

'That's the problem: I can't.'

He'd patted your shoulder and moved on to Dana, your training buddy. She'd already banged out half a thesis on her goals.

'Great, Dana,' he'd said.

Dana also finishes her circuits before everybody else and loudly says, 'I've finished. Should I keep doing squats until everyone else is done?'

You'd crossed out *stop being indecisive* and written:

1. *Decide if Michael is the one.*
2. *Be recognised for being amazing at your job. Be organised with your ambition.*
3. *Reboot your social life.*

Your previous boyfriend, The Hipster, had somehow managed to monopolise and neglect you simultaneously, and you'd let your friendships wither on the vine. You love Mrs Hume and Mrs Kovacic, your elderly neighbours, but really, should they constitute the bulk of your social life?

You'd looked at how concise your goals were. *Right*, you'd thought. *This is your year to pull it together.*

Back in the park, it's getting dark. You're dying to get home. Mrs Hume is expecting her relatives from England this afternoon.

'They're staying with me while they look for a house,' she'd said. She'd rung an hour ago to say she'd been held up and asked you to greet them.

'I just don't want Mrs Kovacic corralling them on the stairs and blathering on about the flats being cursed. They'll think they've landed in some superstitious backwater. I adore Mrs Kovacic, but this curse business is out of hand.'

'No worries,' you'd said. 'I'll conduct an interception if necessary.'

Also, if you're honest, you're desperate to have a look at them. Mrs Hume's relatives are a couple with two children. The father is her nephew, or at least the nephew of her late husband. The mother is reportedly young, stylish and funny. You would like a young, stylish, funny person in the flats to sit around with and throw back margaritas.

It starts to rain. You try your stern voice.

'Porridge!' you yell. 'Come here immediately!'

The breeze picks up as the sun goes down. The temperature plummets. The park is emptying. People sensibly load their pets into their warm vehicles and head home. You turn around and walk in the other direction.

'Porridge, come on, boy. Who wants a treat?'

A woman walks towards you, preceded by a pink raincoat on a lead. Upon closer examination, the raincoat houses a small, neat Pomeranian cross.

'You lost your fur baby?' she says.

You find the term 'fur baby' intensely irritating.

'Yes,' you say. 'Have you seen a large groodle?'

'Um, have we seen a groodle, Trixie?'

The neat Pomeranian sits at her feet. Its paws are placed perfectly in second position.

Why did you get fixated on groodles? Why didn't you adopt a small dog? A dog like Trixie with her ballet paws?

The rain thickens. You're dressed in shorts and a t-shirt because you were only dropping in to the park for 15 minutes, and it was sunny when you arrived. It's now 12 degrees, and you've been here for an hour and a half.

'What colour is your groodle?'

'Like, beige, caramel.'

'What's his name?'

'Porridge.'

'Oh,' she says.

You prepare to launch into the disclaimer that you didn't name him, but it's now raining heavily and you shut your mouth.

'So, is it because of his colour?'

You have no idea why Miriam named him Porridge. You'd asked her on the phone if you could change it. You were thinking of Nolan or Harry.

'No, don't change his name,' said Miriam. 'You want him to come back when you call him.'

'How long will it take him to get used to me?' you'd asked.

'Not long. He's a very well-adjusted, loving family dog. He just might be a bit nervy when he first arrives.'

A bit nervy? The things that unnerve Porridge include plastic bags, men, buckets, his food bowl, cats, hats, sunglasses, your slippers, the lettuce spinner and the car. Specifically, the back seat of the car. You have to physically lever him into the front seat, where he sits with one paw in contact with your leg at all times.

Things that don't unnerve him include roaming over the hills like Julie Andrews.

You'd rung Miriam after a week.

'Yes,' she'd said, 'he just needs time to settle in. He probably misses the ragdoll.'

'Right,' you'd said.

Now, you smile at Trixie's owner. 'Yes,' you say, 'he's called Porridge because he's porridge-coloured.'

'Well, we'll keep an eye out for Porridge, won't we, Trixie? There's nothing worse than not being able to find our fur babies.'

They trot past you, the woman safely ensconced inside her hooded raincoat.

You briefly entertain the notion of going home, leaving Porridge to his own devices. He could catch his own fish from the park pond and eat wild berries, like in an episode of *Alone*. Then you realise he can barely manage to eat from his own bowl, let alone catch his own prey.

It's now dark. You're drenched. The park lights flicker on.

You're going to be late to greet the stylish relatives. Mrs Kovacic will trap them outside her door and unsettle them with her dark theories of angry ghosts that seek revenge on the flats' residents. Mrs Hume will not be happy.

You're standing disconsolately on the path when, through the wet gloom, a lone caramel figure approaches. You squint your eyes. It looks like a groodle shape.

'Porridge,' you call. 'Come on, boy. Who's a good dog?'

It is Porridge, and he is overjoyed to see you. He bounds towards you. He is sopping wet and filthy. He has something disgusting in his mouth.

You want to smack him but, having read a small amount of dog training literature, you have been led to believe that this will dissuade him from returning in the future. Instead, you are meant to praise him for his obedience.

Well, you're sorry, but that's a bridge too far. The best you can manage is to clip his lead on and say, 'Come on, and you're not sitting in the front seat.'

Three minutes later, this threat has turned into a Mexican standoff, with you standing at the open back car door pointing at the seat and him lying down on the ground.

Trixie's owner stops her car next to you and briefly observes the tableau. 'Your fur baby is found!' she says. 'Trixie and I are so pleased.'

She drives off with a little wave in her pleasantly warm car, Trixie looking smugly out the back window.

Lightning and thunder have now commenced. Porridge is lying in an ever-deepening puddle, looking around him like he's at the hardware store searching for the right sort of stainless-steel cement nails.

You drag him to the back seat. 'You're not getting your own way today, buddy', you say.

You're so wet that your hair is stuck to your head, and you're having trouble seeing because the rain is sleeting into your eyes. You put his paws on the seat and lever his back half into the car. He looks back at you, aghast, and immediately climbs into the front, leaning heavily on the door and looking studiously out the window.

You climb into the driver's seat and lean over into the back to find an old dog towel to dry off your hair.

You start the engine and, in the privacy of your own car, you give him both barrels.

'Right,' you say. 'You can look out the window as much you like, but nothing will change the fact that you're a bad dog, a bad, bad dog. Not only are you bad, but you're also a coward. What other dog is afraid of plastic bags and lettuce spinners? Honestly, it's tragic. Also, Susan doesn't like you. The ragdoll cat may have tolerated you, but Susan is a discerning cat, and she's not keen.'

He continues to gaze fixedly out the window.

'I'm giving you back to Miriam.'

He side-eyes you. The threat of returning him to Miriam may have hit home. You adopt a conciliatory tone.

'I'm sorry, Porridge,' you say. 'Next time, if you could come when I call you, that would be optimal.'

He puts his paw on your leg. By the time you get home, you have patted his ears and promised him dinner.

This is why the idea of having children bothers you. You are a total pushover. They'd be roaming all over the park at night, and you'd be standing in the rain, calling helplessly into the dark.

Kat meets a stylish relative

You park the car, haul Porridge out and run through the rain to the flats.

A man is trying to pull open the door to the foyer while dragging two suitcases behind him. This must be the stylish relative. He is tall and square-shouldered, his full head of hair cut short. With him is a boy aged around nine or ten.

The boy looks at you and Porridge.

'Hold the door, Will,' the man says.

'Let me,' you offer.

He sticks his foot in the door and pulls the suitcase through. The boy follows him. The door shuts behind them with you and Porridge still standing outside in the rain.

You open the door, and Porridge lunges at the visitors. Porridge loves new people.

The man turns around and looks at you. He is so good-looking, you feel winded.

'Does the dog bite?' he says

'No, he's very well-adjusted.' You turn to the boy. 'This is Porridge. He's a groodle.'

The boy stares at Porridge. Porridge barks.

'Porridge!' you say. 'Stop it! I'm so sorry.'

'What's the story with the lift?' says the man.

His eyes are extraordinary. Green. You've always found green eyes and jet-black hair very attractive.

'Sorry, our lift is always out of order. Keeps us fit, but let me help you,' you say. 'Give me one of the suitcases.'

'No,' he says, 'I'm balanced. Just keep the dog out from underfoot. Will, come on.' He starts up the stairs.

Keeping a safe distance, you climb the stairs after him.

'Why don't they fix the lift?' he mutters to the boy.

By the time you get to your landing, the man is breathing heavily. Mrs Kovacic has come to her door, tea towel over her shoulder, hands covered in flour.

'Porridge, be quiet,' she says. 'Naughty dog. Come here.'

You release Porridge's lead. He bounds over to Mrs Kovacic and puts his paws on her shoulders.

'Hello,' she says to the man. 'You must be Mrs Hume's nephew.'

He looks at her. 'Yes. Excuse me.' He starts the next flight. The boy trips. The father turns around. 'Careful Will, the last thing we need is another injury.' The child turns around and looks at you. You smile. Nothing.

'I'm in flat four if you need anything,' you call after them.

You hear the door above you open. 'Can you believe there's a big dog in the flat below?' says the man. 'Why do people keep dogs in a flat?'

Mrs Kovacic covers Porridge's ears with her tea towel. 'Don't listen to him, Porridge,' she says.

'You making scones?' you say. 'Maybe he'd like one?'

She raises her eyes to the stairwell, crosses her arms.

'I remember the day the Yees moved in.' She crosses herself. 'That was happy day.'

You cross to her door and take her hand. Your fingers come away dusted with flour.

'I miss him too.' Porridge leans into her leg.

Susan appears and wreathes herself around your legs, then languidly mounts the stairs to Mrs Hume's.

'Mrs Hume should have mentioned her nephew is a god,' you say, watching Susan's progress.

You hope Mrs Hume's handsome nephew likes Susan. You hear the door bang upstairs.

Mrs Hume's handsome nephew does not like Susan. He has descended the stairs holding her by the scruff of her neck.

Porridge puts his paws up on the man's legs. Susan arches her back and hisses.

'Is this your cat?'

'Yes, it is.'

'It keeps coming in the door,' he says, handing her to you.

'Sorry', you say. 'Porridge, get down. I'm sorry, I don't know your name.'

'Alec.'

'Hi, Alec,' you say, smiling and dragging your wet hair back from your face. 'Sorry about me. Porridge didn't want to leave the park.'

He doesn't return the smile. 'I can't chock the door open because he keeps coming in.'

'She's a she,' says Mrs Kovacic. 'She's looking for Mrs Hume.'

'Right,' says Alec. 'Well, can you stop him?'

'Her,' says Mrs Kovacic.

'Also, it scratched me,' he says, showing the underside of his wrist.

'Did you try to move her away from fridge?' says Mrs Kovacic. 'She doesn't like that.'

A voice comes from the floor above. 'Alec?'

Is that the stylish woman?

Alec rubs his wrist. 'My daughter is allergic,' he says, turning back towards the stairs.

'My name is Kat,' you say to his departing back.

He turns. 'Another cat. Do you scratch too?' He continues up the stairs.

'When they find out about the curse, they'll probably go home,' says Mrs Kovacic.

'Mrs Hume says they'll stay until they find a house.'

Mrs Kovacic raises her eyebrows.

'I think she'd rather you didn't discuss the curse with her relatives,' you say.

'What you been saying about me to Mrs Hume?'

'Nothing,' you say. 'But come on, Mrs Kovacic. Mrs Hume has been here for years, and she's fine.'

'Mrs Hume only fine because I put curse remover in her pot plant, but even then, every day, I worry I find her dead. Covid could come back any day and take one of us. Covid is the curse's servant.'

'Right,' you say.

'Mrs Hume said relatives were nice. He's not nice.' She pats her knees. Porridge trots across the hall and sits companionably on her feet.

'Well,' you say, 'he has just struggled up the stairs with two suitcases. They're just off the flight.'

'You going to drop Mickey and go for James Bond?'

'No!' you say.

'Well, why you defending him?'

'It's just in my nature to give people the benefit of the doubt. Also, it's Michael, not Mickey.'

Susan jumps out of your arms, bats Porridge on the head with her paw and winds herself around Mrs Kovacic's legs. 'Sorry, Susan,' Mrs Kovacic says to the cat. 'I'd love to have you, but Mr Cranky says you could get under wheels of chair.' She rolls her eyes towards the inside of her flat, where Mr Kovacic will be sitting in his wheelchair, watching the street from his front window.

You have lived in the flats for six years. After The Hipster left, you bought a new black crockery set, adopted Porridge – inferring to Susan that his stay was temporary – and surprised yourself by not shedding a single tear.

'How is Mr Kovacic?'

Mrs Kovacic shrugs. 'Cranky. He can't stop talking about this concrete cancer in building. He thinks we going to go broke paying strata fees. He driving me crazy.'

'Well, I think we'll find out how much it'll be tonight,' you say. 'It'll be fine.'

You are not remotely sure it will be fine. Mr Sanderson, Strata President, had inferred with some satisfaction that it could be in the hundreds of thousands.

You hear the foyer door open. Footsteps slowly climb the stairs. Mrs Hume is home. Mrs Kovacic leans over the banister.

'They're here,' she says in a loud stage whisper. 'They've arrived.'

'I'm aware of that,' says Mrs Hume, getting to the top of the stairs. 'There's no need to scream.'

Porridge barks joyously at Mrs Hume's arrival. Mrs Hume leans on the railing, pats her hair and looks up towards her flat, breathing heavily.

'Be quiet, Porridge,' she says. 'Have you met Charlotte, Kat?'

Mrs Hume has had her hair done. She usually gets her hair done on a Thursday. Today is Tuesday. And she's carrying her Sunday handbag.

For weeks, Mrs Hume had been preparing for her stylish relatives' arrival. She'd had the carpets steam cleaned, replaced the curtains, bought a new kettle and found English crackers so they'd feel at home.

'We've met him,' you say.

'He's good-looking, like my husband,' she says.

'Wow,' you say. 'Your husband must have been a real knockout. Let me take that bag for you.'

She smiles at you. 'You'll like her,' she says. 'She's absolutely delightful. We've had some Zooms. She's terribly stylish. She's going to rebrand me.'

'She going to brand you?' says Mrs Kovacic.

'*Re*brand,' says Mrs Hume.

'She's going to style her,' you say to Mrs Kovacic.

Susan leaves Mrs Kovacic and rubs herself against Mrs Hume's legs.

'Why? What's wrong with your style?' says Mrs Kovacic. 'You 80. Does she want to make you look like the Kardashian? Anyway, you want a drink of water?' says Mrs Kovacic.

Porridge barks.

'Ignore him,' you say. 'I'm attempting behavioural modification.'

You start up the stairs with Mrs Hume's bag. As you approach the door and raise your hand to knock, you hear a shout from within and a curt answer in reply. You lower your hand, put the bag at the door and head back down the stairs.

Mrs Hume is standing in Mrs Kovacic's doorway, balancing Susan and a drink of water. The door to Mrs Hume's flat opens.

'Aunt Lucy, hello!' calls Alec from the landing above. 'We let ourselves in.' He is leaning on the railing, looking like he's in the middle of a Dior fashion shoot.

Aunt Lucy? You've never thought of her as someone's aunt.

'Hello, Alec,' says Mrs Hume. 'Welcome to Sydney.'

He comes down two steps.

'Do you need a hand?' he says.

Mrs Hume raises her eyebrows at you. 'I can manage a flight of stairs,' she says. 'This is Kat and Mrs Kovacic.'

'Hello.' He smiles, clearly for Aunt Lucy's benefit. His teeth are extraordinary. 'I've met Porridge. Terrific dog.' His smile drops. 'Are you bringing the cat?' he says to Mrs Hume. 'He scratched me.'

'She,' says Mrs Kovacic.

Alec is one of those people whose faces look equally good in repose as when they are smiling.

'You probably tried to move her away from the fridge,' says Mrs Hume, handing Susan to you. 'How's Charlotte?'

'Nose to the grindstone, as usual.'

Mrs Hume puts her hand on the banister and commences the climb, getting to the top where Alec envelopes her in a hug. They disappear into her flat.

'She must have some important job,' says Mrs Kovacic. 'She's only been here five minutes, and she's already nose to the milestone.'

'Grindstone,' you say.

'What?'

'It's nose to the... never mind.'

'I just hope she's nicer than him,' says Mrs Kovacic, wiping her hands on her apron.

You go to defend him, then stop yourself just in time.

eBay calling

You go into your flat with Porridge and change into dry clothes, wondering if the handsome nephew and his family would care that Mr Kovacic has had a stroke, that Mr Yee passed away from Covid or that Mrs Kovacic now believes the flats are cursed.

Your phone rings. You don't know the number, but it might be the store from which you ordered an engraved collar for Porridge. It had arrived bearing the name *Colleridge*. Like you would name your groodle after an 18th century poet. Also, Coleridge has one 'l'.

You pick up.

'Hello, this is Nina from eBay. We're checking on a recent $500 transaction made on your account. Did you make that?'

'A $500 transaction? No. Not that I recall.'

You lower yourself onto the edge of your couch. There was a report on the news last night about a man who'd saved for a house deposit for ten years. Hadn't taken a holiday or been out to dinner. He'd been scammed out of the lot. He cried.

'So that was not you?' she says. 'Okay. Would you mind holding the line while I hand you over to my supervisor?'

'Your supervisor?'

'Yes. He is a fraud specialist who will determine if there has been illegal activity and what you can do about it.'

Your brain goes into panic. *If there has been illegal activity?* You would remember a $500 purchase. Something's not right! What if you've been majorly hacked? Also, Lizzie from work had her identity stolen. It was a nightmare.

'Hello, this is Andrew.'

'Hello Andrew.'

'My colleague tells me that you do not remember making a $500 transaction on eBay.'

'That's right.'

'Well, I'm here to help.'

'How do I know this is a genuine call?'

'I understand your reservations, ma'am,' he says. 'You're right to be wary but I can assure you, this is a genuine call. I work in the eBay fraud team. Would you like my eBay employee ID number?'

Well, you think to yourself, he sounds genuine. But also, hang on, don't be a sucker.

He gives you a number.

'You could be making that number up,' you say.

'Okay,' he says. 'Punch this URL into your web browser and the eBay website will come up.'

You grab your laptop and, yes, the eBay website appears with a photo and ID number. Andrew looks a bit like a young version of your CEO, David Firth.

'Hang on,' you say, 'you could be faking this website.'

He sighs. You begin worrying that he is trying to help and you are delaying the process.

'Okay,' he says, 'let's just confirm your network connections are fully secure. Would that be okay?'

'How do I do that?'

'Open *Settings*.'

'Okay,' you say. 'Open.'

'Click on *Network*.'

'Network.'

'Please click on *Your Connection*, find the *Advanced* button and select *DNS*.'

Click! Click! Click!

'Can you see some numbers?' he says.

'Yes.'

'What we *don't* want are the numbers 192 or 168,' he says.

'Oh no!' you say. 'That's what's here. 192 *and* 168.'

'Both of them? That's not good,' he says. 'Right now, anyone can get into your system.'

Your heart starts to hammer. On top of your Porridge-related park drenching, this is too much.

'Okay,' he says. 'We can stop this. Let's see if anyone is actually targeting you. Please open your *Activity Monitor* and select the *Network* tab.'

'Yes,' you say.

'Tell me if you see the word "NetBIOS" in the list,' he says.

'Yes!' you say. 'NetBIOS!'

'That's them,' he says. 'There're hacking your system right now.'

'What?' you say. 'Someone is hacking me right now?'

'Yes ma'am, right now,' he says. 'NetBIOS is the signature of a Russian hacker syndicate. They pretend to be environmental activists, but they are really just thieves.'

'Is it just my eBay account?'

'No ma'am,' he says. 'They could have access to everything. Including your bank accounts.'

Your legs feel weak. Your stomach churns.

'Can we stop them?'

'We can, ma'am,' he says. 'That's what I've been trying to do.'

'I'm sorry,' you say. 'There's just so much in the news about scamming.'

'Of course, ma'am,' he says. 'You're right to be careful. This is what will happen next: I will send you a link and you will download a security patch that will immediately block NetBIOS hackers from your network and prevent any future hacks.'

'Thank you so much,' you say.

'You're welcome, ma'am,' he says. 'We want to keep our customers safe. Have a nice evening.'

The email arrives as Andrew promised. You download the security patch and install it like an IT pro. You check your bank accounts. Everything is in order.

Porridge comes and puts his head on your lap. You're awash with relief.

'That was close,' you say to Porridge.

No forest green sheets for you

The next morning Michael wakes you. He has inserted a strange device up his nose to stop his snoring. It's not working. It makes him look like a tapir. You lean over and remove the device.

'I'm going to buy the forest green sheet set,' you say. 'And that nose thing makes you look like a tapir.'

You take your phone from the bedside table and open your internet banking account to pay for the sheets.

You sit up in bed. 'No. No!'

Your savings account has been emptied. Susan rouses herself and looks at you.

'What is it?' says Michael.

'I've been robbed.'

'How do you know?'

'Because I went to buy the forest green sheets and my savings account is empty.'

'Check your other accounts,' he says.

You scream. There wasn't much in them, but they too have been cleaned out.

'It's okay,' he says. 'Call the bank. They have a fraud squad.'

'It was the eBay people!'

'The eBay people?'

'The eBay people that rang me last night. They told me I'd been hacked and they would protect me.'

'It's okay, Kat. They have very organised scams.'

'How is this possible?' you say. 'I opened up the eBay website and there was his photo and his ID number. Why am I so stupid?'

'It's okay, Kat. Ring the bank.'

'Oh my god. I'm the worst idiot.' You lie back down and pull the covers over your head. 'I can't afford this right now. We've got the strata fees for the building repairs!'

Michael pulls back the covers. 'Kat, ring the bank.'

'I thought it could have been a scam, but he had an answer for everything.'

'It's okay. They're very sophisticated. Ring the bank.'

'We do training exercises at work where they send out fake scams and see if you'll fall for it. I never have. I thought I was scamming Teflon.'

'Kat,' he says. 'Ring. The. Bank.'

You dial the number. 'They're going to think I'm a total fool.'

The automated voice sounds reassuring. 'In a few words, please tell us how we can help you today.'

'Hello,' you say, 'I'm a complete idiot. I think I've been scammed.'

The automatic voice sounds unfazed. 'Thank you,' it says. 'Hold on and I'll put you through to someone who can help you.'

Michael smiles encouragingly. 'I am a complete idiot,' you say.

'Hello, this is Eva. How can I help you?'

'Yes, this is Kat Mitchell speaking. I've been scammed.'

'eBay?' says Eva.

'Yes,' you say.

'You're the 20th call this morning.'

You don't know if being part of a scammed collective makes you feel better or worse.

YOUR INTERNAL LIE DETECTOR

This tiny slice of Kat's life features dozens of lies with a range of consequences for Kat – from taking ownership of a rambunctious groodle to gifting bank account access to a team of scammers.

Kat's a smart woman. How did this happen? Are human beings entirely defenceless in the presence of lies?

No, we are not. Evolution has provided us with mechanisms that help us detect lies:

- We spot a red flag, smell a rat or sense that something seems fishy.
- Something doesn't quite ring true or stack up.
- We describe someone as acting in a suspect manner or being shady.
- It feels like someone is pulling the wool over our eyes.

In these moments we can tell something's not right – so there is definitely something happening in our nervous system to alert us to the presence of lies.

You may know about the amygdalae: two almond-shaped regions of the brain that light up when we perceive danger. Some lies subject a person to significant danger, so it makes sense that the amygdalae will fire up. But what tells the amygdalae that something is not right?

A neuroscientific study showed the parahippocampal gyrus (PHG) also lights up in our brains when we are told lies.[5] The PHG's primary function seems to be recognising reliable patterns in scenery, landscapes, rooms and furniture. It informs a person about their physical environment and is aroused when something is perceived to be out of place. They showed that the PHGs of test subjects would light up when presented with suspicious information.

The benefit of this function to our pre-verbal ancestors is clear: the presence of an environmental anomaly should have aroused concern. It might be a strange sunset presaging a violent storm. A disturbed campsite could awaken suspicion of a potentially dangerous intruder – animal or human.

When working well, being alert to danger (amygdalae) and sensitive to things being out of place (PHG) combine with other functions to create the mind's internal lie detector. However, like so many brain functions that evolved to keep us safe, the internal lie detector can malfunction. Overly active amygdalae can prevent people from recognising trustworthy sources of information. The inability to trust or feel safe with others under any circumstances is a characteristic of clinical paranoia and anxiety disorders.

But if the system doesn't pick up on the signals at all, or if other brain functions override it, the lies go undetected.

A well-functioning internal lie detector operates in the Goldilocks zone, in which we are not too suspicious yet not too gullible. We can support this vital function by sharpening our critical thinking skills and our powers of observation, reasoning and judgement.

How much is that doggy in the window?

Let's start at the beginning of the chapter, when Kat finds herself the owner of a recalcitrant groodle. Being Porridge's mistress is ultimately a positive experience for Kat, but Porridge is not the well-behaved dog that Kat had anticipated owning. So how did it happen? Why did Kat agree to take Porridge?

Kat has happy memories of childhood days playing with adorable dogs. Kat sees photos of Porridge as a sweet puppy and hears Miriam describe Porridge as 'well-balanced'. Her *perception* is also influenced by emotional drivers that operate beneath the level of consciousness. Deep in her unconscious lies Kat's desire to have a child. She is unaware that the dog is a proxy for the child she wants. (I'm not saying that a dog is a child substitute for most people. It just happens to be for Kat.)

Presented with a picture of an obedient and well-adjusted ex-assistance dog who will leap to her protection when required, Kat constructs a compelling *reason* to proceed. Kat experiences her reasoning as being rational and objective, but it is not. She is oblivious to her unconscious reasoning. That's why it's called unconscious.

She is conscious of several thoughts:

- 'He's a lovely-looking dog.'
- 'It would be good to have a companion for Susan.'
- 'I'd feel more safe and secure with a dog.'
- 'Having a dog will make me do more exercise.'

Kat is convinced by her own arguments and says 'yes' to Miriam.

Humans indulge in motivated reasoning, which means we will reason our way around something to come to the conclusion we want. Being vulnerable to lies about a dog is one thing, but the same kinks in Kat's brain are also in play in other, more risky contexts.

eBay or not?

Online scamming has reached epidemic proportions. How often have you heard someone say, 'I consider myself an intelligent person; I can't believe I fell for it'?

We shouldn't judge ourselves for trusting too easily. Intelligence offers too little protection when we're in the thrall of a professional scam artist.

That said, the scammer's playbook has some common elements. There is an offer that seems too good to be true, coupled with urgency. 'To take advantage of this,' they say, 'you must act now!' If the offer succeeds in triggering desire, our cognitive flaws make us putty in their hands. We think our rational brain is in charge when, in fact, it is our unconscious emotional drivers that are calling the shots. We've all picked up a call and found a potential scammer on the other end. What makes the difference between falling for the scam and not?

Let's take apart Kat's experience of being conned by fake eBay employees. Some of these scams have an impressive shopfront. The original caller, 'Nina', plays her part by sounding like a tech company's customer service officer. When Kat confirms she has not made a recent purchase, the escalation to the supervisor seems like the right thing to have happened.

From a distance, the trick is so simple. 'Have you made a $500 purchase?' It sounds like a genuine question with two possible answers, but 'Nina' knows that Kat will say 'no'.

Why doesn't Kat smell a rat? Well, she does. Her amygdalae and PHG are activated, but the scammers redirect her warning signals. Like many of us, Kat has been primed by her general perception that cybercrime is rife, and it is this very perception these scammers play on. 'You are right to be wary,' says 'Andrew', the 'supervisor'. 'I am here to help.'

What is priming? Priming happens when a person is exposed to certain stimuli that influence future responses to the same stimuli. This is an unconscious process. Words or images can influence our thinking without us knowing.

Kat hears the name of a trusted brand – eBay. She hears the words 'supervisor' and 'fraud team'. She sees what 'Andrew' predicts: the numbers and words he describes are in her operating system. Kat is unaware that asking to see those numbers and words is like asking someone to look inside a car to see if there is a steering wheel.

Even though she begins with a cautious mind, Kat's faulty reasoning makes her vulnerable.

Also, 'Andrew' has the authority of an expert, making Kat vulnerable to the argument from authority logical fallacy.

Argument from authority leads us into the trap of believing something is true because we perceive that the person communicating it is an authority on the subject. Andrew sounds certain. He validates Kat's concerns and praises her for being cautious, which makes Kat feel safe. When Kat feels safe, her amygdalae stand down. She reasons with herself that he must know what he's talking about.

Once she *concludes* that 'Andrew' is on her side, she is lost. The *action* she takes is precisely what the thieves want.

Lie detection

I do hope that doggy's for sale

Notice when you are sucked in by photos of dogs, children, weight-loss products or potential Tinder dates, and be on the lookout for motivated reasoning. Major purchases and decisions, especially those involving animals and relationships with other humans, deserve extra scrutiny.

Are they really on your side?

Be cautious when people, especially strangers, assume the role of your protector.

2

Someone is sobbing in the toilet

You're back in the office. You have completely lost confidence in your view of yourself as an intelligent, thinking woman. You have always been scathing about people getting caught up in scams, and now you have joined their gullible ranks. Some three-person outfit with a computer in a Kuala Lumpur garage convinced you it was eBay.

Despite Michael's reassurances that it could happen to anyone and these scammers were very sophisticated, you're humiliated. The bank has assured you your money will be returned, but you should know better: you work in communications.

You enter the bathroom. Someone is sobbing in the toilet cubicle. You don't know who it is. The sobbing is rising and falling in cadence. With every drop in intensity, you creep towards the exit, only to be drawn back to the sink by another bout of weeping.

The cubicle door opens. Lisbeth, one of your direct reports, emerges. She's dabbing at her eyes with toilet paper.

'You okay, Lisbeth?'

She may have heard redundancy whispers that you've been unaware of. This sets off a highly unhelpful train of thought about the security of your own position.

'What is it?' you ask.

'I hate Ryan.'

There are two Ryans in your team: Ryan Schmidt and Ryan Kraft. It's the cause of much confusion. 'Right. Yep.'

She is now examining herself in the mirror. Her crying has transmuted from a keening to a hiccoughing sobbing.

'I'm angry,' she says, blowing her nose into the toilet paper.

'Right.'

'But I can't access it, so I cry. I cry when I'm angry.'

'Yep, me too.'

'Really?' she says, looking at you keenly through swollen eyes. 'I can't imagine you getting angry.'

You are her manager. You feel that, to have authority, your direct reports should at least be able to imagine you getting angry.

'No, I do get angry. Really angry.'

Lisbeth has lost interest in whether or not you get angry.

'Can you believe that behaviour in the meeting this morning?' she says.

'I wasn't in the meeting this morning. I had a conference call with Melbourne.'

'Well, I walked in, and the meeting went dead silent. I was only five minutes late. What, so nobody else is ever late? So, I look at Ryan because it's his meeting, and I smile, and he stonewalls me. I'm sure they were talking about me. Ryan. And Sarah.'

'Sarah? No.'

'I tell you. I don't think she can be trusted. She's an underminer. I'm going to ask to move teams.'

You don't want her to ask to move teams. It's not good for your reputation. You need to be able to manage problems between your team members.

'Oh, right. Well, Ryan's a bit short-sighted, so maybe he couldn't see you smiling.'

'Two things: not that Ryan, and whose side are you on?'

'Well, nobody's, until I find out what happened.'

'I've just told you what happened. Why don't you believe me?'

Your conflict resolution training flickers at the edge of your brain. You hear Michelle, the trainer, saying, 'Keep your counsel. Do not roll over and immediately agree with the first person's interpretation of the event.'

What would Michelle know? She's not standing in the bathroom with swollen-eyed Lisbeth.

'I'm leaning in your direction,' you say.

'I'm so polite to everybody,' she says. 'If somebody smiles at me, I smile back. How hard is it?'

'Yep, yep,' you say. 'You're super friendly.'

'Yes, I am, and where does it get me?'

You start to answer and then realise the question is rhetorical. You want to leave the bathroom.

The door to the bathroom opens. You are pleased it's Adele, your team's Project Manager. 'Adele. Hi. How's your snake?' you say.

You never thought you'd willingly engage Adele in conversation about her pet snake, but these are desperate times.

'She's great, Kat. Want to see a picture?'

She approaches you with her phone, looks up and notices Lisbeth.

'What's up, Lisbeth?'

Lisbeth shakes her head.

Adele puts her arm around her. You are relieved at the intervention but worried about the lack of safe social distancing.

'Everyone is talking about me behind my back, and Ryan completely ignored me,' says Lisbeth.

'Oh, don't take that personally,' says Adele, giving Lisbeth an encouraging hug before entering a stall. 'He's really short-sighted.'

'Not that Ryan,' you say.

'Ryan Kraft. And Sarah. It was humiliating,' she says, bursting into fresh tears.

'Okay,' says Adele, emerging from the stall. 'What happened?'

You can't bear to hear the retelling again. 'She thinks everybody was talking about her because the room went silent when she entered the team meeting this morning.'

'I don't *think* they were; I *know* they were,' says Lisbeth. 'It was so rude.'

You notice Lisbeth is now successfully accessing her anger.

The door to the bathroom opens again. It's Sarah. Lisbeth straightens.

'Hi guys,' says Sarah. She looks at Lisbeth. 'Are you okay?'

'Yes,' says Lisbeth, 'I'm fine.'

'Okay, good. Look, sorry to be stalking you, but I'm doing a quick whip-around for Ryan,' says Sarah.

'Which Ryan?' says Adele.

'Ryan Kraft. He's having a bad day,' says Sarah. 'He bought his girlfriend an engagement ring. Paid five grand. So much more than he could afford. It's a fake.'

'No,' says Adele.

'It arrived in the mail. Cubic zirconia! Worth about 50 bucks.'

'So, when did you find out?' says Lisbeth.

'In that meeting this morning. You were there; or was it just before you came in?'

There is a sharp intake of breath from Lisbeth.

'Anyway, he's devastated,' she says. 'We all just sat there in silence.'

'Right,' you say.

'So, we thought we could all chip in, buy him something to cheer him up.'

You and Adele catch Lisbeth's eye in the mirror.

'Or you could just give him the cash,' says Adele.

'Yes,' says Sarah.

There is a pause.

'Are you sure you're okay, Lisbeth?' says Sarah.

'Allergies,' says Lisbeth. She gives her nose an enormous blow, throws the toilet paper into the bin, reaches into her handbag, takes out a $50 note and hands it to Sarah.

'This is from us,' she says.

Sarah holds the note.

'Wow, that's so lovely, Lisbeth.'

'From all three of us,' says Lisbeth.

'Thank you,' says Sarah, tucking the $50 note into her plastic zip-lock collection bag. 'Hey, Lisbeth, I think I've got some antihistamine in my handbag.'

'I'm good,' says Lisbeth.

'Okay, thanks!' Sarah exits.

'Poor bloody Ryan,' says Adele. 'It's too easy to get scammed these days. When I bought Emma, the so-called breeder I found online tried to sell me a corn snake.'

'That's outrageous,' you say.

'Thought I couldn't tell the difference between a Stimson's python and a corn snake,' she says, shaking her head.

'Wow,' says Lisbeth.

'Hey, while you're all in the giving mood, my sister asked me to invite people to her place tonight,' says Adele. 'Free wine and food.'

'Free wine?' you say.

'Yep, just a couple of hours,' says Adele. 'You'll discover the life-changing magic of make-up and supplements.'

'Tonight?' says Lisbeth.

'Yep. Come on, Lisbeth. You like a free feed.'

'What about me?' you say.

'And you like free wine. Come on. I'll drive you,' says Adele, smiling at you in the mirror.

'Okay,' says Lisbeth.

They exit, with Adele gently patting Lisbeth's shoulder. The door shuts.

You apply lipstick, pull an angry face. Lisbeth doesn't know what she's talking about: you look quite fierce.

Who wants to be a boss babe?

It's 8.20 p.m. You've been at Jane's for one hour and 12 minutes. Jane lives in a small flat in Lane Cove, north Sydney. Jane didn't want to use her good glasses, so you're drinking wine from small plastic glasses with detachable stems. These stems are problematic as they're prone to detach at inopportune moments, like every time you put the glass down.

'Hi, hon,' Jane says to everyone who enters. 'Grab yourself a wine and a snack. We'll get going when all the other girls arrive.'

Lisbeth does not look thrilled with the snack: Jatz biscuits, cheddar squares and tiny pieces of cabanossi. The other girls are taking their time. Adele is telling you why she chose the name Emma for her snake.

'It's after the girl in the film', she says.

'The old *Emma* or the new *Emma*?' you say.

'The old *Emma*.'

'So, your snake looks like Gwyneth Paltrow?'

'Yes, around the mouth.'

'Your snake should start a Goop empire,' you say.

The arrival of a red-haired girl brings the room to a quarter full. Jane moves and stands in front of the faux fireplace.

Jane is the dead opposite of Adele, who has short, easy-to-manage hair and wears hiking pants, boots and no make-up. Jane is sporting Hollywood hair, thick eyebrows, seriously inflated lips, inch-thick foundation and long, intricately decorated acrylic nails.

She is nervous.

'Welcome, future boss babes,' she says. 'I'm so excited to see you all here.' She looks down at her palm cards. 'Today is the day you can choose to turn your lives around.'

Lisbeth starts chewing the side of her nail. Adele looks at the floor.

'Okay,' says Jane, smiling broadly. 'I can tell you're all fun babes.'

You wish she would stop calling you 'babes'; and Adele is one of the least fun people you've ever met.

'But who here would like to be a boss babe?'

You look around you. The boss babes sit silently in their chairs, gnawing on their Jatz. You feel bad for Jane.

'I'd like to be a boss babe,' you say.

'Amazing,' Jane says. 'You'd like to work part-time from your own home and make a full-time wage.'

You narrow your eyes at Adele.

'Yes,' says Adele. 'We'd all like that.'

'Amazing,' says Jane. 'So, I'm going to demonstrate a line of products developed with women like you in mind.'

'Excuse me,' says Adele. 'Do you have any other crackers?'

'I'm so sorry, I don't,' says Jane, 'but I do have this.'

She sprays something from a small navy bottle into her mouth.

'Who wants to try it?' she says.

'I'll try it,' says Adele, 'If you let me have a look in your pantry.'

Jane looks aggrieved but agrees. She delivers a squirt from the blue bottle into Adele's mouth.

'Wow,' says Adele. 'It's like Aperol without the alcohol. What is it?'

Jane shuffles her palm cards, drops one, bends over to pick it up but cannot get any traction on the wooden floor with her acrylics. It's like watching Edward Scissorhands. After an excruciating 35 seconds, you stand up, pick up the card and hand it to her.

'Thanks, hon,' she says. 'Awesome. So, back to business.'

She holds up the spray next to her cheek. 'This is our post-exercise cellular endurance mitochondrial replacement EC spritz. It's organic and completely biodegradable. There are no parabens or endocrine disruptors. It's incredibly effective and ethical.'

'Wow,' you say. 'Sounds amazing.'

'What's it do?' says Adele.

'What *doesn't* it do?' says Jane. 'The spritz is my star product. It elongates the effects of exercise hours after the workout. The neurotransmitters keep active by redirecting the carbenoid phages to where they're needed. So, it's also an immune booster. It's part of a total post-workout.'

There is silence. Jane punches through.

'I love this so much. It has turned my life around. It's amazing. Imagine having a product this good to sell. Imagine how thrilled your friends will be. Imagine being your own boss babe.'

She grinds to a halt. Adele has wandered off into her kitchen in search of more crackers.

'What are the other products?' says Lisbeth. Clearly, the only way you'll be released from this torture is to encourage Jane to get to the end of her presentation.

'There's an EC whey protein,' says Jane. 'There's hibiscus flower psyllium for fibre gut health. There's a post-workout face toner that prepares your face for the post-workout sun-kissed moisturising emollient.'

'Does that have sunscreen in it?' says the red-haired girl.

Jane looks stumped, then recovers.

'No, it doesn't. Sunscreen contains microparticles and is toxic. The sun is a source of vitamin D. You shouldn't be frightened of it.'

The red-haired girl picks up her plastic mini glass of wine and drains it. She looks out the window.

'Okay, who is ready to turn their life around?' says Jane.

You put your hand up.

'Okay, hon. This is the meeting point between supplements and skin care. You go to the gym, spritz your face and put the sun-kissed emollient on. You're ready to start the day. This is the future; we're knocking everyone else out of the park. These products are your pathway to freedom.'

'Isn't this pyramid selling?' says the red-haired girl.

Jane is ready for this question. 'This isn't a pyramid scheme. Working in corporate is a pyramid scheme.' She rocks back on her heels.

You feel the red-haired girl is readying to take Jane on. You don't want this. You want to go home.

'I'd like to try the spritz,' you say.

'Awesome,' says Jane. You open your mouth. She gives you a short spray. Your mouth starts to tingle.

'Excuse me,' you say, 'I need to go to the bathroom.'

The light in the bathroom is flickering, but you can see enough to notice that your mouth has turned orange. You rinse your mouth out, but the tingling persists. You venture out to the lounge room. You're going into anaphylaxis. You're going to die in the middle of a multi-level marketing pitch in Lane Cove.

Jane is still standing near the fireplace. You grab her arm and whisper urgently into her ear. 'My mouth is tingling,' you say to her. 'I think my tongue is swelling.'

'No problem,' says Jane, handing you a plastic cup of warm wine. You down it in one go. Your tongue returns to its normal size.

'Sorry,' you say. 'All good now.' You take your seat next to Lisbeth. She is sitting with her chin on her hand, scrolling through Instagram.

'Awesome,' says Jane. She addresses the group. 'Now, you're probably having some negative thoughts, like, "Am I a good enough salesperson to sell these products?" Banish those thoughts. Say, "Negative thoughts, be gone!" Okay, who'd like to sign up?'

'Jane?' calls Adele from the kitchen.

'Adele, I'm in the middle of the onboarding. If you want to ask me something, come here.' Jane smiles at her potential boss babes.

Adele appears in the doorway. 'Sorry, but I'm pretty sure you had some Saladas. Any clue?'

'No, I don't,' says Jane tightly.

'Well, there's no need to be snippy,' says Adele.

'Adele,' says Jane, 'if you weren't going to be supportive, why did you come?'

'Because Mum made me,' says Adele.

The boss babes look down at their mostly empty plastic wine glasses. You pull the stem out of your glass and chew on it.

Jane takes a deep breath and smiles.

'If you decide to sign up tonight, you'll become a vital part of the Supplebeauty family. You'll never be alone. We'll support you every inch step of the way. Any questions?'

Who's an empath?

'Your sister is pretty different to you,' says Lisbeth in the car on the way home.

'She's straight, for starters,' says Adele.

'How long has Jane been...?' you ask.

'Flogging Supplebeauty?' says Adele. 'This is pretty new. I've got no idea who she is anymore. She was a software engineer.'

'No!' says Lisbeth.

'Yeah,' says Adele. 'She was at Zambitsy, in the digital payments team. Lost her job. She's super smart; the system was running virtually error-free. Her team loved her.'

'Zambitsy is huge,' says Lisbeth.

'Not as huge as it used to be,' says Adele. 'Gabriel Randall ran a razor through it. Made a name for himself.'

'Gabriel who?' says Lisbeth.

'Gabriel Randall,' you say. 'The DeGreys consultant. The transformation guru who's about to land with us.'

'And now she can't get a job doing what she's brilliant at. She's stuck trying to sell the skin stuff. I shouldn't have made a fuss about the Saladas.'

Poor Jane. You look out the car window. You wish you didn't feel other people's pain so acutely. You had felt Jane's disappointment so intensely that you'd had to sit on your hands to stop yourself from signing up.

Yesterday, you heard a woman at a cafe telling her friend that she was an empath.

'That's the trouble with me,' she'd said. 'I'm an empath.'

'Me too,' the friend had said. 'I'm just so raw. Feel absolutely everything. It's a nightmare.'

It seemed to you she felt everything except the irritation of the first woman for being one-upped in the empathy stakes.

'I think I'm an empath,' you say to the car in general.

'Oh, me too,' says Lisbeth.

'Don't be so ridiculous,' says Adele. 'What even is that? It's a stupid made-up name.'

Adele, as usual, is correct. Sensitivity is not a competition.

SPOTLIGHT ON LISBETH

The lie that inspires Lisbeth to descend into a downward spiral of fury and misery is one she tells herself. She interprets the silence in the meeting as being relevant to her.

The cognitive bias interfering with her capacity to remain more rational in her response is called the spotlight effect. This is the illusion that people are noticing you more than they are. You perceive yourself to be more relevant to the situation than is accurate.

The spotlight effect causes a world of misunderstanding both in our personal lives and in the workplace. It makes us hyperaware of every action that we take, every word we utter and the way we look – and we assume other people have this awareness of us, too. This is, fortunately, untrue. People are as self-involved as we are and are therefore not paying us as much attention as we think.

A small spot on your face or stain on your shirt can feel obvious to you, but it's barely noticeable to the observer. They're too busy wondering if their pants are too tight.

When you're asked a question in a meeting and you fumble through papers to find the data, that moment can feel excruciating to you – but it's hardly observed by the other members of the team, who are all rehearsing what they're about to say in their head.

That disconcerting moment when you walk into a room and the person is cold and dismissive or barely registers your hello is nothing to do with you. Maybe they've just found out their share portfolio tanked.

The sensation of being in the spotlight and therefore judged is highly exaggerated. It's good practice to remind yourself that other people have whole lives of their own with myriad concerns and problems, and the likelihood of you being the centre of their attention is low.

In corporate cultures that are crying out for innovation, the spotlight effect reduces the likelihood that employees will take risks. It encourages a deep conservatism and homogeneity in the expression of ideas.

The spotlight effect also services impostor syndrome. Impostor syndrome is an unfortunately common perception that people will discover you're a fake. It's the disturbing feeling that other people are capable but you don't know anything: that you have been pretending the whole time to be competent. It's believing that any day now the truth will out, and everyone will know you are useless and underqualified. If these sentiments resonate with you, you've been in the grip of impostor syndrome. The spotlight effect only exacerbates this simmering sense of fraudulence.

So, back to the story. Lisbeth, already feeling like she's on the back foot for being late, walks into the meeting and immediately assumes that the silence in the room and the lack of eye contact from her colleagues is related to her. She then nurses the perceived grievance, which means she's not able to turn her focus outward and consider the option that the silence was irrelevant to her. Once Lisbeth is in her heightened state, feeling judged, her capacity to remain rational is greatly reduced.

Lisbeth could have saved herself a lot of upset. She could have noticed that the atmosphere in the room has triggered an emotional response in her. This would have allowed her to take a couple of breaths, giving herself some time to consider the option that she was in the grip of the spotlight effect. She could have further reduced the influence of the spotlight effect by reminding herself of the facts of the situation, saying to herself, 'Hang on here, what's actually going on?' This would have allowed her rational mind to view the situation with clarity. She could have then taken her seat and tuned in to the meeting. At an appropriate moment, she could have asked someone at the table if something was going on that she was unaware of. She'd have then discovered that the silence in the meeting was unrelated to her.

So, next time you want to get up on the dance floor, go for it; and remember: that woman sitting at the next table who seems to be watching you is probably worrying that everyone's noticed how many champagnes she's had – and wondering if she can sneak in another.

Uh oh! Multi-level marketing

Multi-level marketing (MLM) is astoundingly common. Australia has nearly half a million direct sellers. It will be no surprise to you that 77 per cent are women, and that 99 per cent of all participants lose money.[6] Why do we buy it? Because our brains betray us. MLM's lie is that, if you become a boss babe, a world of wealth, autonomy and support will be yours. It works on an *us-and-them* mentality: the losers work for other people, and the winners choose to join the MLM family and be their own boss.

The language MLM peddlers use stimulates you to imagine a future in which you are financially independent and living a carefree life. Once you've agreed that, yes, you *would* like to be rich, rich, rich, they invite you join their happy, supportive organisation. Consistency bias kicks in. You've agreed you want to be rich, so why wouldn't you agree to become a boss babe?

Part of the MLM strategy is to love-bomb you: to be wildly supportive, using language specific to the MLM. This specific language, which infers you are special enough to be part of the 'exclusive' MLM, fires off ingroup bias in your brain.

Jane uses incomprehensible gobbledygook to impress the potential boss babes, hoping they'll believe that the science and research behind the products is valid. The words she uses sound scientific, but they're not. They are used incorrectly and interchangeably. They're designed to give the impression that people in white lab coats have worked long hours to create these amazing products. Be careful when you read or hear these types of words in any context. They are also favoured by Instagram influencers, who are never happier than when they are uttering the phrase 'endocrine disrupters'.

Our brains are easily triggered into ingroup bias. We form into groups very quickly, even if the group is random. If we've been told to sit with a group a people on a program we're attending, those people will, in our brains, become our team; and we will, if required, give them preferential treatment. Our forebears were more likely to survive if they were loyal to a group. If there's an ingroup, there must be an outgroup, and in MLM the outgroup is the people who aren't smart enough to sign up.

Those who do sign up to MLMs will find the delicious support of belonging to the ingroup is withdrawn if they're not hitting the numbers. Many MLM organisations go from being highly supportive to ghosting members overnight. This can be a highly distressing experience for people, especially if they've pinned their hopes on being financially saved.

I should note here that Jane is also a victim of the MLM lie. The Janes of this world – who often enter MLMs off the back of job losses, relationship break-ups or slick Instagram marketing campaigns – often invest money they never recover. Also, intelligence doesn't protect you from being sucked in. Jane is clearly an intelligent and capable woman.

Making quick, impulsive decisions on the back of a feeling leaves you vulnerable to being scammed. No matter how appealing it sounds, if someone is touting an MLM, put your wine glass down, swallow your cabanossi, excuse yourself and leave. Someone at the top of the organisation is rich, but it's never going to be you.

Lie detection

You are not fake news

It's not about you. Watch out for the spotlight effect telling you lies about how relevant you are. Kick impostor syndrome in the posterior. We all feel it. It's rubbish.

Don't be someone else's boss babe

MLM is a big, fat lie. If you're tempted to get involved, go and flush some bank notes down the toilet. It's quicker and less painful.

3

It's a Dyson Airwrap!

The following day you're sitting on the floor outside your flat with Porridge, waiting for Mrs Kovacic to come home. You have locked yourself out. Of course it happened on a morning Michael hasn't stayed overnight.

Mrs Hume's relatives moved in two days ago. Your only experience of them since has been spotting Mrs Hume at the front of the flats explaining to the handsome nephew where the bin should be positioned. You're yet to meet his stylish partner.

The handsome nephew walks up the stairs with Will and an older girl. You scramble to your feet. You wish you weren't wearing your trackpants with the holes in the knees.

The boy stops and stares at you. He leans over and pats Porridge.

'Hi,' you say to the boy.

'He's shy,' says the girl.

The girl is beautiful. She has her father's looks: the same jet-black hair in a thick braid, wide-set green eyes, perfect bow mouth, luminous skin.

She is dressed in Versace sneakers, a Dolce & Gabbana sweatshirt and a Bulgari bracelet. You know because the labelling is all over them.

'Right,' you say. You address the comment to the girl: 'I'm locked out.'

'I'm Willow. At my last school, we had rock climbing as our term sport. They installed a new wall costing £24,000. They had to do a lot of fundraising. I made earrings. They sold for £13.50 a pair. Would you like me to scale the outside of the building and climb through your window?'

'Willow, don't be silly,' says the handsome nephew, pulling Will's hand away from Porridge. Then to you: 'You have a way to get back in?'

'Yes,' you say. 'Yes. Thanks anyway, Willow. That's very kind of you.'

'Anytime, dude,' she says.

The handsome nephew rolls his eyes. 'Okay, kids, keep moving.'

You watch them climb the stairs. The handsome nephew walks in front; the girl next and the boy last. The boy turns, raises himself on his toes and looks at you.

'We should have drinks sometime,' you say.

The handsome nephew turns. 'Sure,' he says. 'Charlotte's going to love you.' He smiles at you. 'Thanks.'

He may be churlish, but to have his smile bestowed upon you feels like the sun breaking through the clouds.

Mrs Kovacic appears on the landing carrying a bag of sweet potatoes. She tuts at you and produces a key.

'Why don't you put spare key on Porridge's collar?' she says.

You open the door. Porridge bounds inside and starts nudging his food bowl around the kitchen.

You sigh. 'Just wait one minute,' you say to him.

'What's wrong with you?' says Mrs Kovacic.

'My bank accounts were hacked.'

'How they do that?'

'I made a mistake and gave my information to a scammer. Be careful if someone rings you and tells you they're from eBay.'

'When the scammers ring me, I pretend to be ignorant immigrant. I string them along. I can't believe you fell for it.' She holds up the bag of sweet potatoes. 'Mr Kovacic dug these from the garden. Mr Yee be so proud. Tonight, I'll bring you and Mickey soup.'

'Oh,' you say. 'Thanks.'

Five minutes later, there's a knock on your door.

'Hi,' says Willow. 'If you're going to walk your dog, can I come? I'm feeling super claustrophobic in that flat.'

'Wow,' you say. 'You've only been home five minutes.' You stand back and wave her in. 'I'm going to walk him in a minute. You hungry?'

'No thanks, I just ate half a packet of Classic Assorted biscuits. Aunt Lucy told me they're discontinuing them, which is criminal. There's going to be demonstrations.'

'Right.'

You go to the fridge where you find yesterday's couscous salad and take three quick mouthfuls. You close the fridge and grab Porridge's lead. Willow is staring at one of your paintings.

'Cool painting. Your flat's super nice.'

'It's the same as your aunt's.'

'Less people and junk,' Willow says.

You go to the mirror above the mantle and tuck your hair into your wool beanie.

'Cool beanie.'

'Your aunt knitted it for me.'

'Oh my god, are they Nike Kyrie sneakers?'

'Um, I don't think so. They were on sale at the mall.'

'Oh my god, you're so authentic.'

'Right.'

In the mirror, you can see her looking at you. You are suddenly aware of yourself seen through her eyes.

You are a cool person able to wear a hat knitted by your octogenarian neighbour without apology. The art on your walls is not the result of your inability to conclude what sort of art you like; it reflects your love of eclecticism.

Eating from the open door of your fridge is not a sign of profound disorganisation and a lack of care for your health; it shows a free-spirited attitude towards food. If you had a stoop, you'd be sitting outside in the cold evenings smoking roll-your-own cigarettes and drinking long-neck beers, which you'd hold by the neck with two fingers.

You are a fully functioning adult. You are in control. You do not care what people think. You can come and go as you please.

You'd like to stay in Willow's sphere of interpretation forever.

'What's this?'

You turn around. 'It's a morse code machine.'

'Like from the war?'

'Yes. My neighbour, Mr Kovacic, gave it to me.'

'I could live with you instead of Aunt Lucy. I tried to move into my new boarding school early, but they said I had to wait until term starts. I told them my whole family had Covid, but they checked. We can be housemates. I've done home economics. I came second in the year. My pancakes are sick.'

'Right, okay. Well, you can't live with me, but we can go for a walk.'

No ordinary hair dryer

You and Willow exit through the foyer door. It's a pristine, late-winter morning. The delicious smell of wood smoke is in the air.

You are buttoning your cardigan when a metallic pink object crashes to the pavement in front of you. You grab Willow and leap backwards. Porridge barks ferociously.

Whatever it is, it's shattered. You look up at the building. There is no sign of life in any of the windows. You still have your arm around Willow. She is breathing heavily, her hand over her mouth.

Porridge continues barking. You and Willow approach the object. Willow nudges it with her foot like it's alive.

'It looks like a hair dryer,' you say.

'That's no hair dryer. It's a Dyson Airwrap.'

You look up at the building again. A head appears. It's Will.

'Oh my god,' calls Willow. 'What are you doing? Charlotte will kill you. It was brand new.'

Porridge is sniffing at the side of the item.

'You could have killed us!' Willow yells.

Mrs Kovacic's head appears at her window. She slides it open and sticks her head out. 'What is crashing noise?' she says.

'It's a hair dryer,' you say.

'It's much more than a hair dryer,' says Willow. 'It curls, waves, smooths and dries hair without extreme heat.'

'Wow,' you say.

'Charlotte's going to kill him. They retail for $800, but Charlotte had a voucher for $100. It was going to expire. So, she only paid $700. Hello!' she calls up to Mrs Kovacic. 'I'm Willow.'

'You daughter of Mrs Hume's nephew?'

'Yes. They won't take me at boarding school yet, and now my brother's tried to kill me with Charlotte's Dyson Airwrap.' She turns to you. 'I was going to try it out tonight, too.'

'You sure it your brother?' calls Mrs Kovacic. 'Could be the curse.'

'The curse?' says Willow.

You sigh. 'Don't worry about it, Willow.'

'Why is there a curse?' says Willow.

'There's not,' you say.

Mrs Yee's quiet

You'd seen her. Mrs Yee.

Her front door had been slightly open, and you'd looked in and seen her sitting in her chair, staring straight ahead.

You had backed away into the hallway, stood uncertainly, like a child, and knocked on the Kovacics' door.

'Something's wrong with Mrs Yee,' you'd said.

Mr Kovacic had pushed open the Yees' door and wheeled himself into the flat.

'I can't cook for one,' she'd said.

He'd taken her hand. 'He never saw the inside of a nursing home, Li Jin.'

It was the first time you'd heard Mrs Yee's given name. Li Jin.

Mrs Kovacic had appeared beside you.

'The curse has taken him,' she'd said and moved past you into the flat. She'd stood behind Mrs Yee and enveloped her in her arms.

'Covid took him,' Mr Kovacic had said. 'He with God now.'

Mr Kovacic had taken both women's hands as they'd sat in silence. Their heads bowed. A triumvirate of sorrow.

You were still in the doorway. You'd loved Mr Yee, but you didn't feel part of this.

To have lived with someone for 40 years and lost them; to have your strong husband confined to a wheelchair – these sorrows were outside the confines of your life. Tragedy had breathed a long, slow breath on their lives and all you could do was bear witness to their grief.

Now, out on the street, you look up at Will. He's still standing at the window.

'Yep, I know,' says Willow. 'He looks so innocent.' She grabs a poo bag from Porridge's lead and fills it with pieces of the hair dryer. Mrs Kovacic leans further out the window.

'Right,' you say. 'So, who else is home?'

'Just Dad. Charlotte was using the Airwrap this morning. It's really improved her curl.'

'Right. And your dad wouldn't have seen Will throwing this Dyson Airwrap out the window?'

'He has to lie down a lot,' says Willow.

'Come on,' you say. 'Let's go and see what happened.'

Porridge is not happy. You pull his lead towards the foyer, but he's having none of it.

'Come on, Porridge,' you say.

He lies down on his side in the middle of the pavement. You long for the likes of Trixie, the small Pomeranian cross who could be scooped up and carried. You would even tolerate putting your small dog in a coat and giving him his own Instagram page if it meant you could pick him up.

You fish out a dog treat and wave it in front of Porridge's nose. 'Come on!' He turns his head away.

'I guess I'll have to go home and save Will,' Willow says. 'Dad won't be happy.'

Willow strikes you as a child who has endured much in her short life. You look into her future and see her ticking off the days until her 18th birthday when she can march out of her parents' home and start life on her own terms.

You want to warn her. There's no new start. There are new people, a new bedspread, a new kettle, different meals, different voices saying, 'Hurry up, I need to use the bathroom,' but you, you remain yourself.

You travel with yourself to your new flat. You are there when you put the key into the lock. You are there at night when you crawl into your new bed you bought with your new credit card. It's your thoughts that wake you in the night. It's you who stares into the half-darkness because someone left the hall light on. It's you who crawls out of bed in the cold dawn to tut at the waste of electricity, only to find your flatmate sitting on the floor with a half-empty bottle of wine in one hand and her phone in the other.

'What is it?' you say.

'I thought he was it,' she says.

It is you who takes the phone from your flatmate and sees the picture of her boyfriend with his arm around someone who is not your flatmate.

It is you who says, 'I never liked him.'

'Kat,' Willow is now saying. 'Porridge won't get up.'

'Apparently he was an assistance dog,' you say.

Willow looks down at Porridge lying on the pavement.

'I guess he wasn't very good at it.'

You are both standing there looking at Porridge when Michael's car rounds the corner. One of Porridge's ears twitches. The car pulls up next to you and Michael gets out.

'Hi,' he says. At the sound of Michael's voice, Porridge leaps up and runs to the car. 'You still need a key?'

'No thanks,' you say. 'Mrs Kovacic let me in.'

'I've bought you a coffee.' He hands you the coffee, kisses your cheek, bends over and pats Porridge's ears.

'Hi,' says Willow. 'I'm Willow. I'm not at boarding school yet, but now I'm not sure if I'll even be able to go because my brother just threw Charlotte's Dyson Airwrap out of the window. It's expensive. Kat has to go and investigate it.'

'Hi, Willow,' he says. 'Who threw a what out of where?'

'Don't go there,' you say to Michael.

Mrs Kovacic reappears at her window.

'Mickey!' she calls. 'Curse cause object to fall and nearly kill Kat and Mrs Hume's handsome nephew's daughter.'

You roll your eyes.

'It's Michael, not Mickey, Mrs Kovacic,' says Michael. He turns to you. 'How about I take Porridge for a walk?'

'He'd love that,' you say.

'You recovered from the scam?' he says.

You shrug. 'Still feel like an idiot.'

'You're not an idiot,' says Willow. 'Will is an idiot.'

Michael takes your hand. 'It's true,' he says. 'You are not an idiot.'

Michael levers Porridge into the back of the car and starts the engine. Porridge has already climbed into the front seat by the time the car pulls away from the kerb.

'Is he your boyfriend?' says Willow, following you into the foyer and up the stairs.

'Yes,' you say.

'Will you marry him?'

'I don't know,' you say. 'Do you think I should?'

'You may as well,' says Willow. 'He seems good with dogs.'

Willow opens the door to Mrs Hume's flat.

'Dad!' calls Willow. 'Will threw Charlotte's Dyson Airwrap out the window.'

The handsome nephew comes to the door. Willow hands him the plastic bag and walks past him.

'He did what?' he says, looking into the bag. 'What is it?'

You lean in and peer into the bag. 'It's the hair dryer,' you say.

'What hair dryer?' he says.

'It's not just a hair dryer. It's the Dyson Airwrap,' calls Willow.

'And he threw it out the window?' the handsome nephew says.

You grimace. 'Yes,' you say. 'It nearly hit us.'

He turns back into the flat. 'Will! Come here!' He picks a piece of the hair dryer out of the bag and examines it.

'Not the $700 hair dryer, is it?' he says. He looks directly at you. His good looks knock you off kilter again.

'It nearly hit us,' you say.

'She's going to want this replaced,' he says. He turns into the flat. 'Will! Come here.'

Willow answers. 'He can't hear you; he's playing a game.'

'Do you have one of these?' he says, holding the bag up.

'Um, no,' you say.

'A $700 hair dryer. Ridiculous,' he says.

'It was $800 down to $700,' calls Willow.

'Also, dangerous,' you say. You stick your hands in your pockets. 'It could have hit myself or Willow.'

'Anyway,' he says. 'That's a year's pocket money he won't be seeing. Thanks, Kitty.'

'Kat.'

'Yep, thanks Kitty Kat,' he says and shuts the door.

You trudge back downstairs, knock on the Kovacics' door and let yourself in. Mrs Kovacic is in the kitchen now, making pasta. You sit at her kitchen table and pull a bit of the hair dryer out of your pocket. You run your finger along it.

'What did father say about hair dryer out window? He agree is curse?' says Mrs Kovacic.

'No, he did not agree is curse.'

Mrs Kovacic purses her lips. She starts cutting the pasta with extra precision.

'There is more things than meet the eye in this heaven and earth,' she says.

'Yes, but we know it was the boy. We saw him at the window.'

Mrs Kovacic shrugs theatrically.

'I guess I should go home,' you say. You head for the front door.

'Bye, Mr Kovacic,' you call out.

As you're leaving, you hear Mrs Kovacic say, 'The curse getting stronger every day, that the problem.'

'Superstitious nonsense. People cause problem, not curse,' says Mr Kovacic. 'Look at trouble I had with Mr Crow.'

Since the stroke, Mr Kovacic's life has closed in on him. There is the lounge room, the view from the window and the slow and never-ending parade through his mind of the injustices heaped upon him by Mr Crow, his boss. He turns the scenarios over and over, finding transitory satisfaction in reconstructing the storylines. In his imaginings, instead of standing mute across the desk from Mr Crow, clever retorts spill from his mouth. He sits, relaxed, his arms crossed behind his head, and his still-functional legs propel his feet upward until they rest on the corner of Mr Crow's desk. He sees the renewed respect on Mr Crow's face; respect tinged with fear.

The reverie is broken by the barking of the stupid dog across the hall.

'Mia,' he calls, 'bring me a Coke and tell Kat she need to take Porridge to dog obedience school.' He tries to return to the pleasant daydream, but the moment has passed.

BELIEVING IS SEEING

Some people perceive tragic events as sad, random and deeply unfortunate. They grieve and then move on with their lives as best they can.

It's also a common human response to look for an explanation for the tragedy. We see this in many contexts. In the face of disaster, people will say things like, 'It's meant to be' or 'It's God's will'. These are understandable human responses to events that are outside our control.

The idea that we exist in a random universe where circumstances can change in a heartbeat is confronting. It is more comforting to imagine superhuman forces in play. These forces can be appealed to, opposed, avoided or railed at. Even if these forces are malevolent, this is preferable to them not existing at all; 'it's better the devil you know'.

We're inclined to believe what our tribe believes. Mrs Kovacic's tribe comes from Brač, Croatia, and has a history stretching back centuries. Her tribe is steeped in a belief that curses are causal in adverse events.

It's easy to look at Mrs Kovacic and think that her belief in curses is archaic. Still, for all of us, our sense of self, our very identity, is tied up with our tribe's beliefs. If you believe that events are caused by something from an unknowable realm, you're playing in the same ballpark as Mrs Kovacic – whether your beliefs are connected to a religion or a new-age sense of spirituality. You get to belong to a tribe of people who see the truth that the rest of us are unaware of. You are part of a population that understands there are things in play that are not of this world.

There is comfort in social tradition – in centuries-old beliefs that explain why seemingly random events are not random at all. To believe there are dark forces at work means you can employ strategies to combat those forces. You do not have to feel victimised by errant events outside your control. Instead, there is a pattern to the occurrences; and a pattern means, at some point, the occurrences will stop.

Mrs Kovacic's thinking is hijacked by motivated reasoning. This is where you decide what evidence to accept based on the conclusion you'd like to reach – just like Kat does when she agrees to take on Porridge despite evidence he is a tricky animal. If the conclusion you'd like to reach is that the flats are cursed, you'll search your internal database to support this belief and seek out people who are also of this opinion. You can then happily go on your way, safe in the knowledge that there is a reason things are going awry.

Confirmation bias is also in play. This is a bias we *all* fall prey to constantly. It ensures we only notice information that supports our position, and we discount data that is antithetical to what we already believe. In Mrs Kovacic's case, anything positive that happens is automatically discounted or not even noticed, but every negative occurrence in the flats is confirmation that a curse is at play.

Availability bias is a pervasive brain flaw where we rely on information that most readily comes to mind. As Mrs Kovacic grew up with people who believe in curses, it's the explanation she thinks of when something goes wrong.

Magical thinking is the belief that our thoughts or wishes will have some effect on the external environment. Mrs Kovacic puts a curse remover in Mrs Hume's pot plant to keep her safe. The fact that Mrs Hume is still alive proves to Mrs Kovacic that her magical thinking is working. Mrs Hume has indeed lived unharmed while the curse remover has been in the pot plant; however, this doesn't prove the curse remover is responsible for Mrs Hume's ongoing survival. Again, confirmation bias kicks in to confirm the curse protection technique is working.

It's accurate to say that errors of perception and reasoning travel in packs. They support and encourage each other. They enable and vouch for each other.

It's easy to look at Mrs Kovacic and judge her for her superstitious beliefs; but every time you touch wood or make a wish over a birthday cake, or avoid walking under ladders or stepping on cracks in the footpath, you're indulging in magical thinking.

What's Kat really like?

The way we see the world is a complex process. We do not simply look out into the world and make a clean assessment of what we see. Neuroscience now tells us that the way we see things is predictive. Our perception is like a mosaic of our past interpretations, experiences and feelings; what we see is a composite of these things.

We use heuristics – mental shortcuts – to enable cognitive speed. (The term 'heuristic' was coined by economist and cognitive psychologist Herbert A Simon.) An object shaped like a tennis racquet is easily identified as a tennis racquet, even if you've never seen that particular make of tennis racquet before. If we didn't have heuristics, we wouldn't be able to function. The downside is that heuristics mean we're assumptive about people. We make lightning-quick assessments of people based on obvious external factors that may or may not be accurate.

When you meet someone, your brain does a quick search of its database to come up with similar attributes in people you've come across before. These could include their voice, their haircut, their clothes, the vocabulary they use, the way they tilt their head or the curl of their lip when they smile. Your unconscious then throws all these impressions into a mixing bowl, gives it a quick stir and, without you being aware of the behind-the-scenes action, you have what we refer to as a gut reaction.

Now, gut reactions can, of course, sometimes be unerringly accurate. It's this dazzling accuracy in *some* situations that leads us to conclude that our gut reaction is accurate in *all* situations – but a lot of the time it's way off the mark.

Our intuitive response to situations and people has unfortunately been elevated to an almost mystical level. Women especially are sold the message that our intuitive response should be trusted – but this is a message sold without context or nuance. Gut instinct is usually based on previous experience – good or bad. Then confirmation bias kicks in, which doesn't allow us to consider the facts of the situation rationally.

It gives us a sense of control to think that we have a mental algorithm we can rely on to assess other human beings. Unfortunately, we don't. Willow interprets Kat. Kat interprets Willow. Kat makes an assessment about Willow's future based on her own past. Willow interprets what sort of person Kat is based on the films she's watched and people she's met during her short life. We are incredibly assumptive about people.

Why does it matter? Because assumptions are dangerous.

You may think you make considered assessments of who people are based on concrete evidence, but you don't. Think about the last time you met someone at a party or a work event. Chances are, afterwards you said something like, 'I met Evan; he was so nice,' or 'I met Evan; he was awful.'

The truth is, you have no idea who Evan is. Consistency bias is a cognitive flaw whereby, once we've decided what a person is like, we're likely to skew our thinking to support our original decision. If added information comes along that may challenge our initial impression, we are likely to discount it using confirmation bias to bring us back in line with our original impression. After all, being right and feeling we can trust our intuition is important to our sense of self.

If you've decided Evan is 'awful', you may miss the positive contribution that Evan could make to your life. If you've decided Evan is 'so nice', you'll probably interpret his motives in future interactions as honourable. You'll trust him, and this may or may not be in your best interest.

Label laws

Why do we care about labels? How do marketers get into our brains and convince us that we will be happier if we have the right shoes, the right sweatshirt, the right holiday, the right kettle, the right diet? I don't need to tell you we are bombarded with advertising. Our brains absorb it like sponges, and we unconsciously trust the people who are selling to us.

We are tribal creatures. Fitting in and having status is built into our DNA. There is a strong survival drive to be the dominant person. When I was in Switzerland recently I visited Château de Chillon, where the medieval duke once received his guests while lying in bed as a way of communicating his social standing. Nothing has changed. Being able to open your Prada handbag to retrieve your Montblanc pen while tapping the heels of your Louboutins fires off a part of the brain that is linked to survival.

Our brain is striving to ensure that we survive, that our genetic line is ensured. How does a $6000 handbag safeguard our genetic lineage? It doesn't. But we rely on parts of our brain that have been functioning for thousands of years to make sense of our new and complex world. Being able to show that we can afford the expensive shoes, the expensive house, the expensive car or the seat at the front of the plane sends a message to others that we are someone who matters.

Once we have bought the luxury item, confirmation bias kicks in. We need to justify our purchase. So of course the $1000 shoes were worth it. We can feel the quality as soon as we slip our feet into them.

These trinkets conveying status are also attached to our children. If we feel our children reflect ourselves, then it's important they attend the right schools, wear the right clothes and visit Aspen on their school holidays – all reproduced on social media so our social standing is verified, of course.

We also have a bias around loss aversion. Once we have a discount voucher in our grasp, we feel a strong desire to use it. If we don't use it, our brain feels we have lost something – as if the money really *was* in our pocket. It feels like wastage. Marketers play on our deep fears around scarcity, plugging in to our atavistic anxiety around dwindling availability. Competing for scarce resources was a reality in our deep, dark past; but our anxiety around loss is not so useful when we're driven to buy a $800 hair dryer for $700 just because we fear the voucher will run out.

The bandwagon effect is also huge in influencing our purchasing decisions. We *perceive* there to be social proof that an item has value if it has gained popularity. Just having been exposed to something increases the likelihood we'll want to own it, drink it, eat it or wear it. Once our visual cortex has perceived an image, it is stored in the brain; then, the next time we see it, it's familiar. Sporting brands spend buckets of money advertising their gear at sporting events for this reason. And of course, as every exhausted parent at the supermarket knows, it's a constant battle to combat the assault of junk food on children's brains.

IT'S A DYSON AIRWRAP

Lie detection

A curse on both your houses

Believing in curses, the universe giving you lessons or bad things coming in groups of three is your brain's way of making you feel there's order in the world. There's probably not. Believing in higher forces can muddy your cognitive waters and get in the way of you analysing situations with clarity.

I know who you are

Your brain makes lightning-quick assessments on who people are. You are clueless. That person could be the love of your life or they could be Melissa Caddick.

I have to have that handbag

No, you don't.

Lydia is the worst boss

On the days you work from home, you wake up later and later. Less travel time has encouraged more late nights watching Netflix and eating delicious snacks from the fridge. You regularly stumble out of bed at 8.25 a.m. to join 8.30 a.m. Zoom calls.

You hate your boss. You feel bad about this, but the truth is incontrovertible. You'd assumed working remotely would mean less contact with Lydia, but Zoom is like cocaine to her. It's given her unfettered access to you and your entire team at any tick of the clock.

This morning she has scheduled an 8 a.m. Zoom meeting with you and Darsha from HR to talk about your ever-diminishing team.

Your team is ever-diminishing because Lydia is so difficult. In your opinion. Actually, not *just* your opinion. Zac left last week. On his last day, you'd asked him what work he had lined up.

'I don't have anything lined up,' he'd said, 'but I'd rather be an actor than work here.'

'An actor?'

You'd found this to be an unusual example of a bad career. You'd always fancied the idea of treading the boards. You'd said this to him.

'Treading the what?' he'd said.

You'd realised Zac was only 24. 'Never mind. So, why not acting?'

'My parents are both actors. They've survived the last 30 years doing chicken commercials, and they're vegan. It's ugly.'

'Right.'

Now, on the Zoom call, Lydia asks you if you know why Zac left.

'I think he's gone to take up an acting career,' you say.

'Oh, that doesn't surprise me,' says Darsha from HR. 'Both his parents are actors. I went to school with his mum. She was in the last KFC ad. She was very convincing.'

'I did a few commercials myself,' says Lydia, 'but they were more modelling. If I were going to be an actress, I would have wanted character roles.'

'I think it is *actor*,' says Darsha.

'I'm sorry?' says Lydia.

'It's the non-gendered *actor*, not *actress*.'

Lydia thins her lips.

'Darsha,' she says, 'what is HR going to do about staff turnover? Clearly there's a problem with hiring. We've lost six people in the last two months.'

You see Darsha inhale and look down.

'We've been collating the exit interviews, and there seems to be a common theme,' she says.

Lydia looks directly at Darsha down the barrel of the camera.

'There seems to be a theme of team members feeling they're being micromanaged.'

'By?' says Lydia.

'Um,' says Darsha. 'By you, Lydia.'

There is a long, cavernous silence.

'What do you think about that, Kat?' says Lydia.

You tuck your hair behind your ear and do a rapid-fire calculation involving your moral courage, your desire to stay on the right side of HR, the degree to which your answer will affect Lydia's micromanagement, the amount of misery Lydia can create for you and the inconvenience of finding a new job.

'I think,' you say, 'in the current climate, as the business prepares to upgrade, the need for disruptive innovation will drive and leverage adjacent synergies, necessary as they are to ensure our deliverables are maintained. If modernisation means looking at our value-adds through fresh eyes, so be it. Not everybody gets that, though, right?'

Lydia nods at you. 'I think Kat's right, Darsha,' she says. 'It's a very disrupted space. Not everyone gets that. Maybe this could be made clearer in the onboarding process.'

Darsha looks at you. There is a slight twitch at the corner of her mouth. 'Of course,' she says. 'Thanks, Kat.'

'Anyway, Kat,' says Lydia, 'we're short on bodies, so it's all shoulders to the wheel until HR gets its house in order.'

'Sure,' you say, wondering how long you can avoid running into Darsha in the communal kitchen.

We'll meet again

When the pandemic hitched a ride into Australia, you packed up your desk, set up your computer on the dining table and switched on Zoom, not realising you wouldn't be turning it off for two years. In the beginning there was a sense of wartime camaraderie. While the chaps at the Home Office strategised in drawing rooms on how to fight the blasted thing, cigars clamped between their teeth, you and your team would bunker down in your shelters and fight the good fight.

The solidarity has long faded. Zoom has become a permanent feature of your work existence. You find yourself trapped in the early chapters of a dreary post-apocalyptic novella that should never have been published in the first place, and you suspect the end will be awful.

Lydia, however, was made for a global pandemic and its aftermath. A warlike footing meant the line between the end of the workday and the beginning of home time was non-existent.

Lydia, as the Executive General Manager for Corporate Affairs and Communications, works 24/7. In the hundred million Zoom calls you've had with her you've seen no signs of life in her home – except for an incredibly restrained bearded collie called Ghost, who has an unnerving habit of looking directly at the camera with his one blue eye and one brown.

Lydia considers it permissible to contact you by any device available. If you don't answer her email, she texts you. If carrier pigeons were available there would be one bearing Lydia's corrections in its little canister, tapping at your lounge room window. Constant phone pings and rings now punctuate your dinners with Michael.

'Hope I'm not interrupting, Kat,' she says.

She *is* interrupting. Michael is standing at the fridge, waving a tub of caramel ripple ice cream at you. You give him the thumbs up.

'All good,' you say.

'I texted Adele, but she is feeding dinner to her snake,' says Lydia.

Of course Adele is feeding her snake. Adele has no trouble saying no to Lydia. 'Just because Lydia works relentlessly doesn't mean we have to jump every time she calls,' Adele once told you. 'God, Kat, you're the worst pushover.'

It's easy for Adele to say. She has one of those straight-up personalities. She's the sort to tell an Uber driver to go the shorter way or to send back a tepid coffee. You do not send coffee back – half-concerned you'll look painful and demanding, half-concerned the barista will spit in it.

You want to apply for another job, but last time you asked Lydia for her support she was less than helpful. The conversation had taken place over a Zoom call. Lydia was in her home office, Ghost at her elbow. You'd been on the call for ten minutes before noticing you only had make-up on one eye. Porridge was still wet from lying in the pond at the park and had chosen to jump up on your lap in the middle of the call. He had barked repeatedly and knocked your tea off the table. Ghost had sat perfectly still, evaluating Porridge's Zoom performance.

'So, how are you going adjusting to life post-Covid?' Lydia had said, ticking off the mental health question.

'I'm fine,' you'd said. 'Though it's not really post-Covid, is it? It's going to be around for years.'

'Well, I don't know, Kat. I'm sick of thinking about it. We have to learn to live with it.'

Living with it. Saying that made it sound easy. You weren't finding it easy. You'd been having terrible headaches.

'That would be stress-related,' the doctor had said. 'If you're working from home, take breaks between calls. Once in a while, go and look out the window for a couple of minutes.'

Last time you'd looked out the window, a couple from the units across the road were having a massive row on the street. She threw a shoe at him. She was wearing two shoes, so she must have had an extra one secreted about her person, which you'd found intriguingly pre-emptive.

'Okay, so, you are coping well. Good,' Lydia had said. 'So, why do you want to apply for this new position?'

Your interest in moving to the Transformation team is due to working for Lydia being like working as a surgical nurse to a tetchy surgeon. You proffer Lydia the appropriate instrument, only to have her knock it from your hand, roll her eyes at you from behind her mask and select her own.

Last week, she gave you the task of simplifying the company value statements. You had shortened one of the sentences from:

We learn from our experience by evaluating the data, proposing hypotheses and testing through action.

To:

Evaluation of Actionable Data Drives Learning.

You'd wondered if capitalising the main words was overkill.

Lydia didn't like it. Her only comment: 'Simpler.'

What kind of feedback is that? What kind of *simpler*?

And then she was asking why you want to change positions. It was pretty simple.

'I'm passionate about change,' you'd said.

'My concern is that you might not meet the selection criteria,' Lydia had said. 'I think you should consolidate your skill base in your current position before you go off to Transformation. I'd like to see you working on not second-guessing yourself so much. Let's take Transformation off the table until you've got this position under your belt.'

Off the table? Under your belt? You'd wanted to scream at her: 'Your use of mixed metaphors is appalling!'

That was two months ago. Things have not improved. The work week is now seven days. Weekends are non-existent. She'd called you last week from a boat. You were in the cinema. She'd called you right at the climax. You had taken the call. In the background, you could hear the clinking of yacht rigging. Someone had asked, 'Another prawn, Lydia?'

Now it's Saturday night, 8.30 p.m., and you are in another unscheduled Zoom call with her.

You're drinking wine from a teacup.

'You're still missing the point,' she says.

You sigh inwardly. 'You said you wanted it in plain language,' you say.

The door behind Lydia swings opens and Ghost pads into the room.

'I'm going to bring Norbert in, just to get his input,' she said.

You don't want Norbert's input. Norbert has been at the firm for about 4000 years. Nothing is ever conservative enough for Norbert.

'Great idea,' you say.

'Okay, I'll get Mabel to book a conference call with the three of us for 7.30 a.m. Monday. Norbert likes an early meeting.'

Of course Norbert does. He probably needs an afternoon nap.

'Mum?'

A small head comes around the door. Lydia turns around.

'Mummy's on a call. Remember I told you if the door's closed, it means don't come in.'

The child – *Lydia's* child – reaches up and twists the doorknob.

'There was a noise.'

'It's the wind, Nathan.'

'I don't think so,' says the child.

'If you have to go, that's fine,' you say hopefully. 'We can reconvene on Monday.'

Nathan eyes his mother hopefully. 'Where's Dad?' he asks.

She looks at you directly. 'Well, that's another question,' she says.

Ghost shifts slightly and looks up at his mistress.

'Let's talk at 7.30 Monday. Expect an invite from Mabel.'

Poor Mabel. She was probably sitting down to *The Crown*.

'I could just text Norbert,' you say.

'It's okay, Mabel doesn't mind.'

'Mum?'

Lydia never exits Zoom calls; she just leaves the room. You watch her stand and move towards the child. There's the sound of a door banging somewhere in her house.

'It's all right, Nathan,' Lydia says, taking his hand. 'It's just the wind.'

Maybe she smiles at him; maybe she doesn't.

The door closes behind them.

You exit the call and drain the last of the wine from the teacup.

Your mental picture of a solitary Lydia dissolves. A child is now in the frame. And a father. An absent father? Absent this evening or more permanently? There could even be another child secreted in the house who will materialise at the door on another Zoom call, asking for juice.

Either way, Lydia has a family. And that, surprisingly, is one up on you.

THE BIG LIE OF EMPOWERMENT

An empowered workforce dripping with discretionary energy. That's the goal, isn't it? We want employees who understand their job description and are given the autonomy to enact it. However, far from being empowered, many employees struggle to wrest authority from their managers.

Empowerment has become little more than a husk of a notion.

The dictionary definition of empowerment is: 'The authority or power given to someone to do something'. It sounds obvious, but to give someone something you must let it go. If you are giving someone a gift, the moment you hand it to them you must release your grip.

This simple action of letting go, or not letting go, is at the centre of so much drama, churn and loss of productivity. It's the focus of a thousand backroom conversations.

Why can't managers let go? It's not as if empowerment isn't front and centre of their corporate values. They walk through foyers every day, past mission statements proclaiming customer-centric cultures fuelled by empowered workforces.

They can't let go because the structures under which they operate won't allow them to.

Lydia may well have a highly controlling perfectionistic character – but behind every perfectionist is a person afraid they're not going to do well enough. The thought of being perceived to be underachieving is like death to a perfectionist. So, who manages Lydia? How many performance reviews is she receiving a year?

Are they high-quality conversations? Because, if the person managing Lydia has low skills when it comes to giving constructive feedback, Lydia is going to leave her performance reviews feeling diminished and criticised without improved understanding of the impact of her behaviour – or, worse, under the impression that everything is going fine.

Lydia herself is unaware that she is driven unconsciously by her issues around control and perfectionism. She has post-rationalised her reaction to Kat's request.

We all post-rationalise constantly. We make an emotional decision in the unconscious part of our brain (the limbic system) then post-rationalise it in the conscious part of our brains (the prefrontal cortex). This is a quick, unconscious process, and being smart doesn't ameliorate the danger we're in from going with our gut response. In fact, having a high IQ often simply means our post-rationalisation sounds more convincing to ourselves and others.

Lydia genuinely believes her own justification for not supporting Kat. She thinks Kat is underconfident and won't back her own judgement, so moving to another area is premature.

Kat has a problem with power

Kat struggles to be clear and succinct in communicating her wants and needs. She is aware that she is intimidated by Lydia and feels unable to stand up to her, but how valid is this perception?

We humans are highly responsive to the unspoken power dynamics that are played out between us every day. We may not be able to exactly explain why, but some people intimidate us, while some people present no threat. In some relationships, the power imbalance is always present. One person is always dictating the outcomes. Other relationships are more fluid: the power balance moves back and forth. We're not consciously aware that we're responding to an unspoken power dynamic, because it happens in the unconscious part of our brain; but, before we know it, our conscious brain has justified the reaction we've had to the power imbalance.

This is what has happened to Kat. She is aware that she can't hold her ground, but she has justified her reaction. It feels right. In her mind she's just not the sort of person to push back. But feeling right is not the end of the story.

Kat needs to apply some critical thinking to her reaction to Lydia. She never gets beyond the fact that she can't hold her ground. She never questions why, or what she can do about it.

If she could eyeball the power imbalance with clarity, she might feel able to take back some of her own power for herself.

Authenticity, really?

If you find yourself in one of these situations where you're struggling to stand up for your wants and needs, look at someone else who can hold their ground and ask yourself how they do it. Kat observed Adele saying no to Lydia and put it down to Adele having a tougher personality. This is of course true to some degree, but the idea that we can't learn to incorporate new behaviours into our own personality is untrue.

We often hide behind the idea of authenticity. We are told to be ourselves. But who are we? Are we the same at the age of 20, 30, 40, 50? No, we're not. We grow and develop. We automatically adapt and adjust to our circumstances and environment. We can be deliberate in what we choose to incorporate into our personality.

The thought of saying no to Lydia makes Kat extremely uncomfortable. But in this situation, the feeling of discomfort should not be the arbiter of whether or not she holds her ground. This goes to the point of being able to discern which intuitive reactions should be listened to and which need to be questioned. Kat's feeling of discomfort is also fed by confirmation bias. She has never been good holding her ground, so why would that change? The instances in which Kat *has* held her ground are automatically discounted in her mind.

For Kat, the thought of ignoring Lydia's calls or telling her it's the weekend and she's happy to talk on Monday feels dangerous – but it's a feeling, not the truth. The only way through these situations is through them. Kat needs to sit in the discomfort, say no to Lydia and then notice that the world doesn't fall apart. Lydia is used to having Kat on tap. She may buck at the change in power dynamics but, once she gets the idea that Kat has boundaries, she may just well adjust.

Challenging the power dynamics, either in a one-off situation or an established relationship, is not easy but it's not impossible.

Lie detection

Hand me the reins, please

If you're being told that you are empowered to do something without being handed the authority to do it, lay down on the floor and have a tantrum.

No, don't.

But you can say, 'To be accountable for this, I expect to have the authority to make these decisions' (for example, expenditure, hiring locations, access to data, being kept in the loop).

Be reasonable and practical. Keep it simple without losing accuracy. Most delegation fails when there is ineffectual assigning of power.

And then ask, 'Please tell me, do I have authority over these things?'

Keep asking until it's clear. Don't buy the lie that you're telepathic, or such an empath that you can read your manager's mind about which decisions are yours and which are not.

The authentic self

Trying to be yourself is a road to nowhere. Which bit? At what age? In which context? Work on your critical thinking skills instead. It's a much better use of your time.

An accident with a wheelie bin

Porridge has been agitating for a walk. 'Okay,' you say, 'let's visit the garden. See if Amelia's laid anything.'

You notice that all the bins are out except for Mrs Hume's. It is still in the bin store, overstuffed with the added refuse of Mrs Hume's stylish relatives. You hear the rumble of the garbage truck.

You slide Porridge's lead up to your elbow and reach for the bin's handle. You give it a tug, but it won't budge. You grip the handle with both hands and give an almighty heave. It remains stuck fast.

'Come on, Kat.'

You give it all you have. The bin violently breaks free, frightening Porridge, who wrenches the lead from your arm and skitters out of danger. In the microseconds it takes for you to fall back, you drag the hard edge of the handle into your forehead. Before you know it you are lying on your back, covered in rubbish.

'Kat, Kat!' Mrs Kovacic has witnessed the incident from her flat.

You hear the garbage truck arrive.

The driver – 'Just call me Neville, love' – climbs down from the cabin and crouches next to you. 'Are you right?' Your eyeline is level with Neville's yellow steel caps.

Willow appears. 'Kat, you have literally saved my life. Aunt Lucy asked me four times to put the bin out.' She pulls a scrunched-up tissue from her Tommy Hilfiger trackpants and dabs at your face. The tissue comes away red.

'You'd better stay lying down,' she says, pushing you into the recovery position next to the bin. 'You're experiencing blood loss. You might faint. I did first aid at school.'

Your face is lying in a bed of tea leaves and orange peel.

A woman appears behind Willow, holding Porridge's lead.

'Are you okay?' she says.

Even through the tea leaves, you can see the woman is immaculate.

'I'm Charlotte,' she says.

'She's experiencing blood loss and may be concussed,' says Willow.

'I'm okay,' you say.

'Oh dear, Willow, give me a tissue please.' Charlotte speaks with the clarity and cadence of a BBC newsreader. She hands Porridge's lead to Willow, crouches in front of you and applies the tissue to your forehead. 'There's a bit of blood, but it doesn't look too deep.'

Mrs Kovacic arrives. 'Kat! Is she alive?'

'A bump and a little blood,' says Charlotte, 'but she seems to be alive.'

Mr Kovacic is at the Kovacics' window. 'She okay?'

'She okay,' calls Mrs Kovacic. 'She covered in rubbish, but eyes open.'

'Probably second-degree concussion,' says Willow.

'I'm okay,' you say.

'She's okay, Bartol,' calls Neville to Mr Kovacic.

'Thank you, Neville,' calls Mr Kovacic.

Mrs Kovacic eyes Willow and Charlotte.

'You Mrs Hume's niece? I'm Mrs Kovacic, from level 2.'

'Yes,' says Charlotte. 'Hello, Mrs Kovacic. Lovely to meet you at last.'

'This is Katrina,' says Mrs Kovacic. 'She also on level 2.'

'Katrina,' says immaculate Charlotte.

Mrs Kovacic turns her attention back to you. 'Curse in full swing. You lucky to be alive.'

'I'm guessing this is your dog?' says Charlotte.

'Yes,' you say. 'Thanks for your help, Porridge.'

'He was halfway down the street,' says Charlotte scratching behind Porridge's ear. 'Rather determined to get to a cocker spaniel, weren't you, fella?'

'Oh yes, that's Daisy. Half the street's in love with her,' you say. 'She must have some serious pheromone action. Honestly, she's not that attractive.'

Charlotte smiles compassionately. She probably assumes you have a head injury.

The scene is now expanding. People are sticking their heads out of windows. Another woman arrives and stands next to Mrs Kovacic.

'I saw the whole thing,' she said. 'I was on my way home from the shops when I looked up and saw her falling backwards. That's life for you. One minute you're putting out the bin, the next minute you've lost an eye.'

'I know, Riya, she lucky to be alive,' says Mrs Kovacic.

Traffic is building up behind the truck, which is blocking the road. Cars are beginning to toot.

'Keep your pants on,' says Neville in the general direction of the traffic. 'I'll take the bin, Miss. Looks like you've got all the help you need.'

'Bye, Neville,' calls Mr Kovacic. 'See you Thursday.'

'Kat,' says Charlotte, 'Come up to our flat. Let's clean your face up.'

'It's quite bad,' says Willow. 'Hope you don't scar. You're very pretty.'

You get to your feet. 'I'm okay.'

Charlotte takes you by the elbow. You climb the stairs to Mrs Hume's. Charlotte opens the door, guides you into the bathroom and closes the door behind you. You look at yourself in the mirror, pull some tea leaves out of your hair and wash your face.

The humiliation feels worse than the knock. To be found lying in garbage on the driveway, bleeding, having clocked yourself with a wheelie bin, was not how you wanted to meet Mrs Hume's stylish niece. You had wanted to hand her a glass of dry white over a perfectly set table while she complimented you on your canapes and the relaxed curl of your hair.

'Are you okay, Kat?' calls Willow through the door. 'If she's fainted, I'll pick the lock.'

'No, I'm fine,' you say, opening the door.

Willow takes you by the hand and steers you towards the couch.

Charlotte approaches with a cup of tea. 'Let me know if this is too sweet.'

She's pretty, but you can't tell. Her face is perfectly made up in the understated way you covet.

You put your hand to your face and feel the cut. You are ridiculously close to tears.

'I think Kat's going to cry,' says Willow.

'Willow,' says Charlotte. 'Be a darling and get the orange balm from my dresser.'

'On it,' says Willow.

'I'm not going to cry,' you say.

She sits next to you and touches a tear in the leg of your linen pants.

'If I was wearing those amazing trousers and I'd torn them, I'd be inconsolable.'

'They're brand new,' you say. 'I spent so long agonising over the colour, and this was their first outing.'

'Sob away.' She takes one of your hands. 'I'll light a candle and we'll have a requiem for your trousers.'

Willow returns with the balm. Charlotte dabs at your face with her perfectly manicured hands. Willow produces a thermometer and points it at your forehead.

'I nicked this from my old school,' she says. 'They took our temperature every day. It was stupid.'

'I don't think Kat has a temperature,' says Charlotte.

'Infection can cause a spike in temperature,' Willow says. 'We may need to immerse her in an ice bath.' She looks at the thermometer. 'Except we won't because she's 36.4.'

Charlotte raises an eyebrow and smiles at you.

'We can get those trousers invisibly mended. I'd kill to look that good in chartreuse.'

'You should lie down and elevate your feet,' says Willow.

The rising sob dematerialises before it has a chance to escape and is supplanted with an intense feeling of warmth.

Charlotte and Willow's ministrations are redolent of a long-forgotten childhood memory when illness kept you from school and you were allowed to stay in your pyjamas, drink Milo and watch TV.

'What's on TV?' you say.

'We don't have one,' says Willow. 'Aunt Lucy doesn't like them.' She picks up her phone. 'But look, Mrs Kovacic's friend has posted a TikTok of you and the bin. It's hilarious. Do you want to see?'

'Who's done what?' you say.

'Mrs Kovacic's friend.'

'Riya's posted a TikTok of me and the bin?'

'Wow,' says Willow. 'She's got good TikTok skills for an old person. You want to see?'

'No, I'm good thanks.'

The warm feeling is dislodged by humiliation.

'Poor Kat,' says Charlotte. 'Nothing's private anymore.'

'Time for me to go.'

'No, Kat,' says Charlotte. 'Stay as long as you like.'

'You've been too kind.'

'At least take the balm. It'll help prevent scarring.'

You trudge downstairs and re-enter your flat. Porridge greets you at the door with a sock in his mouth.

You sit on your couch, your hands dangling between your knees. You are bereft. You wish you'd stayed on Mrs Hume's couch. It's like you were in a basket of puppies and someone has picked you up by the scruff of your neck and tossed you outside.

You look up towards the ceiling, hearing Willow and Charlotte's footfalls. You long to be upstairs in the flat of healing balms and people who know that yellow-green is chartreuse.

You hear a key in the lock, and Michael enters.

'Oh god,' says Michael, 'what happened to your face?'

'I banged my forehead retrieving Mrs Hume's bin.'

He puts his backpack down and gingerly touches your forehead.

'That's a nasty bump. What's that orange stuff?'

'That's Charlotte's healing balm. It's going to stop it from scarring.'

'Your lovely face,' he says. 'What happened?'

You sigh. 'I had an accident rushing to put Mrs Hume's bin out. Willow had forgotten to do it.'

'And you were trying to save her from Mrs Hume's wrath.'

'I'm an idiot.'

'You're a community-minded heroine,' says Michael. 'That's what I love about you.'

'Do you?'

'Do I what?'

'Love me?'

It must have been the near-death experience with the wheelie bin that allowed these words to spill from your mouth.

'Oh, well, yes, of course I do,' he says.

You had imagined this moment. You thought it would happen on a romantic weekend, which Michael had organised without you showing him an article titled 'great last-minute getaways' on your phone. It would happen mid-hike on a clear morning, the mist rising through the valley. You would stop at a panoramic lookout to catch your breath and offer him a cheese sandwich you'd carefully packed. No, take out the cheese sandwich. Go back. You'd be at the panoramic lookout, pausing to take a breath, when he'd take your hand. 'I love you, Kat,' he would say.

In this scenario, you wouldn't have to ask him if he loved you after you'd given yourself a head injury.

'You've never told me.'

'I thought you knew.'

'Well, I do now. I love you too,' you say.

'Good.'

A sensation of lopsided happiness rises in you, a goofy sense of joy. You could roll around on the ground with your hand over your mouth laughing. This is not like being loved by The Hipster, which had a shining, glittery quality to it. That was an obedience trial of a relationship, with meaningless obstacles and scraps of reward for dutiful compliance. Michael loves you because you know Willow will be in trouble if the bins don't go out.

'Anyway, I met Charlotte,' you say. 'She was super nice. I'd like to live with her.'

'Okay... Porridge and I are going to run you a bath.'

It's while you're in the bath, with Porridge leaning his head on its lip, that your mind trawls over the morning's events of the day.

'Hey Porridge, guess what?'

Porridge cocks his head.

'Michael loves me.' He cocks his head in the other direction.

'Yes,' you say, 'I think Daisy loves you, too. She just can't quite find the words to tell you.'

Enter Mrs Belleri

The next morning there's a knock on your door. Before you can answer it, Mrs Kovacic opens it and ushers in a heavily bejewelled woman in her late 60s. It's winter, but the woman is mopping at her forehead with her handkerchief.

'This is Mrs Belleri,' says Mrs Kovacic.

'What happened to your face? That staircase is a killer,' she says, 'What's wrong with your lift?'

'It's out of order,' you say.

'You should fix it,' says Mrs Belleri, pushing past you into your flat.

Without asking, both women take up positions on your couch. Porridge is thrilled; he loves strangers. He leaps onto the couch and deposits his 40-kilo frame into Mrs Belleri's lap.

'I'm sorry,' you say, pulling him by his collar. He's immovable.

'It's okay, he likes Mrs Belleri,' says Mrs Kovacic.

'Yes, he likes me,' says Mrs Belleri. 'This is a good sign.'

'A good sign of what?' you say.

You're starting to wonder how you allowed this incursion to happen.

'When a dog comes to me and sits on my lap it's a good sign,' says Mrs Belleri.

You don't want to tell her that Porridge will sit on anyone's lap.

'So, what's this a good sign of?'

'Taking off the curse,' says Mrs Kovacic. She puts her arm around Mrs Belleri's shoulders proudly. 'She's cheapest and best.'

'Cheapest and best?'

'I just told you she take off curse. I happy to throw in some money.'

'What do you mean you'll throw in some money? Who's paying?' you say.

She looks at you. 'You are. The curse move onto you. Is causing you most trouble.'

'I'll give you a good price,' says Mrs Belleri.

'Look,' you say, 'Mrs Kovacic thinks there's a curse. I don't. She brought you here under false pretences.'

'What do you think caused your face trouble?' says Mrs Belleri.

'I fell trying to get a bin out,' you say.

'Yes, but why?' she says.

'It was stuck,' you say.

'It's not just bin,' says Mrs Kovacic out of the corner of her mouth. 'There's all the other stuff I told you about.'

'You think these things just happen out of the blue?' says Mrs Belleri.

'Yes.'

She shakes her head. 'Also, I can stop the Covid curse visiting the flats again.'

You sigh. 'Anyway,' you say, 'It was lovely to meet you. I was about to go and walk Porridge.'

'What if you're wrong?' says Mrs Belleri. She examines the ring on her right index finger.

'Well, I'll have to live with that,' you say. You go back to the door and get Porridge's lead. Normally this evokes a flurry of excitement, but now he just looks at you from Mrs Belleri's lap.

'How bad would you feel knowing you could have prevented it and you didn't?' she says.

'I don't believe in curses.' You lean forward and pat your knees. 'Come on, Porridge.'

'It doesn't matter what you believe. I can remove the curse and nothing more bad will happen,' she says.

You walk over to the couch and grab Porridge by the collar.

'So, you'll remove the curse, then nothing will happen. So, if nothing happens, I can assume it worked. It seems like you can't lose,' you say.

'Well, isn't nothing happening a good thing?'

The woman's convoluted logic is killing you.

'Yes, but how do I know it was due to you? What if nothing was going to happen anyway?'

You're trying to clip the lead into Porridge's collar. He's jiggling his head, making it difficult. Leaning over him has hurt your face.

'Porridge, settle down.'

Mrs Belleri leans over, takes the lead out of your hand, holds Porridge's face and clips the lead on his collar.

'Thank you.'

She folds her arms across her ample chest. 'You've had trouble with a man in the past. I see it.'

You roll your eyes.

'Wow,' you say. 'Media alert. Woman has trouble with man.'

'This man sleeps with another woman behind your back. You cry and ring his phone a lot. He takes your remote and tea set. You take him back, even though he's bad.'

'You've just described the story of pretty much every female over 25,' you say. 'Also, clearly you've told her everything about The Hipster,' you say to Mrs Kovacic.

Mrs Kovacic looks aghast at the suggestion.

'This man will come back to haunt you,' says Mrs Belleri.

'We're off,' you say to Mrs Kovacic. 'Let yourselves out.'

Mrs Belleri turns to Mrs Kovacic. 'She's impossible,' she says.

'Okay, Kat,' says Mrs Kovacic, reaching up and taking your hand. 'There's the passing of Mr Yee.' They both cross themselves. 'There's Mr Kovacic's stroke. There's the scam business. There's the near-death experience with the hair dryer. Then you were nearly killed by a garbage truck.'

'I fell,' you say. 'I was nowhere near the garbage truck.'

Mrs Kovacic tuts and turns to Mrs Belleri. 'She was nearly blinded,' she says. 'Charlotte, the angel from upstairs, saved her sight.'

At this point, Susan comes in through the window.

'This is a sign of the curse,' says Mrs Belleri. 'The cat knows.'

'This curse business seems to have a lot of animal involvement,' you say.

Mrs Kovacic is torn. She wants to stay on Mrs Belleri's good side, but she also wants to defend you.

'She good girl really. She just doesn't understand curse.'

'She'll understand soon enough. Something bad's about to happen to her,' says Mrs Belleri.

She picks up her handbag, rummages inside, pulls out a roll of lollies, takes one, puts the lollies back in her bag, pulls out her hanky and mops her forehead. Eventually she stands.

You go to the door and open it. Mrs Belleri lumbers across and out onto the landing.

'Fix the lift,' she says after descending two stairs, 'or I won't come back.'

Mrs Kovacic stands next to you, waving at Mrs Belleri.

Willow sprints down the stairs from Mrs Hume's.

'So?' says Willow. 'What's the curse-removing lady like?'

'She's a charlatan,' you say.

'Kat,' she says, pulling out her phone. 'It's a real thing. Curses have blighted humanity since the dawn of time.'

She shows you a picture of a medieval peasant with bats and frogs coming out of his mouth. A portly woman stands behind him, waving her hands above him while her eyes roll back into her head.

Susan wreathes herself around her legs. Willow bends down to pat her.

'And cats are very implicated,' she says.

'Hang on, your dad said you were allergic to cats.'

'Only allergic to curses. Anyway, I forgot, Charlotte sent these down.' She hands you a moisturising balm and a bottle of red. 'Charlotte said to use it twice a day. The balm, not the red wine.'

'That's very nice of your mum,' says Mrs Kovacic.

'Okay, but she's my step mum, like, not in an evil way, but in a fairy godmother way. Like, she's super cool. She bought me this.'

She pulls her wallet out of her pocket, unzips it and produces a MECCA gift card.

'Wow,' you say, '$100. What are you going to buy with it?'

'False eyelashes,' she says.

'Good plan,' you say.

'Are yours natural?' she says.

'So, where's your real mum?' says Mrs Kovacic.

'Yes, all mine,' you say.

'Wow, they're long,' she says. She turns to Mrs Kovacic. 'She died.' She zips the gift card back into her wallet.

'Oh,' you say, 'I'm so sorry, Willow.'

'Yep,' she says.

You look at her face, wondering what her mum looked like. You look at the slope of her nose, her wide, green eyes.

'Do you remember your mum?' says Mrs Kovacic.

'She died three years ago. Of course I do,' says Willow, slinging her bag over her shoulder. 'Her name was Laura, and she was a linguist.'

She stares at her phone. Mrs Kovacic puts her hand on her shoulder. She looks up.

'My mum thought food would fix everything. Will liked that. She would have loved Susan. I miss her, but Charlotte's nice.'

'She is,' you say, 'she's very nice. Anyway, you should ask your dad and Charlotte if they'd like to come and visit our community garden sometime.'

'Can I come too?' she says. 'Will there be food there? I can make haloumi dippers. We learned it in food tech. Anyway, I have to go.'

She throws her arms around you, then Mrs Kovacic.

'See ya,' she says. 'I'm off to MECCA.'

She trots down the stairs and you hear the foyer door closing behind her.

'I surprised,' says Mrs Kovacic. 'Her father looks like Christian. Maybe her mother who dies was Muslim?'

'Not Mecca the holy city; MECCA the make-up chain.'

'Why they call it MECCA?'

'I don't know. It would have been nice of Mrs Hume to let us know that Charlotte was the stepmother.'

'Yep. Now we put our feet in it.'

Porridge appears with a sports sock in his mouth and stands between you. He looks down the stairs. You lean on the banister. 'I wonder how her mother died?' you say. 'Please don't say it's the curse.' You rub your shoulder.

'Lucky I give you blue eye protection, otherwise garbage truck kill you. Curse knows no boundaries.'

You shake your head. Porridge barks.

'Porridge knows the truth,' says Mrs Kovacic.

He looks up at you, the sock dangling from his mouth. If there was ever a dog who knew less than Porridge, you'd like to meet him.

HELP, IS THERE A PSYCHIC IN THE HOUSE?

Mrs Belleri presents herself as the saviour of the flats. She is the traditional face of the scammer. Her technique may be more rustic, but she uses some of the same tricks that the modern-day scammer uses.

Just like 'Andrew' the eBay scammer, Mrs Belleri uses argument from authority. She speaks with certainty and conviction. This infers validity to what she's saying. Mrs Belleri has been sprung on Kat, but generally people approach a psychic of their own volition. If someone has approached a psychic, they want to believe – just like a person hoping that the financial scam they are flirting with will deliver on its promise. The person seeking out a psychic is complicit in the lie. They want to believe that the psychic has a hotline to the future and an explanation of the past.

Humans also come under the thrall of the Forer effect. The psychic will use generalities then make them sound specific. This is the same trick that astrology uses.[7] Think of the following phrases and how many people in your life they might apply to:

- You have had a loss in the past.
- You give a lot and feel that other people take advantage of you.
- You are tired.
- Sometimes you love company; other times you yearn for solitude.

- You don't suffer fools gladly.
- You are trusting, yet you have a sharp eye for the disingenuous.

Everything a psychic says is phrased in the positive. You are unlikely to agree that you're intolerant and bloody-minded when challenged, but you are likely to agree that you have firm views and defend them vigorously.

The list of attributes and past circumstances a psychic pronounces will apply to everybody, but the psychic describes them in such a way that we believe they have special insight into our lives. We like to be understood, admired and recognised, and to have our supposed qualities reflected back to us. We want to believe that there will be a positive resolution to our issues, and that there is a reason for our past problems. We want certainty, an explanation and some reassurance that there is a plan for our lives, and this is what psychics prey on.

Psychics use cold reading techniques to give the buyer the impression that they have a hotline to the other world. A person schooled in this technique can glean a great deal of information simply by observing the person's body language, the way they dress, their hair and the way they speak. They can obtain information by having a casual conversation with the person before they start the reading. People will often let on why they want the reading in this preamble chat. This disclosure is, of course, unconscious. The buyer is then amazed when the psychic uses high probability guesses to feed back to them what their issue is: they've had a close relationship with someone whose name starts with 'S'; they have recently lost their job; or a person with blond hair has bullied them. The psychic then watches the person's face to see if this is accurate. We all have micro expressions that cross our faces. We may not be aware of these, but psychics are extremely sensitive to them and use them to their advantage. If a micro expression appears on the buyer's face that tells them that 'S' is wrong, or they haven't lost their job, or a blond person has not bullied them, the psychic will say, 'Hang on, I am getting another message through,' and change their story. The buyer is, subconsciously, a willing participant in this process.

Then, our old friend confirmation bias will kick in. The buyer will leave the psychic reading only remembering the accuracies the psychic mentioned. As time goes on, the more glowing their memory of the experience will be.

Lastly, we are driven by motivated reasoning: 'I want this to be right so my future will be better,' or, 'I want the money I've spent to have been worth it, so it must be accurate.'

Kat, like all of us, has different vulnerabilities in relation to being fooled. She fell for the eBay scam but is on the money with Mrs Belleri.

Lie detection

Just say no to psychics

If you're tempted to go a psychic – or, worse, a psychic show – don't. Or at least understand what it is you are paying for.

Spanakopita

You are standing in the Kovacics' lounge room staring at a crack running up the wall.

'I've got one just like it,' you say.

'Soon we all be out on the street,' says Mrs Kovacic.

'Why will we be out on the street?'

'The repairs to building going to kill us. You heard what Mr Sanderson say. We all up for thousands.'

It has been a week since the strata meeting, and you still have no idea how you'll find the money. The meeting had been held in Mr Sanderson's lounge room. He's currently the Strata President – a title he relishes. Mr Sanderson is a small man in his 70s whose hair looks like it has been drawn on with a whiteboard marker. He favours Old Spice cologne and brightly coloured shirts depicting fish and bird scenes.

There had been about 20 people in the room. Mr Sanderson had addressed the other residents from his Jason recliner, his West Highland white terrier, Peanut, on his lap.

'Right,' he'd said. 'Let's get this underway so we can have a nibble and a tipple.'

You hadn't wanted a nibble and a tipple. His flat smelt mouldy.

'Shall I open a window?' you'd said.

'Not on your nelly,' he said. 'Unlike you high risers, you may have noticed I live on the ground floor. Theft is rife.'

'Who is going to climb in your window with 20 people in the room?' you'd said.

'Well, Mr Sanderson,' said Mrs Hume. 'The repairs to the building. How much are we up for?'

'The remedial work is agenda item two,' said Mr Sanderson. 'Agenda item one is animal behaviour. Molly, we've had a complaint about your macaw.'

'Adonis is a parakeet,' said Molly. 'Who's complaining?'

'I am not at liberty to say,' said Mr Sanderson.

'Mr Sanderson, we would appreciate an indication of the projected costs,' said Mrs Hume.

'It's you, isn't it, Mr Sanderson? You're the one complaining about Adonis,' said Molly.

'I'm merely passing on a message, Molly. Your macaw has been pushing things off the balcony and screeching. Repeatedly.'

'Susan pushes things off my bookshelf,' you'd said.

'He is not a macaw,' said Molly. 'Macaws are gigantic, destructive, furniture-chewing beasts. Adonis is a gentle bird and he's not screeching. He's asking for spanakopita.'

'Spanakopita?' said Mr Sanderson.

'He's rehomed,' said Molly, 'from a Greek family.'

'It doesn't sound like he's saying spanakopita.'

'It's his accent. The family was from Macedonia.'

Agenda item one is going nowhere.

'I rehomed Porridge,' you'd said.

What is wrong with you? you'd asked yourself. *Who cares if you rehomed Porridge? How does that get the conversation back on track?*

'Porridge isn't really a proper name for a dog, is it?' said Mr Sanderson.

'Why is it less proper than Peanut?'

'I would have thought that to be self-evident.'

'Mr Sanderson,' said Mr Kovacic, 'you can discuss animal issues after you tell us how many dollars we need!'

'Anyway, if we could ensure that all pets are responsibly managed to ensure the comfort of all residents,' said Mr Sanderson.

'What we up for, Mr Sanderson?' said Mr Kovacic.

'Mr Kovacic, I am merely following the agenda.'

Mrs Hume had stood up. You'd noticed she was holding Peanut.

'Mr Sanderson, if you don't tell us how much, right now, you may find you get up one morning and Peanut is missing.'

He'd smiled at Mrs Hume. 'I like a woman capable of making threats.'

She'd rolled her eyes.

'Item two. Cost of building remediation: $30,000 each.'

There was a silence. Eventually Mr Kovacic had said, 'Each as in *each*, or each as in *together*?'

'Each,' Mr Sanderson had said with some satisfaction. He'd picked up Peanut and put him on his lap. 'Alright, on to agenda item three.'

'How many more items are there to discuss?' you'd said.

'Twenty-three,' he'd said. 'I'm assuming you read the agenda, Katrina. I did send it to you.'

'Of course I read it, Mr Sanderson. I printed it out, memorised it and ate it.'

Peanut had barked.

'Keep that up, Katrina,' said Mr Sanderson, running his hand across his hair, 'and I'll get Mrs Hume to dispatch Porridge.'

'Who put him in charge?' you say to Mrs Kovacic. You're still looking at the crack.

'He is power hungry,' Mr Kovacic says as he rolls out of the bathroom. 'Like my old boss, Crow.'

Mrs Kovacic doesn't want to talk about Crow. 'Curse is causing concrete cancer,' she says.

'She stands at her sink, filling her kettle. She leans her forearms on the sink.

'I keep telling her, Kat, curse is nonsense,' says Mr Kovacic. 'All her friends from Brač, they all believe in rubbish.'

'Leave my friends alone,' says Mrs Kovacic.

'You're not from the same place?' you say.

'No, I grew up on the fifth floor. In Split,' says Mr Kovacic.

'You no better than us, Bartol. We all came over on the same boat. We all seasick together.'

'Too many people from Brač on that boat,' says Mr Kovacic.

'Where did they all go?' you say.

'Mona Vale,' says Mrs Kovacic.

'Okay, well, I'm glad you came to Sydney,' you say.

'How we going to pay for repairs, Bartol?' says Mrs Kovacic.

'I'll check the account after Kat has gone,' says Mr Kovacic.

'It's okay,' you say. 'You can check now. You want me to bring you your computer?'

'It's okay, later fine,' he says.

'His "account" is suitcase of money he keeps under the bed,' says Mrs Kovacic.

'I can hear you,' says Mr Kovacic. 'I have stroke, I'm not deaf. Anyway, where's my paper? And my Coke?'

Mrs Kovacic opens the fridge. 'Coke coming,' she says.

'I have to go,' you say. You cross the landing into your flat, wishing you had a suitcase of cash under your bed.

What will I wear?

Transformation guru Gabriel Randall has arrived from DeGreys. The first opportunity to behold him in the flesh is at a special executive leadership team meeting. Gabriel Randall has the relaxed charm of someone who has lived his life in R.M. Williams and whose father bought him a Land Rover for his 18th birthday.

He is 188 centimetres and speaks with a cadence that suggests unassailable self-belief. You hate him on sight.

Lydia has asked you to attend and take notes.

'Oh, okay. What will I wear?' you'd said. Lydia didn't get the joke.

'Just take notes,' she'd said. 'Just on matters relating to Corporate Affairs and Comms.'

At the head of the table, Gabriel Randall must have whispered something terribly funny in CEO David Firth's ear, because they are giggling like a couple of schoolboys.

'I am delighted,' says David, 'to introduce to you all the transformation guru himself, Gabriel Randall. Gabe, welcome to WorkWellbeingSure.'

'Thank you, David,' says Gabriel Randall. 'I am delighted to be here.'

David sits back in his chair and clasps his hands on his stomach. 'Gabe, what can the team expect?'

Gabriel Randall takes a moment. He makes meaningful eye contact with every person in the room.

'Team, there are three things you can expect from me,' he says. 'Authenticity. Accountability. Innovation.'

He lets that sink in.

Lydia speaks up. 'Gabriel?'

'Call me Gabe,' says Gabriel.

Lydia has never warmed to being corrected. She starts again.

'Gabriel,' she says, 'can you give us a sense of what is going to happen with the business? I'm sure you've formed a view on the priority areas.'

'Thank you, Lydia. Straight to it,' says Gabriel. 'I have no hard-and-fast plans for the business, yet. Today marks the beginning of my listening-and-learning tour. I plan to immerse myself in the operation and establish a guiding coalition before shaping a vision for WWS 2.0.'

'You must have some idea,' says Lydia. 'We've all heard about your success steering Zambitsy through Covid.'

'That's right Lydia. Zambitsy came through it very well. It came down to whether or not the business viewed Covid as an opportunity or a threat. I was firmly in the opportunity camp.'

Of course you saw it as an opportunity, you smug bastard, you think to yourself. *I bet you didn't have a Mr Yee in your life, who succumbed to Covid after 11 days.*

Lydia looks at him, her expression indeterminate.

'Lydia,' he says, 'every organisation is different, yet there are some reliable truths.'

Gabe clearly feels the repeated use of a person's name infers intimacy and a good working memory.

'Successful businesses are driven by customer-centric, accountability-first cultures. The goal of every business is to cultivate an environment where everyone does their best work; to have the right people in the right roles doing the right stuff at the right scale.'

Ralph Femio, Executive General Manager of Marketing, looks out the window, flicking imaginary lint off his pants.

Gabriel surveys the room with a benevolent authority. David flutters his eyelashes.

'What are you asking of this team, Gabe?' says David.

'I'm asking this team to get behind a journey of judicious right-sizing,' says Gabriel, 'to deliver optimal productivity while building a customer-centric, accountability-first culture.'

Norbert Hyems, the Chief Operating Officer, raises his hand. 'So, Gabe, are you talking about running leaner?'

'Potentially,' says Gabriel. 'Do you think this business could run leaner?'

'I think it could,' says Norbert.

'Do we need six floors of prime CBD real estate?' says Gabriel.

Lydia looks down at her hands, twisting her wedding ring.

Oh god, you think, *he's going to can the office space*. You'll be 100 per cent working from home. You'll never be able to escape Lydia's constant need to engage.

'Not everyone wants to work from home,' you say.

Lydia looks at you and narrows her eyes.

'Well, I don't want to do a spin class at 5 a.m. every morning,' Gabriel says, 'but I've signed up to the Peloton Challenge, so I do it.'

'Let me rephrase that,' you say. 'Not everybody works as well from home.'

'I'm sorry, what's your name?'

'Kat Mitchell,' you say. 'Internal Comms. I'm on Lydia's team.'

'Kat Mitchell, do you remember when hot-desking was introduced?'

'Yes, I do,' you say.

'We all resisted. "Where am I going to put my plant and photos? How am I going to concentrate without a permanent cubby hole?" Now it's just the way things are.'

'Hot-desking was a total—'

Gabriel cuts you off.

'So you don't want people to work from home,' he says, 'and you don't want them hot-desking. Perhaps everyone should have a corner office with a private butler.'

Everyone laughs except you and Lydia.

Gabriel smiles at you. 'I know your instincts are to keep our employees happy, which is admirable. I've been working with sales teams that have been hot-desking for three years. It's perfect.'

'I don't just want to keep our people happy,' you say. 'It's about being—'

'You are right to want to keep your people happy and productive,' says Gabriel. 'And the key to that is attitude. It's mindset.' He slows right down. 'It. Is. Culture.'

'Culture eats strategy for breakfast,' says Norbert.

Gabriel smiles at Norbert. 'Top of the class, Bert.'

Why is he calling Norbert Bert? Norbert is Norbert. Norbert *hates* Bert.

Except today. He's smiling broadly.

Gabriel is now sitting on the corner of the conference table. He turns his attention back to you. Damn Lydia for bringing you here.

'I know you use the Myers-Briggs tool,' he says, leaning forward, his forearm on his crossed knee. 'Do you know what your profile is? I've got a theory.'

Oh god. Myers-Briggs. You've done that workshop. What are you? You're at an executive leadership team meeting and you can't remember your Myers-Briggs type.

Ralph is looking at you. He nods imperceptibly.

'Um, I think I'm an AWOL or something.'

You look at Ralph. He shakes his head.

'No. No, I'm an ENPL.'

Gabriel gives a short, sharp laugh. David Firth doesn't get the joke but, regardless, joins Gabe with a giggle combined with a shake of his head.

'Okay,' he says, 'getting closer, but there's no L in Myers-Briggs.'

'L is the *learning* type, isn't it, Kat?' says Lydia. 'You've always been a good learner.'

'You, Kat Mitchell, are an INFP,' says Gabriel, straightening up and crossing his arms across his chest.

'Right.'

'Of course, there's no right or wrong with personality profiles. INFP. You're a Mediator. You strive to make the world a better place, which is incredibly valuable.'

'That's true,' says David. 'You do.'

This is the first compliment you have ever received from David Firth – or, in fact, from anyone at WWS. Lydia has never suggested the way you see the world is valuable. Maybe you hate Gabriel less than you thought.

'Hot-desking might work in sales, Gabriel,' says Lydia, 'but it's never worked for Corporate Affairs and Comms.'

'And you would be our ISTJ,' says Gabriel. 'The Inspector.'

'The Inspector,' says David. 'That's you to a tee, Lyds.'

'And our CEO,' says Gabriel, 'is an ENTJ. The Commander,' says Gabriel. He nods at David. 'Proud of you, mate.'

David looks like he's about to cry. 'Thanks, mate.'

'And that, ladies and gentlemen,' says Gabriel, 'is gratitude. That's the culture we want to instil. You want to know about direction, Lyds – can I call you Lyds?'

'Lydia is fine,' says Lydia.

'No worries, Lyds, that's the culture that we're building, and mindset is key. Let's circle back on all of this once I've completed my listen-and-learn.'

'Great idea, Gabe,' says David. 'Welcome to the team.'

'Hear, hear,' says Norbert.

Ralph packs up his computer, winks at you in a conspiratorial way and exits. Lydia leaves without a word. You pack up your computer and head for the door.

Gabriel is waiting for you. He opens it and walks out with you.

'I hope I didn't talk over the top of you,' he says.

What are you meant to say to this? Of course he talked over the top of you.

'No, all good.'

'I'm just the new kid on the block, and I'm sort of excited.'

'Well, I guess that makes me a local gang member.'

'Uh oh, is there some sort of ritual initiation?'

You're unsure of his tone – if he's being flirty or just trying to appear more approachable. Whatever; it's not working.

'Anyway, Kat Mitchell, Comms. David Firth tells me he's struggling with the ingrained negativity in the culture, and I'd like your input.'

'Shouldn't Lydia be part of this conversation?' you say, looking down the hall to see if Lydia is in earshot.

'Kat Mitchell, we have an absolute burning platform. I prioritise progress over hierarchy any day.'

'Okay.'

'Right, so I've said to David, to heal the dysfunctional, disengaged culture he speaks of, we're going to pilot a positivity program – something that incorporates mindfulness, gratitude, mindset, that sort of thing. See if we can turn the ship around. Get some serious wellness happening.'

'Okay. I think the negativity may have something to do with everyone being exhausted after the pandemic. It's been year after year of uncertainty.'

'Yep, I hear you, but you're talking about the past. It's time we support people to take control of the now.'

'Right.'

'It's the only thing we can control. I want Comms and HR in the pilot workshop, and I want you to tell me what you think.'

'Right.'

'Champion, expect an invitation to the workshop; and also, you need to put some neem oil on your face.'

'Excuse me?'

'Some neem oil. For that cut on your forehead, it'll help with the healing. It's Ayurvedic.'

'Right,' you say, pulling your fringe over the scab. 'Just so you know, my vision of the next six months does not include losing half my team.'

His phone rings and he takes the call. 'Billy, my man, wassup dawg!' he says. 'How's it hanging, my brother?'

You stand in the corridor for another minute, wondering why white men have to talk to each other like they're doing drug deals on the mean streets of Chicago.

WHAT'S WITH ALL THE MEETINGS?

Poor Kat. She has lurched from one unsatisfying meeting to another. Human beings seem to reserve some of their most irritating behaviour for meetings. And we have *so many* of them. How often do we hear the words, 'I can't get back to you until the end of the day. I'm in back-to-backs'?

I wonder, how many of these 'back-to-backs' result in progress made? The fraudulent promise of meetings is that, by bringing interested parties into the same room, you make progress. It's possible this happens, but unlikely. So, why do we spend so much time in unproductive meetings, and what can we do about it?

Without discipline, people will speak about whatever is relevant to them – their *perception* of the agenda. This is because agenda items are often open to interpretation. We look at life through an autobiographical lens. This includes our perspective on work issues. People are often infuriated because their perspective is not being considered or discussed. This relates to the illusion of transparency. This error of perception leads us to assume that, because our emotional and intellectual perspective on an issue is so obvious to us, it must be to other people. Of course, it's not. They are too involved in their own perception of the issue.

To achieve the best possible outcome in a meeting, everyone should be aware of what they're going to discuss before they arrive. All meetings should be preceded by a written agenda of clear, unambiguous questions to be addressed. Note I've said *questions*, not *statements*. Once the agenda items are phrased as questions, disagreements will arise. Disagreement is too often perceived to be obstructive, which sends people into passive, defensive or aggressive behaviour. Disagreement is not obstruction. It's the opportunity to explore the different contexts from which people address the issue being discussed.

The meeting owner should pre-consider the differing perspectives that will likely arise from the questions and be prepared for the potential querying and debate. They should decide on the importance of each agenda question and start with the most pressing first. As is the way with so many minor bureaucrats, Mr Sanderson frustrated his fellow residents by insisting on discussing the 'macaw' issue before the more salient question: the money required for the building remediation.

Myers bridge too far?

There's a lot to unpack with Gabriel. I deal with corporate speak in another chapter; first, I'd like to look at psychometric testing – specifically Myers-Briggs, which is still widely used.

A lot of psychometric testing is fundamentally a lie. People's careers and decisions are being based on loopy made-up non-scientific frameworks.

Myers-Briggs, if you're interested, was created by Katharine Cook Briggs and her daughter Isabel Briggs Myers. Both dabbled in writing fiction and opinion pieces before turning to human personality and behaviour. They based the tool on Carl Jung's psychological testing. Myers-Briggs is not called a test; it's called an 'indicator', which saves it from needing any robust psychological analysis.[8] The mother-and-daughter team had a kind motivation for creating the tool: to help women evaluate their strengths when entering the workforce during World War II. As most women had been homemakers up to that point, Myers and Briggs thought a tool would help to ease them into jobs that were new and possibly intimidating.

Myers and Briggs then tried to sell their model as a psychological tool, but psychologists – realising there was no scientific validity – were not interested. However, those working in the early incarnations of management consulting were. In the 1940s Isabel Briggs was working at a consultancy in Philadelphia. The consultancy sold the tool to big organisations for a number of different purposes. It was primarily used to evaluate candidates in the interview process, but it was also used as a self-assessment tool for CEOs – and, astoundingly, by insurance companies to assess whether they should charge people with certain profiles higher insurance premiums.

In the 1980s its use exploded. Business was suddenly extremely invested in the tool. The big Wall Street firms bought into the notion that people's personalities were highly relevant to how they would fit into business. ESTJs (Extroverted, Sensing, Thinking, Judging) are supposedly brimming with confidence, so this particular profile became a marketing tool for self-promotion.

In fact, Myers-Briggs measures precisely nothing – but it's still a multimillion-dollar industry, with organisations using it to test potential and current employees. In her book *The Personality Brokers*, Merve Emre says the tool was even used by the CIA and the US military.[9]

And yet there is zip evidence supporting its relevance or accuracy.[10] You can get a different outcome when taking the test twice only hours apart. Some of the 'psychological preferences' that are set up as polarities, such as sensing or intuiting, are not: you can absolutely have a tendency to both sense and intuit.

So how did we get here? There are a number of biases at play. First is consistency bias. Once we have started doing something – in this case, using the tool – we convince ourselves that it must be useful. Our brains are strongly disinclined to change course.

Then there is social norming. We are social creatures. If the tribe does it, and the tribe has been doing it for a substantial period, it must be right. We assume that, if a tool has been used in a widespread fashion for an extended period, due diligence must have been conducted. Myers-Briggs has the benefit of the bandwagon effect, whereby we do something primarily because other people are doing it. We understand humans have herd mentality in more basic situations, like whether our eyebrows should be thick or thin – but it can occur just as readily in the upper reaches of the corporate world.

There is also nothing more delicious to us than being able to claim an identity: I'm a Capricorn, I'm an empath, I'm an ENTJ. Some identities are benign; but if hiring decisions are made and teams constructed according to Myers-Briggs types, that's a problem.

'Don't take my MB type off me!' I hear you say. 'I like being an ISTJ.' If you feel it validates some part of your personality and you find comfort in that, fine. It's just good to remember that saying you're an ISTJ is in the same ballpark as saying, 'I'm a Pisces.'

Halo. Halo. Halo.

Gabriel is living the halo-effect life.

It goes like this. You've seen an actor in a film or on TV and then they appear in a commercial, spruiking a product. Let's call the actor Roxanne Rowe. Roxanne's promoting a wellness supplement. You think, 'I really liked her in *Avengers: Annihilation*. I'm going to buy me one of those curcumin detox kits.'

The reason you're more likely to buy Roxanne Rowe's detox kit is that you're under the thrall of the halo effect. Because you admire someone in one context, you assume they have the goods in another. An employee arrives from Apple or Google and everyone assumes they're going to be a valuable addition.

Good looks can also lead us to come unstuck. Gabriel is running the halo effect trifecta: he's good-looking, tall and brings the aura of a highly successful consultancy with him. We are incredibly biased around height. We subliminally assess tall people to be smarter, more talented, more charismatic and better leaders.[11]

If someone is good-looking, we assume they're going to be a good, decent, intelligent, caring person.[12] I probably don't need to tell you how incorrect this assumption is. I offer you Ted Bundy as evidence. (No, I'm not saying all good-looking men are serial killers.) Good looks mean zilch when it comes to decency. Unfortunately, however, our brains under the thrall of the halo effect do not acknowledge this incontrovertible truth. Add a glass of wine to this brain bias and we're in serious danger of making an inaccurate assumption.

Lie detection

Make a meeting work, always

Unless an agenda of questions has been circulated, don't go to the meeting. You have the best excuse now. Practise saying this: 'Sorry. I didn't get an agenda of focus questions.'

You can use a button in Teams to reject meetings, they tell me. I don't know how to do that, but I believe it's possible.

Imagine how much extra time you'll have to drink coffee and eat croissants.

Identity theft

Don't let your need for an identity put you in a box you don't belong in.

Don't let your halo slip

That good-looking guy at the end of the bar could be a running a charity for the homeless, or he could be running a Ponzi scheme. Either is possible.

7

Mr Yee's garden

You are walking en masse to a nearby allotment that locals have transformed into a community garden. Will pushes Mr Kovacic's wheelchair ahead of you, Mrs Kovacic and Charlotte. Michael, Alec, Mrs Hume and Willow are bringing up the rear.

Charlotte, who looks like someone who never lets carbs pass her lips, is wearing jeans and a half-tucked white shirt. You've previously tried the half-tucked look but have only succeeded in looking half-dressed. Charlotte has insisted on bringing champagne.

You are delighted by the bond that seems to be emerging between Mr Kovacic and Will. Even though you are yet to hear a word from Will, he seems to have taken to the role of Mr Kovacic's lieutenant.

'They get on so well,' you say.

'Yes, perfect for each other,' says Mrs Kovacic. 'Will never talk, which means Mr Kovacic can bang on. Works for me, too. Less chitter-chatter when he get home.'

'It's a big adjustment for Will,' says Charlotte, 'but he's doing rather well, I think.'

'How are you, Shallot?' says Mrs Kovacic.

'Just marvellous,' says Charlotte. 'I love it here.'

Alec puts his hands on Charlotte's shoulders. He is deeply tanned, wearing a white polo shirt. The two of them look like they have just stepped off their private Mediterranean yacht. He smiles.

'Her name's Charlotte, not Shallot,' he says to Mrs Kovacic. 'A shallot is a vegetable.'

Mrs Kovacic looks mortified. 'Oh, I'm sorry,' she says.

'It's okay, Mrs Kovacic,' says Michael. 'I thought Charlotte was a cake.'

You think you register irritation on Alec's face. You are quietly mortified. What is wrong with Michael? He sounds gauche, unsophisticated. You can forgive Mrs Kovacic. English is, after all, her second language, but why would Michael say he thought Charlotte was a cake?

You wish he wasn't wearing the t-shirt that says, 'I might look like I'm listening to you but actually I'm thinking about buying more chickens.' When he first wore it, you'd said, 'You don't own chickens; and not only is that t-shirt intensely daggy, but the statement is stupidly long.' He'd frowned and looked down at the t-shirt. 'It was a present from my sister,' he'd said by way of defence.

Willow runs to the fence. 'This is totally sick,' she says. You follow with Mrs Kovacic and Mrs Hume.

'We had a garden at school. We grew Japanese turnips,' says Willow. 'I hate them. Why does this sign say Mr Yee's Garden?'

'Mr Yee was a very kind man,' says Mrs Kovacic. 'After stroke, Mr Yee push Mr Kovacic down here every day. He show him how to grow bok choi and snow peas. Then Mr Kovacic get better. Also better for me. Mr Kovacic was huge sorry sausage to live with.'

'Where is Mr Yee?' says Willow.

'We lost him to Covid,' you say.

'And, no doubt, the curse,' says Mrs Kovacic. 'It was second strike.'

'Oh, that's so sad,' says Charlotte. 'Did he have a wife?'

'Yes,' says Mrs Kovacic, 'she is my friend. Mrs Yee comes to garden still, even though she lives in God's waiting room.'

'It's not God's waiting room,' you say. 'It's assisted living.'

'Same thing,' says Mrs Kovacic.

'Maybe don't mention it to Alec,' says Charlotte. 'He's sensitive about Covid.'

Willow turns to where Gail and Amelia, the head honcho chickens, are scratching ruminatively in the dirt. 'I love the chickens,' she says.

'Amelia ready for the pot,' says Mrs Kovacic.

'Why would you say such a thing?' says Mrs Hume. 'Amelia is laying well. When I get too old, would you put me in the pot?'

'You already past it,' says Mrs Kovacic.

'What's over there?' says Willow.

'That's the old bowling club room,' says Mrs Hume. 'Willow, you are standing on what used to be green number one, where I won the 1997 club championship.'

Willow looks to the fence east of the plot where the vacant building sits.

'This place is brill. If you had that bit of land, too, you could have more plants and horses and goats and alpacas and llamas. I can ride horses. I learned at school. We could have a riding school. I could teach kids with autism on the weekend. It's really good for them.'

'Right,' says Mrs Hume. 'That sounds very altruistic, but don't get your hopes up. There's talk the whole area is about to change.'

'What you mean?' says Mrs Kovacic.

'There's a proposal before council to redevelop the site,' says Mrs Hume. 'Premium townhouses.'

'Awful,' says Michael, appearing beside you with some lemons he's plucked from the tree. 'More stock for the Airbnb market.'

'That's disgusting,' says Willow. 'No one cares about the autistic kids.'

'Arm of curse now reach to take away our garden,' says Mrs Kovacic. 'Nothing safe.'

'I think it's more the arm of developers,' you say.

Charlotte turns to look at you. 'With the rubbish out of your hair, it is magnificent. I bet it falls like that naturally.'

'I don't know,' you say. 'I thought the tea leaves gave it texture.'

'Michael,' says Mrs Hume. 'I saw your car parked out the front of the flats. Be careful you don't get booked. It's been over an hour.'

'How do you do it, Mrs Hume?' you say. 'Your mind is like a steel trap.'

'Willow,' says Mrs Hume. 'Let's see how close we can get to the clubhouse.'

'Cool,' says Willow, and they head towards the fence.

'Your aunt is amazing,' you say to Charlotte.

'I'm giving her supplements,' she says. 'Should keep her well and dementia-free for as long as possible. Who knows, maybe she'll get a letter from the Queen.'

'King,' you say.

'Oh yes, of course. King.'

'It's a shame the Queen couldn't get her hands on some of your supplements. She could have sent herself a card.'

Charlotte's very smooth forehead moves imperceptibly. A slight furrow appears between her eyebrows. You worry she is a staunch monarchist and you've upset her. She is British, after all.

'Not that I don't think the Queen is terrific,' you say. 'Or *was*.'

She smiles at you. 'It's alright, Kat. Signs are the monarchy may have had its day.'

You breathe a sigh of relief.

'Can I have some of these supplements?' says Mrs Kovacic. 'I beginning to look as old as Queen.'

'You look amazing, Mrs Kovacic,' says Charlotte, 'but I will get you some very special face cream. It takes ten years off.'

'Ten years,' you say. 'I'd like that.'

'Ha, you look 12!' says Charlotte. 'Alec tells me there was a near miss with my Airwrap. I'm so sorry.'

Will is levering Mr Kovacic's wheelchair down the path between the broccoli and the spinach. Alec calls to him. 'Will, I don't think you've properly apologised to Kat.'

Will keeps walking.

'Honestly, it's fine,' you say.

'She had bigger fish to fry with the garbage truck nearly killing her,' says Mrs Kovacic.

Alec follows Will down the path, grabs Will's arm and drags him over to you.

'Will would like to say sorry, properly,' says Alec.

'Alec, darling,' says Charlotte, 'I think Kat's moved on.'

Will looks at you, his expression indecipherable. He nods.

'Thank you, Will,' you say. 'It's totally fine, but thank you for such a nice apology.'

Alec smiles broadly, releases Will's arm and ruffles his hair. 'That's my boy,' he says.

No wonder the child doesn't speak. You know bullies. You lived with The Hipster.

'Hey, Will,' calls Mr Kovacic, 'I need your big strength to pull this one up.'

'Can I help?' says Michael, and he and Will troop over to Mr Kovacic.

Charlotte pours champagne into Mrs Hume's crystal sherry glasses. 'So, Kat, besides having incredible hair, what other talents do you have?'

'Don't know about talents, but I have a job, a dog, a cat and a boyfriend.'

'Not in that order of importance,' Charlotte says. Charlotte watches Michael. 'He seems lovely.'

'He is,' you say. You feel guilty about wishing he wasn't wearing the chicken shirt.

'How did you meet?'

'We met when I was climbing over a balcony to escape my old boyfriend.'

'Oh my god!'

'I was hanging off the edge of a balcony with a Great Dane breathing in my face. Michael saved my life.'

'Mickey is good boy,' says Mrs Kovacic.

'How far were you off the ground?' says Charlotte, quaffing her champagne.

'First floor. I was saved by Michael and a conveniently placed wheelie bin.'

'What is it with you and wheelie bins?' Charlotte throws her head back and roars with laughter.

'Curse of the wheelie bins,' says Mrs Kovacic, which makes Charlotte laugh even harder.

You don't know if it's the champagne or the winter dusk, but you suddenly feel intensely happy. You look around the allotment. Mrs Hume and Willow. Mr Kovacic, Will and Michael. Mrs Kovacic, Charlotte and the handsome nephew. For a moment in time, everyone is smiling. You surprise yourself by clutching Charlotte's arm and leaning into her.

'Welcome to the flats,' you say.

'Right,' says Mrs Hume. 'Time to go home.'

'Who'd like turnip soup?' says Mrs Kovacic.

Michael bravely raises his hand. 'Love some.'

Poised for positivity

You are sitting in a semicircle of colleagues from Corporate Affairs and Communications and HR. Lisbeth, Sarah and both Ryans are chatting with Darsha and Chen, the new girl from payroll. Meredith and Timothy have been released from archives and are sitting drinking tea at the back of the room. You look over at Adele; she is scrolling through posts on what looks like a subreddit about snakes.

Lydia sits at the end of the row, looking like she's waiting for medical results. Barry the dog is sitting at the front of the room in a shopping trolley, propped up on cushions, one paw hanging out, breathing heavily. He is accompanying Michelle, the trainer who is running this 'Poised for Positivity' wellness session. Gabriel Randall has insisted that everybody attend Michelle's session, as positivity seems to be in short supply.

'Barry is joining us today,' says Michelle, scratching him under his chin, 'because there is a lot of research that pets help to relax you. They lower blood pressure and increase happiness. Though we don't need research to tell us that, do we, Barry?'

Barry looks disinterested in whether he's helping lower anyone's blood pressure. Also, Michelle must have decided her natural voice is too shrill for a wellness environment, as she's layered some whispering over the top. She is difficult to hear.

'So please, over the course of the session, take advantage of Barry's presence and give him a blood-pressure-lowering pat. Dogs are also very good at helping you develop a positive mindset, aren't they, Barry?'

Barry emits a low sigh.

You hope she isn't going to address too many more comments to Barry. You find people who spend large portions of their conversational capacity talking to their dogs dispiriting. Your discussions with Porridge are of a different calibre. Barry is some sort of ancient bulldog-cross-staffy mutt. His general demeaner doesn't really speak 'positive mindset', but he's clearly been around for so long that retrenching him would be cruel.

Michelle more than makes up for Barry's lassitude.

'We're all aware that WorkWellbeingSure has a strategy to upgrade and modernise the business. The only way we'll get there is by building our customer-centric, accountability-first culture.'

'I've heard about it,' says Chen, the newish girl.

'To build that culture, we are going to unleash your undiscovered superpower.'

Adele looks at you and twists her mouth.

'And that superpower is gratitude. So, let's start in a positive frame of mind. In situations like the post-pandemic environ we find ourselves in, it's easy to focus only on the negative – but today's the day we're going to break that habit. Who's with me?'

There are a couple of desultory murmurs.

'Come on, we can do better than that!'

'I'd like to break that habit,' says Chen.

You don't think Chen has a negativity habit to break, but maybe it's her enthusiasm for these sorts of programs that has fuelled her perky positivity.

'In the pre-work,' says Michelle, 'you've been asked to fill in your gratitude diaries.' Michelle lovingly holds up one of the said diaries: an exercise book decorated with grateful cartoon characters hiking up a pastel rainbow.

'Let's open our diaries', says Michelle, 'and take the next few minutes to pause and reflect on our entries, adding anything that we're grateful for since our last entry.'

You open up your book. You have three entries:

1. *Woman at David Jones make-up counter said I had even skin tone.*
2. *Michael cleaned up Porridge vomit.*
3. *Not pregnant.*

You look over at newish Chen. She's just asked Michelle for a second book as she's already filled in the entire first book. You see she has small, neat writing. You wonder what she has to be so grateful for. You'd heard she has two small children and her husband lost his job months ago.

Later, at morning tea, Adele corners you near the coffee pod machine.

'I'll be grateful when this program is over so we can get back to work,' she says.

'Me too,' you say.

'Also, doesn't Chen drive you mad?' she says.

You shrug and insert a coffee pod into the machine.

Adele tears open an individually wrapped mini quiche. 'I knew what she'd be like on day one, when she brought her own gloves and bleach to clean the kitchen.'

'Oh yes, I remember.'

'She was here till 7.30 last night, apparently, so who's looking after her kids? I won't even leave Emma alone for too long. She frets.'

'How do you know?'

'She won't acknowledge me. Gives me the cold shoulder. Snakes are very loyal.'

'Snakes don't have shoulders.'

'It's a metaphor, Kat.'

Michelle rings a bicycle bell and you reluctantly reconvene.

'Thank you, everyone. On the board I've written some positive qualities. In your triads, discuss the qualities you believe you bring to your job.'

Oh, this is going to be good, you think to yourself. Your position in the semicircle puts you in a triad with Adele and Lydia. Michelle notices this combination has resulted in an awkward silence. She steps forward to facilitate.

'Why don't you start, Kat?' says Michelle.

'Okay. I'm a Mediator.'

Adele makes a low grunt. Lydia looks at you and smiles tightly.

'That's great,' says Michelle, beaming at you. 'That's a really good, specific, positive quality.'

'I think the other side of being the Mediator is a tendency to sit on the fence,' says Lydia. 'To avoid saying what you think. Maybe that's just me. I'd be interested in Adele's perspective.'

Before Adele can offer her perspective, Michelle cuts in.

'To be a Mediator is a wonderful quality,' she says. 'It helps you see the positives on both sides of the argument.'

'What if there *are* no positives?' says Adele.

'There are always positives,' says Michelle, 'if you look for them. Even in challenging life events, you can find the positives. When you can find the positives, it enhances your resilience and compassion.'

'What about the pandemic?' says Adele. 'What was positive about that?'

Oh god, you think to yourself. *This will provoke Michelle to talk about quality time at home and cooking sourdough from your own starter.*

But no. She throws the question back to the room.

'Who can think of something positive to come out of the pandemic?'

All you can think about is Mr and Mrs Yee. This was supposed to be their time in the sun. The pandemic robbed them of that.

There is a long silence. Eventually, Chen says, 'Well, I have enjoyed more quality time with my kids. I have been able to take an active role in their education.'

You look at Chen. You secretly agree with Adele. You find Chen irritatingly perfect. She is uber efficient and never wears rayon, and you suspect she styles the back of her hair for Zoom meetings. She has photographs of two perfect children on her desk. They're both at selective schools.

'Great, Chen,' says Michelle. 'Anything else?'

There is an even longer silence.

'We fostered a cat,' says Ryan Kraft.

'Right, great,' says Michelle.

'People died,' says Adele. 'People got sick. People lost their jobs. In what way is that positive?'

'Well,' says Michelle, 'those people aren't here, so I can't ask them.'

'The fact they're not here would have to be a negative thing for them, don't you think?' says Adele.

'I'm not saying bad things don't happen,' says Michelle. 'What I'm saying is you can view them through a positive lens. It's our *response* to the situation that causes our unhappiness, not the situation itself. At the end of the day, we can't control what's outside ourselves, but we can control our attitude.'

Adele rolls her eyes.

'Also, how do we know that being retrenched didn't open up other possibilities for those people? Wellness is multifaceted, and one important pillar is a resilience mindset. If you develop a positive attitude to this pandemic, you'll be prepared for the next.'

Michelle looks pleased that she's successfully pivoted the conversation.

'It's a once-in-100-year event. I'll be 132 by the time the next one happens,' says Adele.

The muscles around Michelle's mouth tighten. 'Well, there'll be other events that living through the pandemic will prepare you for.'

'I'm finding lots of positives,' says Chen. 'I'm finding the gratitude diary really helps.'

Adele rolls her eyes and mouths to you, 'Told you she's a pain.'

'That's fantastic, Chen,' says Michelle.

Michelle then launches into a well-practised monologue about her own 'Positivity Journey'. She was a bookkeeper when the company she was working for enrolled her in a positive thinking workshop.

'It was the best afternoon of my life,' she tells the group. 'It set me on my wellness journey. Actually, it was the best afternoon besides my wedding. Though when I think about it, they were neck and neck.' She winks.

'Gee,' whispers Adele, 'must have been a crap wedding.'

After that one workshop, Michelle had packed up her books and opened her corporate training company: Poised for Positivity. Her laptop cover and phone feature matching unicorn branding.

'In times like this, when we're all challenged, it's good to be able to develop a mindfulness practise,' Michelle says. 'To find a way to be present in the moment and not project into the future or ruminate about the past. Being negative is easy. Who would like to wake up in the morning feeling refreshed and ready to meet the day – regardless of what's going on in your life? It is possible.'

Michelle had hit her persuasion sweet spot. We were all now picturing ourselves climbing enthusiastically out of bed, flicking on the kettle and calmly but purposefully striding out to meet the day. Adele looks at me and crosses her eyes.

Michelle produces a bag of raisins, offering one to each of us. 'Now, in the spirit of remaining in the present, I'd like you all to shut your eyes and hold this raisin in your mouth. If your attention wanes, just gently bring it back to the raisin. Avoid swallowing the raisin. Just *hold* the raisin. Be present with the raisin.'

You begin quite well. You instruct yourself not to swallow the raisin but to roll it around in your mouth, exploring the texture of it with your tongue. However, as Michelle had forewarned, your attention begins to wane. You bring your mind back to the raisin, but not swallowing the raisin has turned into a mammoth task. You *have* to swallow the raisin. It's beginning to feel enormous in your mouth. If you don't swallow it, you may die. You sneak one eye open to see who else is struggling with this simple task when a noise like a drowning person taking in their last desperate breath rents the room.

You open your other eye. Chen is doubled over, holding her ankles, like she's in a brace position on an aeroplane.

'Chen,' you say, moving to kneel in front of her. 'What's wrong?'
You pry her hands from her ankles.
She looks at you.
'I don't want to be in the present. I don't like it.'
'Okay.'
'They've cut my hours.'
'Right,' you say. 'That's very tough.'
'By two thirds. My position may not last the month.'
'Right.'
'I swallowed the raisin,' she says.
'That's okay,' calls Michelle. 'They're organic.'
'I know. I did too. It's very difficult not to,' you say.

Chen looks back over her shoulder and puts her hand to her neck.

'He's gone,' she says, very quietly.
'Gone? Who?'
'Ray,' she whispers. 'Ray. Ray.'
'Gone? Like *gone* gone?'
'Yes, he left us. Four months ago.'
'Oh Chen. No.'
'Ray's left you? Oh my god,' says Adele. Adele has hearing like a bat.

Adele stands and turns to Michelle. 'Spin this one, Michelle. Chen's husband's left her during a pandemic. Work is cutting her hours and she has two small children. Are you behind on the mortgage, Chen?'

'Yes.'
'And she's behind on the mortgage,' says Adele.
'I don't know if that's helping, Adele,' you say.

Adele moves behind Chen and puts her arms around her neck.

'You and the kids can stay with me, Chen. If they're frightened of snakes, I'll put Emma in the cupboard. She's very understanding for a python.'

Michelle tries to wrest control back.

'I'm not saying that what's going on for Chen isn't terrible,' she says. 'It sounds unimaginably hard, but nothing stays the same and everything is an opportunity for growth. We just don't know it at the time. And isn't it a good idea to have stress management techniques when you're under stress?'

'Yes, yes,' you say.

Adele snorts.

'Maybe,' says Adele, 'they could cut the wellness programs and use those funds to give workers more hours. More money would be better for Chen than rolling a raisin around in her mouth.'

'What can we do to help you, Chen?' you say

'I would like to pat Barry,' says Chen.

Michelle extricates Barry from his trolley and puts him in Chen's lap. He growls at the disturbance. You can't help thinking that a Labrador puppy would better represent a positive mindset.

'We were going to get a dog,' says Chen, scratching Barry behind the ears, 'but with Ray gone...'

You look at Michelle. You wonder if this counts as a bad day for Poised for Positivity. You wonder if she will take Barry home and say to her husband that people are difficult and demanding and resistant. That maybe she should have stuck with the bookkeeping.

Maybe her husband will pour her a glass of merlot and reassure her she's on the right path. Or maybe he'll say, 'I told you so,' and go back to watching *Border Security*.

Who knows what goes on in people's lives?

The room is silent. A semicircle has formed around Chen. She is staring into the middle distance. We all look at her. We have collectively lost our nerve. Our positivity has faltered because calamity has entered the room. She is a palpable presence. She is sitting in the corner, filing her nails, wondering who to point her finger at next.

Michelle packs up her bag and puts Barry back in his trolley.

'I know today was difficult,' she says, 'but a positive mindset steers us through life. I'm so sorry to hear about your situation, Chen. I hope everything turns out for you. We all deserve to have a happy, well life.'

She walks to the door, smiles tentatively, then pushes Barry's trolley through and closes the door behind her.

She is a nice and decent woman.

You hope husband number one is waiting for her at home.

WHAT ACTUALLY IS WELLNESS?

Nobody is quite sure what wellness actually is. It certainly sounds appealing. Wouldn't we all like to be well? Adele has an intensely negative reaction to the positivity workshop. Is there any validity to her standpoint?

These programs, led by soft-voiced practitioners encouraging us to 'be in the moment', are proliferating like mushrooms across corporate training rooms and, thanks to Zoom, people's lounge rooms. But what are leaders actually trying to achieve by offering these programs? Like so much in the overcrowded canon of corporate speak, wellness and her offspring mindfulness have crept into our communications – but we haven't examined what we're actually talking about.

Ostensibly, we're talking about stress reduction, learning to manage our anxiety, sharpening our focus, improving our productivity, showing resilience in the face of challenge, living mindfully and focusing on the here and now. These are all valuable skills but, as with everything, context is king and oversimplifying is unwise. People and their anxiety, depression or stress are without a doubt complicated, especially in this post-pandemic environment.

The problem with the wellness approach is that there's a strong implication that our response to the situation is causing our misery, not the situation itself: that the problem is our attitude.

Really? Tell that to the woman with a toxic manager who feels unable to report him to HR. Or to the senior executive who's juggling childcare while turning up to 7 a.m. meetings with her male team members for whom childcare is not an issue. Or to the young lawyer working 75-hour weeks because that's the way it has always been done. Or the call centre operator who goes home every night to a domestic violence battlefield.

Should we be encouraging them to cope better, or should we be challenging the social underpinnings that create the stress in the first place? Managing stress is of course an extremely helpful skill to develop, but care should be taken that an undue amount of responsibility is not allocated to employees' internal responses to stress, rather than addressing the underlying workplace stressors.

Gratitude practices are correlated with increased satisfaction and happiness, but there is no current evidence that they lower stress or anxiety. The philosophy itself has value but, in the hands of women who tend to be submissive, it can mean pasting a layer of gratitude over a deep well of trouble. Twisting yourself in knots to be grateful instead of looking at your situation with clear-eyed pragmatism is wildly counterproductive.

I don't think wellness sessions are always deliberate attempts by employers to whitewash workplace stress, but it's worth talking about how we arrived at corporate wellness and mindfulness, what it is and whether it actually works.

The answer to that, by the way, is: we don't know. Wellness is so amorphous and broad, we don't actually know what it's made up of. There's a lot of anecdotal reporting that mindfulness is almost miraculous in its healing benefits, but the hard evidence is lacking.[13] The hype has leapt ahead of the science.

Things such as mindfulness and meditation have value, I'm sure, but it's the packaging, the overpromising and the monetising that has begun to smell. Sure, if mindfulness wants to buy you a drink after a hard day at the office, go for it; however, if she offers to sit with you till closing and solve all your problems over a bottle of scotch, I'd move down the bar.

In focusing so much on helping people manage their stress we are missing the opportunity to investigate and perhaps ameliorate the issues, inequalities, ideologies and flawed systems that cause the stress in the first place. Flawed systems are the main offenders. We're trying to optimise our businesses while we're weighed down under obsolete methodologies and questionable ideologies. If we're not going to address the conditions in which they operate, is it fair to help people to adjust and better cope with those stressful conditions?

This is very salient for women; we're already bombarded with unhelpful messages about acceptance and gratitude. We don't need more motivational maxims. We need to ensure our workplaces are uncompromisingly safe, equal and stimulating.

If you find mindfulness or meditation works for you, that's great. Just be aware of the hyperbole from the intensely flexible practitioners sitting in their yoga pants in all their clear-skinned gorgeousness. Are they really going to make you well, or are they unwittingly encouraging compliance – urging you to shut down your natural resolve to right the wrongs you encounter?

Chen and the raisin

Chen gets up Adele and Kat's noses. Adele has a negative gut response the first time she meets Chen, then confirmation bias kicks in to confirm what she already thinks. First impressions can be disastrously wrong, as we addressed in chapter 3. It's an example of how heuristics – mental shortcuts – can get us in strife.

Kat could recognise that Chen irritates her. She could realise she is in the grip of a spurious unconscious bias about impossibly neat and organised Asian women (Marie Kondo, anyone?). But she doesn't. Adele's commentary aids and abets Kat's faulty *perception*. In the thrall of these cognitive errors, Kat misses the possibility that Chen is under pressure and perhaps her perfectionism and relentless positivity is a coping mechanism.

There is a flaw in our perception when it comes to evaluating negative behaviour in other people. It's called primary attribution error. Listen up; it goes like this. If you are late or angry, you forgive yourself. You understand your own circumstances and why you're late or angry intimately. You are late because your dog vomited in the car on the way to doggy day care. You are angry because you've left six messages for your ex-husband and he refuses to pick up.

If somebody else is late or angry, you are not privy to the background or their circumstances and, therefore, put their behaviour down to a character failing. They are late because they are disorganised. They are angry because they can't control their emotions.

Kat assumes Chen's behaviour is a character flaw instead of a situational response. The lesson is: if you have a strong emotional reaction, whether it's positive or negative, you need to put it on ice until you can analyse the situation with some accuracy.

By the way, primary attribution error is an absolute corker in your intimate relationships. Your behaviour is understandable. Look at the pressure you're under! Your partner's behaviour, however, is a character flaw. Very disappointing.

Lie detection

Well, well, well

The word 'wellness' is now everywhere. Ignore it. It's on the tissue box I'm currently looking at. Really, my tissue is going to make me well?

The community digs it

If there's one in your area, join a community garden. They're wonderful. Or, even better, start one yourself.

How good are margaritas?

You are up at Mrs Hume's having a margarita with Charlotte in the kitchen. Your dream of stylish margarita-drinking neighbours has materialised. It's 5.15 p.m. on a Wednesday – only 45 minutes before permitted drinking time commences.

'They didn't make you suck on a raisin, did they?' says Charlotte. 'I went to a wellness retreat once. All the women were trying to lose weight. I was very thin at the time. They all thought I had cancer, and they were still jealous. I had to share a room. I would lie under my duvet at night looking at my phone and drinking scotch. My roommate reported me. They came and tried to take my scotch off me. "What's your problem, Melissa?" I said to my roommate. "It's for your own good," she said.'

'Snitch,' you say.

'I snuck to my car that night. Went to the next village and booked into the pub. The landlady served me up a stew and a Guinness. It was the best meal of my life. I left the scotch on Melissa's bed with a "see ya" note on it. I worried later she might have been there for alcoholism.'

'I have a friend who went on a wellness retreat where you fast for five days. You get bone broth. That's it. It was $5000 a week.'

'What's $5000 a week?' Alec comes in the door.

'Just a retreat a friend went on,' you say.

'Don't get any ideas, Charlotte. We can't afford it. Also, did you buy a $500 dress?'

'Yes,' she answers, winking at you. 'But it was on sale, down from $1000.'

'Charlotte, we can't afford it. I had another call from the car finance guy. He was really unpleasant.'

She opens a bag secreted in a cupboard and shows you the dress.

'It's okay,' she calls out to him, 'I took it back.'

Your eyes widen.

'Anyway, you want a drink? I'm just pouring another one for Kat.'

'No. Isn't it a bit early? I'm going to have a lie down. Stop shopping.'

You hear the bedroom door shut.

'Anyway, another margarita, Kat? And don't worry, we totally *can* afford it. He grew up with a mother who knew ten different ways to cook mince. He's never adjusted to the reality that things are good now.'

'What happened to Alec's first wife?'

She leans on the kitchen bench, pulls her hair into a ponytail and clips it.

'She caught Covid. It was the first wave. She didn't look all that sick, then she suddenly passed away. Terrible. She was 43 years old.'

'No!'

'Yes. Alec was devastated, as were the children. '

'No. God.'

'They were incredibly happy. Apparently, she was lovely. It happened early in the pandemic. She was one of the first young ones to die.'

'Oh god.'

'Yep. She was terrified of them all getting it. She used to disinfect the groceries before they were allowed in the house.'

'Fair enough. We didn't know then how it was transmitted.'

'Well, she was an anxious person, quite fearful, before the pandemic. She must have been off the Richter once it hit. Don't think that helps.'

'How do you mean?'

'Well, I think your state of mind has something to do with it. It's not the whole story, obviously.'

'Something to do with what?'

'Something to do with whether or not you get sick or die from Covid.'

'Huh?'

'Obsessive worrying doesn't help anything. That's all I'm saying.'

'Mr Yee was the most optimistic person I've ever met. It took 11 days to kill him.'

'I just think being negative and fearful doesn't help. We know stress lowers your immune system.'

It's a microbe, you think to yourself. *How's your emotional state going to affect that?*

'Our health is complicated. Mind and body are interconnected. How positive you are, how fit you are, the food you eat – it all affects whether you allow disease into your body,' says Charlotte.

'Allow disease?'

'Anyway.'

The front door opens and Will appears. He puts his school bag on the dining table.

'Hi, baby boy,' says Charlotte.

He goes to the fridge and pulls out a Coke.

'Say hi to Kat, Will.'

He looks at you and raises a hand.

'Is that the best you can manage?'

He shrugs and leaves the kitchen.

'Well, that will have to do.'

'I was a shy child,' you say.

'Well, there's shy and there's Will. Alec has taken him to every child psych. They say he has social anxiety. Traumatised by losing his mother. Trauma seems to be the new black. My wondrous childhood came to an abrupt halt and I don't have social anxiety disorder. Everybody has some bloody disorder these days, don't they?'

'Well, I get a bit anxious,' you say.

She makes a dismissive gesture with her hand. 'Well, you'd never know,' she says, 'so, go you.'

You make a quick mental note to never share your anxious thoughts with Charlotte. This sets you on a labyrinthine quest through your friends and acquaintances to examine who you might have shared your anxieties with, and who may be now be sitting in judgement of you.

'Why an abrupt halt?'

'Pretty average story. I lived the high life with my parents, went to the best public school – what you'd call private school. Best parties, best holidays, until Dad laid his eyes on my mother's tennis coach. He left us. Had a brand-new family. My mother fought him to keep the house, which she did, but he completely cut off the funding.'

'How old were you?'

'Twelve. Guess what the tennis coach's name was?'

'Tiffany.'

'Oh my god, how did you know?'

'I guess it fits the whole clichéd nightmare. Did she have a blonde ponytail?'

'Yes! Of course she did.'

You both laugh and high five each other.

'So, my poor mother, who was born with a silver spoon in her mouth, had to, for the first time in her life, work out how to survive.'

'How did she?'

'We opened up the house to tours. I didn't mind it so much – being an only child, I quite liked the company – but my mother is not designed to collect tickets and make scones.'

'Wow.'

'Anyway, it made me completely self-reliant, and determined. I will not be making scones for strangers at 50. Anyway, enough of the pity party. Do you like these jeans?'

She holds her phone in front of you.

'Yes, I do, but they're $700.'

'Yes, well, look at the cut.'

You look down at your own jeans. You bought them on sale at the mall. You like them because they're soft and stretchy.

Charlotte pinches the fabric. 'Aunt Lucy wears these. I'd be anxious too if I was getting about in elastic-waisted jeans. What are you, 80?'

She hands you another margarita.

'I don't know, it's 5.56. That will be two drinks before 6 p.m.'

'Oh, for god's sake. What are you going to do? Sit about in your elastic trousers and wait for six o'clock to have a sherry?'

You both roar with laughter.

Demiurgic

The following day you're wishing you'd been more judicious with the margaritas. Lydia instructs you to rewrite WWS's values statements in the morning. You barely limped through an afternoon of aimless meetings by drinking an organic version of Red Bull that Lisbeth swears by. You're preparing to escape for the day when Gabriel launches himself out of the lift and bounces across to your desk.

'So, how was the workshop?' he says. 'Feeling grateful?'

'It was very positive,' you say. 'The group was—'

'I've got a job for you,' he interrupts.

'Right.'

'I'm about to email you a presentation.' He looks over his shoulder. 'Very confidential. Entitled "Pathway to Success". I want you to WWS it.'

'Right.'

'It shouldn't take long. Basically, swap out the Zambitsy logo for WWS, change the dates on the timeline to next year, change the colours and the fonts, change the title to "Roadmap to the Future" and change the subtitle to "Our Digital Upgrade". Change "Our Manifesto" to "Our Creed"; "Horizons" to "Cycles". So, "Cycle One", "Cycle Two", "Cycle Three".'

God, you think. 'Right.'

A tinkling sound emanates from Gabriel Randall's pocket. You think it might be his phone until he produces a pair of enamelled balls that he rolls around in the palms of his hands.

'These are Baoding meditation balls – my own personal wellness app,' he says, in answer to a question you didn't ask. The tinkling sound is affecting your bladder.

'Lydia said you'd been working on the values?'

'Yep.' You hope he's spoken to Lydia about this. She hates disruptions in the chain of command.

'Where it says "Principles", swap it out for "Values" and put your stuff in there, and I think we'll be good. Can I have that by tomorrow morning?'

You really wish he'd stop the health-ball jingling.

'Yes.'

'And one last thing. You'll need to write this down.'

You take up your pen.

'Demiurgic.'

'Demiurgic?'

'Make that the sixth value.'

'What?'

'Make "demiurgic" the sixth value. That's what sets us apart.'

'Demiurgic?'

'Yes.'

You perform a quick search on 'demiurgic'.

'Demiurgic. Relates to a gnostic deity who is the creative force.'

'Yes, if you are being literal; but being our favourite comms girl, you know better than that.'

You smile at him. Comms girl? Gnostic deity? Jesus.

'I'll send the prezzo now. It's great having you on the team.'

He heads to the fire stairs and flashes a winner's smile. 'Ambient exercise,' he says, before bounding up the stairs to the executive level.

You sit for a moment looking at your notepad. *Demiurgic*.

You grab your bag and head for the lift before Gabriel comes back and asks you to insert floccinaucinihilipilification into the mission statement. You run for the bus and just make it.

The woman sitting opposite you looks to be in her mid 40s. She pulls a pair of runners from her bag, takes her stilettos off, briefly rubs the underside of her right foot then puts the runners on. Without socks. You doubt the lack of socks is intentional. Maybe she was getting a child ready for school and she left the socks on the bed. You wonder how far she has to walk when she gets off the bus. You wonder if she questions the culture of the company she works for – a culture that demands she wear painfully high heels. You wonder if she hates her job.

Does Michael get it?

That night you are sitting at the dining table making progress on Gabe's presentation. Michael is cooking again. Something involving grilled haloumi. Porridge has retreated to the bedroom. Susan has taken to ambushing him from the back of the sofa. He's now more anxious than when he arrived.

Demiurgic. Okay. Gabe wants it in. It's in.

'What do you think of this?'

'Don't ask me,' says Michael. 'I don't understand the dark arts of corporate communication.'

'Have a look.'

Michael wipes his spatula and scans the presentation.

'Demiurgic is your sixth value?'
'You familiar with the word?'
'No, are you?'
'I am now.'
'What's the point of it, if no one knows what it means?'
'Well, you and I aren't everybody. Gabe knows what it means.' You stretch your arms above your head and yawn. 'And he's Harvard.'
'You need a Harvard degree to understand your sixth value?'
You sigh, leaning your head on your palm.
'I am so tired. It means creative and powerful,' you say.
'So, why not say that?'
'Because that's three words, versus one word. Demiurgic.'
'I told you I'm the wrong person to ask about that stuff. I really know nothing.'
'You know how to get spiders out.'
He follows your eyeline to a large huntsman crawling up the wall near the window.
'I do.'
'Go about your business, my good man, and leave me to my demi-urges.'

Now you've been exposed to the word for several hours it is growing on you. You don't bother looking it up. You decide for yourself that there must be a noun, and that's you, a true demiurge.

OF GNOSTIC GODS AND CORPORATE VALUES

You may laugh at the notion of inserting the word 'demiurgic' into corporate values, but is it so different from 'selflessness', 'passion', 'frugality' or 'value-centricity'?

The idea of being guided by mission statements, vision statements and values is laudable, but somewhere along the line we've lost connection with what the language means and even what we're trying to achieve via these statements.

If passion, loyalty, accountability and respect are articulated in the values, that's great – but how are these traits communicated and enacted? How do we bridge the gap between the corporate value and employee behaviour? How often do we even ask this question?

Gabriel's instructions to Kat to amend the presentation might seem like a literary flourish I'm using to put the character of Kat under pressure, but actually, I've seen similar situations unfold in countless organisations.

The problem with Gabriel Randall and his ilk is that they use language to throw a net over their audience. Whether it's an audience of one or 2000, they are caught in a swirl of stultifying confusion. Language should be used to communicate clearly – to inspire, to motivate, to warn. Instead, corporate speak obfuscates, confuses and distracts, all while the speaker hopes to impress.

Gabriel Randall is a charming narcissist. His main driver is to be admired. His capacity to truly connect to another person is low.

But due to the halo effect, as we saw in chapter 6, his good looks, square jaw and reputation from his previous placement mean those in charge are unable to see the flaws in Gabriel's approach. The potential ramifications of his unfettered control of the business are manifold. His impenetrable language means nobody understands what's being asked of them.

Covid? Who needs it?

There is no doubt that chronic stress is deleterious to the human body due to the effects of raised cortisol and adrenaline, among other chemical changes.[14] We know that living with constant anxiety and depression is not good. There is also no doubt that the food we consume is either helping or hindering our health. It's well documented that diseases such as diabetes, cancer and heart disease are on the rise because of poor diet and a lack of physical exercise.[15] We also know that yoga and meditative practices *can* have a positive effect.[16]

So, chronic stress is bad for us. The research is clear. The lie occurs when this message is oversimplified. It begins when the evidence that stress is bad for us is picked up by the alternate medical brigade and resold as 'stress causes all disease'.

The perception that a positive attitude, stress management techniques, eating properly, detoxing regularly, taking vitamins, exercising and doing yoga is all it takes to protect ourselves against disease is not true.[17] It's a lie. That your health can be guaranteed by you applying yourself to maintaining it is a simplistic con. Covid tells us this is not true.

This lie results in a sort health superiority. If I am well, it is due to my own efforts. If I am sick, it is due to a dereliction of duty on my own behalf.

The complexity of diseases like Covid, genetic factors and the virulence of the strain are all rendered insignificant once someone has jumped on the 'I'm in complete control of my health' bandwagon. Plenty of people who could lay claim to a healthy lifestyle have fallen victim to Covid. Some are still laid low.

'Surely it's okay to detox,' I hear you say. Yes: your liver and kidneys detox you every day. No amount of green juice or lemon detox kits will do it for you.[18] Dietary interventions may or may not afford you a healthier system. What they definitely won't do is protect you against a virus.

Alternate medicine's tendrils are so far-reaching that it's easy to assume its message is valid. Influencers have now wrapped their toned arms around alt med. With a flick of their post-yoga ponytails, they dispense health advice that's endangering consumers' lives. The bandwagon effect kicks in. A lot of people believe it so it must be true. Anecdotes abound: 'Sally went off gluten and cured her autoimmune disorder.' We don't know *why* Sally got better, or even *if* Sally got better, but our brains, under confirmation bias's influence, ignore any evidence that throws doubt on the enthusiastic narrative.

I keep reading that food is medicine. This is not true. Food is food and medicine is medicine. Of course we would like to grow older without the use of medicines. None of us want to age pickled in pills. We would all like to avoid diabetes, heart disease and cancer and give ourselves the best chance to stay well. At the same time, if we need pharmaceuticals, we need them. Science has a lot to offer us so we can remain well for longer.

Lie detection

Watch your language

Be the refreshing change we are all hoping for. Stun your listeners by using the same language you use when out with friends!

An apple a day might help, but you should still see the doctor

When it comes to health advice, don't believe untrained influencers with swishy ponytails.

Why aren't you in Morocco?

You wake feeling proud of what you accomplished the night before. You had made all the substitutions and additions to the presentation, as requested, and even juiced it up with some animations. You'd sent it to Gabe and saved a copy to the shared drive.

Having risen to the demiurgic challenge, your brain is now serving up images of a mortgage-free life, riding high on the crypto wave. Somehow, in this scenario, Porridge is perfectly behaved, can hold his ground with Susan and is a pleasure to take out in public.

By the time you arrive at work, you're light of step and filled with optimism. One could say you were feeling positively demiurgic.

First up is the end-of-week alignment meeting with what remains of your team. You buy coffee for everyone and hand the oat cap (no chocolate), extra hot three-quarter latte and almond decaf flattie to the correct recipients.

By 8.55 a.m. you're all sitting around a table. Adele has the project dashboard on the screen.

'Let's confirm what we've achieved this week,' you say. 'What's outstanding and what will be our priorities next week?'

'Before we do that,' says Adele, 'can you please explain this "Roadmap to the Future" presentation?'

'That was something Gabe asked me to do for him. You found it?'

'It was on the shared drive,' she says. 'Is it a draft or something?'

'Gabe wanted it for a presentation this morning. That's all I know.'

'It's being presented today?'

'I think so.'

'There's a lot of new information in that presentation.'

'Right. Don't worry about it.'

'If we're going to be aligned as a team, don't you think we need to talk about it?'

You lean on the table and look at her.

'Do you want our buy-in or not?' says Adele, her face setting into granite.

Damn those management training sessions. The phrase 'buy-in' always featured heavily.

'Yes, of course I do.'

Adele crosses her arms. 'Well, you should have let us in on the scope of this earlier.'

'I only found out about it last night, Adele. What's your question?'

'It doesn't address the mission statement.'

At 2.38 a.m. the following morning you'll have a brilliant retort to this, but now you pointlessly say, 'That's not a question.'

'Okay: why doesn't it address the mission statement?'

'You've just said the same thing but rephrased it.'

'I think what Adele is trying to say is that there's no mention of the mission statement,' says Ryan Kraft.

'Yes, I get that, Ryan,' you say, 'but the substance of the mission statement is now articulated in the creed.'

'How does that work?' says Adele.

'Since when did we have a creed?' says Lisbeth. 'Do I need to update the website?'

'I don't know that a mission statement and a creed are the same thing,' says Ryan. 'Sorry; statement, not question. How can a creed be the same thing as a mission statement?'

You clutch the back of the chair. Why is your team being deliberately obtuse? You're now regretting the optimism-fuelled coffee generosity.

'You can't seriously be questioning me about the relationship between a mission statement and a creed.'

'We can,' says Adele, 'because you didn't ask us for our feedback.'

You want to throw your iced mocha at Adele, but this type of behaviour was frowned upon in management training.

'I didn't ask you for your feedback?' you say instead.

She raises her eyebrows at you.

'You can't be serious,' you say. 'Gabe asked me to put this together. Last night.' You're hoping this will end the conversation.

'This is a whole new story,' says Adele. 'There are campaigns with timelines.'

You sigh, feeling like a long-suffering detective talking to a squad of rookie cops.

'I know there are timelines,' you say. 'I wrote it.'

'Then can you tell me what "demiurgic" means?' she says.

'To be demiurgic is to be forcefully creative,' you say.

'Okay, it says here, "A demiurge is a gnostic deity",' says Ryan.

'Oh my god,' says Adele. 'Has Lydia seen this?'

'I expect Gabe has shared it with her,' you say. 'They are probably discussing it as we speak.'

You unplug your computer. You are outraged. Prior to today, you have over-communicated with your team. You hate everything.

You look at them. Adele is staring at you. Lisbeth is looking at her phone and Ryan is smiling at you nervously. Why are you surprised? They are all younger than you and, typical of their generation, they are incapable of staying abreast of fast-moving scenarios. They have to be spoonfed, it seems. Their lack of discretionary imagination is breathtaking.

'Kat?'

You realise Ryan is speaking to you.

'Yes?'

'I just asked if we could take the weekend to absorb everything and meet again on Monday? To give us time to respond?'

'I don't need time,' says Adele. 'It's pretty clear we're not inside the tent.'

'Right,' you say. 'Well, this isn't a camping trip, Adele. There's no tent. I did what I was asked to do. And anyway, that presentation isn't going to change the course of history, okay? It's a roadmap.'

The table was silent.

'Kat,' said Lisbeth, 'I don't think Lydia is in today.'

'There's no way she's seen this. We'd have heard about it,' says Adele.

'I've tried all the search engines,' says Lisbeth, 'and I can't find a definition of "demiurgent" anywhere.'

You look at your watch. It is only 9.15 a.m.

You imagine yourself arriving home, telling Michael what a nightmare your team is and how they hate you. He'd say something anodyne, like, 'I'm sure they love you, Kat.'

Michael has no idea about the difficulties of dealing with people. He's a park ranger, hence his skill at managing spiders in the flat. 'I guess,' you'd said to him last night, 'compared to the deadly snakes you must encounter daily, spiders are a piece of cake.'

'Kat, the snakes are not the wildest things I have to deal with. It's either the nudists or the perverts spying on them.'

'Oh.'

Later, you are standing outside the office waiting for Michael the park ranger to pick you up. It's been 32 minutes and he still hasn't arrived. Why did he decide to leave IT and the comforts of a city office to become a park ranger? He has further to come to pick you up, and less money. Not that he's worried about the money. He loves working outside, he's always saying. Well, you don't like being outside. You're standing freezing on the street while a man with teeth like broken fence palings pushes his injured shopping trolley around and talks loudly at you about the new world order and how Trump was robbed.

You want to move away but don't want to be seen as judgemental, so you stand there staring hopefully down the street for Michael's car. Minutes pass. The street is emptying and darkening.

The man moves closer to you. You can smell his unwashed jacket. You begin to sweat with fear. You mutter the word 'Covid' and take two steps away from the man. He follows you, pushing his trolley into your leg. You ricochet between berating yourself for your lack of compassion and worrying your sister will give the eulogy at your funeral and use the opportunity to show off.

You are thinking how Michael will spend the rest of his life haunted by those critical 32 minutes and your sad, untimely death when the car pulls up. You rip open the door and throw your bag in.

'I've got to go,' you say apologetically to the man over your shoulder, like you are leaving a meeting early.

Michael smiles and squeezes your knee as he pulls away from the kerb. Your heart is hammering out of your chest.

'That man frightened me,' you say.

Michael glances at him for five seconds in the rear-view mirror.

'What, him?' he says. 'He's harmless.'

You sit rubbing your hands together near the heated vents. 'I was also very cold,' you say.

'You should have waited in the foyer, Kat,' he says, smiling.

Three hours later, after he's run roughshod over your obvious distress with his perky offers of wine, and anecdotes about hilarious

John from work and his incredible impression of Trump, you've had enough of waiting for him to ask if you are okay.

'That scary guy with the shopping trolley, who I thought was maybe going to murder me, thought Trump was robbed,' you say.

'Oh, classic, absolute classic. Murder you,' Michael chuckles. 'You're an absolute classic, Kat.'

You don't feel yourself to be a classic. You feel yourself to be the unacknowledged victim of a near-crime. You rise from the couch.

'Well, goodnight,' you say plaintively.

'Goodnight, Kat,' says Michael, giving you a little wave with his fingers bent like a toddler.

You maunder off to the bedroom where you lie on the bed thinking you are living the wrong life. If you were fabulous and independently wealthy you wouldn't have to think about corporate values or Michael's lack of sensitivity or the word 'demiurgic' or Adele's face. You'd be in a Moroccan riad drinking mint tea with other wealthy people having razor-sharp conversations. 'Anybody know what "demiurgic" means?' you'd say. 'No,' they'd reply. 'It sounds like a stupid word anyway.' You'd laugh and chink mint tea glasses.

You pick up our phone, open Instagram and find yourself back on Charlotte's profile. You don't know why you keep doing this. Comparisons are odious, you say to yourself. You know Instagram reflects nothing more than people's curated lives, but you can't seem to stop yourself. She's been everywhere. All over Europe and Asia. In the most recent pictures there must be a nanny just out of shot. Sometimes she and the handsome nephew are with the children, sometimes without. This weekend they're in the Barossa. Alistaire, who owns several wineries, has his arm around Charlotte. The sun is setting on the vineyard. One of his wines, 'Charlotte's Guess', is named after Charlotte. They were neighbours in England. The people in her photos are always intensely glamorous. In some of the pictures, Alec is smiling. He should do it more often. It suits him. Another picture is of a massive waterfront house they are looking to buy in Sydney. It has a circular driveway.

Michael appears in the doorway. You switch to email.

'I've brought you a cup of tea.' He sits on the bed and takes your hand. 'Sorry I didn't listen to you. I'm sorry you were scared.' He smiles at you. 'You still okay to go to Elouise's beachside idyll tomorrow?'

Oh god, you think. *I forgot.*

'Yep! Really looking forward to meeting your work friends.' You leap out of bed and rifle through your wardrobe.

'What are you doing?' says Michael.

'What will I wear?' you say.

'It's just a casual weekend at the beach, Kat. You can wear whatever you want.'

What is wrong with men? Just because they can wear the same t-shirt and pair of shorts to the beach and their wedding doesn't mean you can.

'Go away. I need to select.'

'Okay, but I think you look good in anything.'

Jesus, you think. *Men.*

Fish in the bucket

You arrive at Elouise's beachside idyll. It's a shack.

This is a lovely rustic residence, you say to yourself as you step over a bucket with a still-alive fish in it. It looks at you with one eye as you pass.

'Wow,' says Elouise, three seconds after you've arrived. 'How did you get that scar on your face? It's really cool.'

'She fell over the rubbish bin,' says Michael.

'Hey guys, this is Ham, my bro,' says Elouise.

Ham swivels around at the kitchen counter.

'Hey,' he says. 'Look at these beauties.' He holds his hand out. 'Beadhead prince nymph. The best.'

'That's Ham's way of saying, who's up for some fly fishing?' says Elouise, handing you a glass of wine. Elouise has clearly been having a good go at the wine bottle prior to your arrival.

'Mikie, look at you,' she says. 'Why didn't you tell me your girlfriend was so pretty?'

Michael, who trucks in the literal, begins to reply.

'I think it was rhetorical,' you say.

'And she's smart, too. Congrats,' says Elouise, like he'd won you in a competition.

'Anyway, hope vegan's okay,' says another man in the kitchen, flinging a tea towel over his shoulder.

'Oh yes, this is Scott. He's trying to save the planet,' says Elouise. 'So no lamb chops for us.'

'Hey Scott, all good,' says Michael. 'I find lamb too fatty.'

'What if we catch a trout?' says Ham. 'Trout's not vegan.'

'Scotty can eat tofu', says Elouise, 'while we tuck into the trout.'

You smile encouragingly at Scott. 'Do you need a hand?'

'No, he doesn't,' says Elouise. 'Scott is the king of the kitchen. You may not enter. You do, however, need a top-up.' She refills your barely touched glass.

'Elouise,' says Scott, 'did you buy aubergine?'

She rolls her eyes at you. 'Scott thinks he's back in the motherland. Do you mean eggplant?'

'Ah, yes.'

'No, I didn't.'

'That's okay, I can use courgette.'

'Zucchini, Scott, for god's sake.'

'Okay,' says Ham, 'let's get dinner happening. We have an early start tomorrow.'

The following morning, Michael sets off early with Ham. Standing in waders is his idea of heaven. Elouise sits in the lounge room and morosely smokes, and you head outside to sit on the beach with Scott. Scott is a poet. He sits on his towel, jotting things into a notebook.

'Do you know what "demiurgic" means?'

'Um, yeah, he's a figure responsible for fashioning and maintaining the physical universe. Greek. Plato.'

'Right. My boss wants to make it a corporate value,' you say.

'And in the corporate sector the demiurge creates / While floors below him, the workers' fears abate,' Scott says.

'Wow, a demiurgic poem. My boss would love you.'

'Come and look at my labyrinth. It's very meditative and, unlike a maze, you can't get lost.'

You follow him off the beach into the bush. Arriving at the labyrinth, you realise you don't need reassurance that you won't get lost. It is flat and about two meters across.

You follow Scott around the labyrinth while he chants and hums. Some teenagers appear from the bush and ask if they can join in.

'Not today, guys. We have reached our optimum vibration. Come tomorrow, 2 p.m. Happy to show you the ropes.'

Later, at dinner, Elouise became progressively drunker, more unhappy with Scott and more intent on blowing cigarette smoke into your personal space. You have never smoked and find the process of it repulsive.

After sitting through a hilarious but viscous monologue detailing Scott's continued failure to get his driver's license, you escape to the bathroom. When you emerge, you find Elouise standing in the hallway smoking another cigarette. 'I'm pregnant,' she says. 'The problem is, I don't know if it's Scott's.'

'Right.' You've only known her for 24 hours. Surely she had a closer friend to disclose such intimate problems to.

'I feel I could tell you anything,' she says, curling her arms around your neck and resting her head on your shoulder.

You are mortified. What if you are harbouring Covid and are spreading it to her unborn child? Also, you're tempted to tell her to maybe stop drinking and smoking while she thought about who the father could be, but at that moment Michael appears. You look at him over Elouise's shoulder and enact a small mime, hoping he will assist in your extrication. His response to this is to let out a yell, run towards you and throw his beer over your head.

In the car on the way home, Michael apologises for the fact that Elouise set your hair on fire with her cigarette. 'But,' he says, banging his hand on the steering wheel for emphasis, 'she is a classic, isn't she? That Elouise, an absolute classic.'

'How would you know what she's like? You were standing around all day in giant galoshes catching no fish.'

'Well, he seems a decent bloke, that Scott.'

After the incident, Scott had made you sit on the side of the bath while he carefully cut out the burnt bits of hair. He was seriously one of the nicest and most dazed people you'd ever met. You were perplexed as to how he was in a relationship with Elouise.

Elouise had stood in the doorway, smoking and watching. 'Who knew we had a hairdresser in our midst, Scotty?'

Scott had looked up at her and smiled.

'I thought all hairdressers were gay,' said Elouise.

'Mine's not,' you'd said.

'Right, well, it would explain a few things about Scott,' she'd said, drifting up the hallway.

'Why do you stay with her?' you'd said.

He'd held a strand of hair and clipped it efficiently.

'She's very nice when she's sober,' he'd said.

'Is she sober much?'

He'd shrugged.

'Not a lot.'

Burnt hair

The burnt-hair aroma has stayed about your person for the entire week. It doesn't seem to matter how often you apply shampoo. It has now accompanied you to a meeting you're conducting at your desk with Adele around post-Covid protocols.

Adele has coughed twice so far.

'Can you smell something burnt?' she says.

'It's my hair.'

'Your hair? What?'

'It caught on fire on the weekend.'

'How?'

'With a cigarette. I'd rather not talk about it.'

'I didn't think you smoked.'

'I don't. I hate it.'

She coughs again. What if she has Covid? You don't want it again. She should go home to her snake. Snakes can't get Covid. She could cough all over Emma.

'Kat, stop looking at me. I test every morning.'

Joel has arrived. Joel has a cold. Joel is the Transitioning Out of Covid Protocol Team Leader. 'Can anyone else smell something burnt?' he says.

'It's her hair,' says Adele, nodding towards you.

Joel raises an eyebrow.

'It's something to do with a cigarette, but she doesn't want to talk about it.'

'You shouldn't smoke,' says Joel.

You wipe your keyboard down and offer the hand sanitiser around. Joel refuses it. Adele tips half the bottle into her hand.

'Thanks, Joel. I'll definitely try to give up.'

'Anyway, I had to wait 12 and a half minutes for a lift this morning,' says Adele. 'I mean, I get it. Management is just trying to keep us safe. I'm all for social distancing, but I was late for a meeting.'

'Yeah, I know,' says Joel. 'It's ridiculous, but management has drunk the Covid Kool-aid so this is what we have to do.'

Joel produces a laminated checklist and prepares to start ticking.

'It's important,' you say. 'I'm glad we're taking the risks seriously.'

Joel snorts. 'You get in a car, don't you? You go swimming? You get in planes? They all have risks. This is all just hysteria created by the media.'

Joel leans over the top of your desk, putting his elbows on the back of your computer.

'The whole thing's a beat-up. Covid is no worse than the flu. It's ridiculous. And nobody is making me wear a mask. I need my oxygen, thanks very much.'

You wish he would wear a mask. You wish he used fewer plosive consonants. Why is everybody suddenly enunciating so clearly? What happened to the great Australian tradition of speaking through a half-closed mouth?

You stare at your feet, noting you're wearing one brown boot and one black.

'There's a lot of evidence it's a beat-up, spread by 5G,' says Joel.

'Hang on,' you say. 'How can it be a beat-up and also spread by 5G?'

'Kat,' says Joel, 'there is no way I'd be putting that vaccine into my body. It's a rush job. It's all about big pharma making money. Look around you. Did you notice the number of vaccinated people getting sick and dying from Covid? Have you heard of natural immunity? Gates wants to vaccinate you so he can microchip you and control the whole world. Stop being such a sheeple. Educate yourself.'

'I thought you were our Covid Protocol Team Leader,' you say. 'How did you get that job?'

'I applied,' he says.

'Joel,' says Adele, 'you're sounding like a dopey conspiracy theorist.'

You are beset by a deep lassitude. You run your hands though your hair, releasing burnt-hair molecules into the air.

'Kat is recovering from her cigarette incident, Joel. Calling her a sheeple is unkind, plus it's a stupid term. Anyway, we're here to sort this out, so let's get on with it. Agenda point one: optimising workplace practices to ensure employee safety during staged transition from home to office,' Adele reads.

'Right,' says Joel. 'So, accessibility to hand sanitiser stations and encouraging people to handwash. Can you believe people need to be babied and told to wash their hands?'

'Yes I can, Joel,' says Adele. 'The general population is very non-compliant.' She shakes her head at him. 'As you're unvaccinated, I'm going to remove you from Emma's birthday party list.'

'I don't want to come to your stupid snake's birthday party,' says Joel.

You bite your lip.

'It's okay, Kat. I know you're fully vaxxed. You're welcome to come. No presents required.'

You look out the window and pull some of your burnt hair away in your hand. You wonder if you could survive outside of the corporate world. You look at Adele, imagining her going home to Emma. At least, you think to yourself, your pets have legs.

SNAKES AND BURNT HAIR

Here we are again, swimming around in the illusion of transparency where we wildly overestimate how well people know what is going on for us emotionally.

Because we are so exquisitely aware of our own internal reality, it's easy to assume that other people are aware of it, too. We are self-focused and the centre of our own universe, so we imagine our emotional reactions and thoughts are evident to others as we move through the world. We assume there is some magic vibe that transmits our thoughts and emotional state to those around us. We feel things so acutely and we are so intimately involved in our own narratives and emotional reactions that it seems impossible those around us are unaware. Yet, to an astoundingly large degree, they are.

The result of the illusion of transparency is that we expect people to mindread. We arrive at decisions having completely hidden the thinking that went into the decision from those who are affected by the outcome. We then wonder why we don't get buy-in. The process Kat went through putting together the presentation for Gabriel was so all-consuming to her, she assumed she was communicating the whole picture to her team. She forgot that things that are obvious to her, due to the amount of time she spends talking about them or working on them, are not magically communicated to her team members.

When Kat realises her team is not responding in the manner she expects, she could take a deep breath and check to see if she's assumed she has communicated clearly, rather than allowing the desired outcome to stay closeted in her own mind. Employees feeling left out of the decision-making process are likely to start fomenting unhappiness and becoming obstructive. Kat is immediately defensive when her team members question the strategy. She responds to a strong feeling of outrage. Sometimes our feelings are accurate, and sometimes they're not. Kat's response to her feeling is to dig herself further into her standpoint that she has communicated clearly and her team is being deliberately obstructive.

Primary attribution error, which we also saw in chapter 7 in Kat and Adele's negative responses to Chen, is also playing out. Kat is buying into the tendency to attribute personality flaws or character failings to other people's behaviours or mistakes, rather than looking at the possibility that the situation or environment may be influencing them. At the same time, in Kat's mind, her own behaviours and mistakes are not due to her character failing but are a result of the situation she is managing. In other words, Kat believes that her team members are at fault because they are young and unmotivated – a fundamental character flaw – whereas her mistakes are due to the prevailing circumstances: she is busy, trying to manage Gabriel Randall on top of everything else.

If you start to look for this error in your thinking, you'll see it operating in all contexts in your life. You'll find you are much more forgiving of yourself than of other people. You might also see that you jump quickly to offense when you are labouring under the illusion that the other person knows what's going on for you and is being obtuse or uncaring.

This phenomenon also extends to how well we think we understand what other people are feeling or thinking. Relying on flawed assumptions and errant instincts, we can be quick to project an emotional state or story onto another person. If we have a close and well-established relationship with a person, we may be close to the truth; but making assumptions about what other people are thinking is dangerous. With strangers and acquaintances, the likelihood of our assessment being accurate is very low.

Kat, what are you doing?

Trust your instincts if you sense you're in danger.

Regardless of whether the trolley-toting man is dangerous or not, Kat feels he is. This is when our instincts should be categorically respected. We are gifted with a primitive instinct regarding danger. The limbic system in our brain senses danger in the unconscious first, then organises some handy chemicals to be released into our system to prepare us to go into fight, flight or freeze mode.

Sometimes our instincts are on the mark, and sometimes they're not. But, when it comes to personal safety, a false positive – where we assume something is dangerous but discover it's a false alarm – is a better option than a false negative – where we ignore the signals telling us we're in danger and open ourselves up to threat.

Kat should listen to her instincts and move away from the man. She doesn't have to do this in an offensive way. Women especially are schooled that manners are more important than anything. There is no reason why she has to stand on the street feeling threatened when she could move back into the foyer, or somewhere else that is better lit and more densely populated.

We know this propensity to ignore warning signs – either in one-off situations, like Kat experiences, or in intimate relationships – puts women in danger. There is now evidence that nearly all violence in intimate relationships is preceded by coercion and control.[19] Women need to be supported in recognising these warning signs and leaving these relationships. The red flags are always there early on and women ignore them due to confirmation bias. They don't need their thinking cluttered with the current crop of gratitude memes, misconstruing the controlling behaviour as love or falling into the trap of being nice.

Kat also needs to be much more direct with Michael. Waiting for him to notice that she is upset and has been feeling unsafe clearly isn't working. Her internal reality, no matter how acutely she experiences it, is not evident to Michael – only to her. Because she isn't backing herself about her fear or being clear about its effect on her, she allows Michael to diminish her concerns, which then leaves her feeling unsupported and uncared for. This can become a game, where one person waits for the other person to discern they're upset; then, when they don't, a new upset is loaded onto the original issue. And on it goes.

It's a conspiracy, stupid

Denial is a very natural and common response when people feel threatened and emotionally overwhelmed. Events and situations such as pandemics elicit a very normal response in us to being out of control. We want to feel that things are understandable and that we can affect what is going on around us.

Some people are truly unconcerned in these unsettling situations. Others are aware of the risks and put risk-management protocols in place in their lives. Others become so frightened they go into denial, and they may unconsciously move towards motivated reasoning – deciding what evidence to accept based on the conclusion they'd like to reach. (We saw this with Mrs Kovacic in previous chapters, where each disaster at the flats is proof of the curse.) Confirmation bias ensures we only notice information that supports our position and discount data that is antithetical to what we already believe. Then availability bias kicks in, causing us to rely on information that most easily comes to mind. For Transitioning Out of Covid Protocol Team Leader Joel, it's wacky conspiracy theories that are top of mind and easiest for his brain to access.

We are also tribal and highly influenced by social norming. Our sense of self, our very identity, is tied up with the beliefs of our tribe. Conspiracy theorists believe they belong to a tribe that is not ordinary. Their tribe is a special group: the only people who can see the truth, who are intelligent enough and brave enough to ditch the societal line. They get to feel in control.

If mask-wearing is not an accepted practice in your tribe, you're less likely to do it. To go against the socially normed practices of your tribe is to open yourself to up to mockery, to be rejected.

We also know our brains are fundamentally innumerate. Large numbers just bounce off our brains. It's why charities stopped talking about millions of starving children and began telling the story of the struggles of one child who has a name and a face, and a 14-kilometre walk each day to get water.

It's the same with Covid for a lot of people. They're more likely to be affected by a story of that one friend-of-a-friend who had a bad reaction to the AstraZeneca vaccine than a statistic from the government stating millions have died.[20]

The internet amplifies conspiracy theories. When Covid began, the anti-vax network and other purveyors of wacky anti-science formed a febrile cohort and are still happily spreading their pseudoscientific beliefs.

You may be wondering why we should care what a bunch of paranoid, science-denying individuals think. It's because, thanks to the internet, their beliefs are spreading into the more moderate ends of society. They're undermining and sometimes outright rejecting health messages that are critically important.[21]

Believing in a conspiracy theory is, of course, an unconscious process, which is why trying to argue with a conspiracy theorist is extremely frustrating. Their beliefs are based on unconscious emotions, not logic. People who have widespread belief in conspiracy theories are often low in agreeability and have a general distrust of science. Personal alienation and anxiety also contribute.

Once people believe in one conspiracy theory, they're more likely to believe in others. The spread of conspiracy theories such as QAnon shows us the ease with which dangerous, baseless ideas can thread their way through societies, with disastrous consequences.

Conspiracy theorists have a nice, comfortable basis to reject health findings. Social distancing, mask-wearing, getting vaccinated – they don't like it, and their tribe rejects it, so suggestions of overreaction feed into implicatory denial. They reject the findings because they don't like the implications.

Lie detection

How could you not know I was upset?
Because I'm not you. People aren't mind-readers.
Put everyone out of their misery; tell them what's going on for you.

Dark carparks, lifts, walkways and parks at night
If you sense danger – ever – take action. Get out.

Googling is not 'doing your own research'
It's just googling. Research takes years and an understanding of scientific method.

10

Lydia is no longer the worst boss

WorkWellbeingSure (ASX:WWS) today announced an upgrade of compliance governance structures resulting in a change in the senior executive team. That change is: Ms Lydia Vaughan, currently Executive General Manager for Corporate Affairs and Communications, will step down from her role today.

WorkWellbeingSure's CEO, David Firth, said:

'I want to thank Lydia Vaughan for her 18 years of service to WWS and her unwavering commitment to our values. The company is far more authentic, accountable and innovative because of Lydia. We wish her well.'

Enquiries: Saxby Simms
E: hello@saxbysimms.com
Instagram: @saxbysimms
Facebook: @saxbysimmspr
Twitter: @saxbysimms

Oh no. Poor Lydia. You go straight to her desk. She is packing her things into a box. She turns to you.

'I'm apparently not what the business needs right now.'
'What does the business need right now?'
She shrugs. 'Not an Inspector.'
Lisbeth arrives at Lydia's desk.
'Sorry, Lydia. What bastards. Saxby Simms? What do they know about the Australian market? They'll cost the business a fortune.'
'Thing is,' says Lydia, 'what no one noticed is that I was going to quit. I can't stay and watch Gabriel Randall destroy the place.' She packs the last notepad in her briefcase. 'Because of him, I nearly threw away my redundancy. How dumb would that have been? Eighteen years.'
'So, you're okay?' you say.
'Of course I'm okay. Go for an operational role, Kat,' she says. 'Internal services isn't the place for you if you want a future.'
'We'll miss you, Lydia,' says Lisbeth.
'Don't be ridiculous,' says Lydia. 'No, you won't.'
'Who will ring me on a Saturday night to ask me to update the corporate values?' you say.
'I'm sorry I made your life difficult,' she says. 'I think you're very talented.'
You want to hug her, but as you've never so much as patted her on the back, you don't.

The Hipster again

That night you are home, making lasagne with Mrs Kovacic.
'So this Lydia gets the boot,' she says. 'You better be careful they don't get rid of you.'
'I'm okay,' you say. 'The senior leadership team is safe.'
'With curse here, nobody is safe.'
There's a knock at your door. You open it. A man is standing there.
'Yes?'

'Hello, I'm Detective Bradley from the Surry Hills crime squad.' He flashes his ID. 'Are you Katrina Mitchell?'

'Yes.'

'I wonder if I could have a chat. May I come in?'

You motion towards the living room. Mrs Kovacic is standing at the entrance to the kitchen, wiping her hands on a tea towel.

'This is a private matter. It might be better if I speak to you alone.'

'A private matter in regard to what? Is my family okay?'

'Yes, it's not about your family.' He looks at Mrs Kovacic.

'It's okay, she's my neighbour. She doesn't speak English.'

Mrs Kovacic looks at you.

'Okay. I've been given your name in relation to a Noel Simpkins.'

The sound of his name is like a punch to your chest.

'Right.'

'So, you do know him?'

'Is he dead?'

'Why, do you have information that he might be?'

'I've had nothing to do with him for more than two years.'

'Why would you assume he was dead?'

Susan jumps in your lap.

'I just thought that's why police came to your door. Not that I'd care. I mean, I'd care to the degree that he's a human being, but apart from that...'

You wish the detective would go away. Whatever The Hipster has done, you don't want to have to think about it.

'Mr Simpkins is a suspect in a financial crime investigation.'

Mrs Kovacic clasps her hand across her mouth.

'Right,' you say. 'He's upgraded from being a gaslighting narcissist.'

'It appears that Mr Simpkins was in a relationship with,' he pauses, looking down at his notes, 'a Rebecca Lacombe. He has disappeared, and it appears he has taken with him money from Ms Lacombe's bank account and her Range Rover.'

Mrs Kovacic's eyes widen.

So, Rebecca from The Real Estate has copped it in the neck. You don't believe in karma, but it would seem justice has been served. She took your boyfriend. He took her car and the contents of her bank account.

'What's this have to do with me?'

'Rebecca Lacombe gave us your details.'

Mrs Kovacic clicks her tongue.

'Oh, did she?'

'I understand you had a relationship with Mr Simpkins.'

You point to your lap. 'This is Susan.'

'Okay.'

'She's his cat. He walked out two years ago and left her. That's all you need to know about him.'

'So, he left his cat, but did he rob you in any way?'

Mrs Kovacic exhales heavily, leaning back on the couch.

Only of my sanity, you think to yourself. You don't want the past clawing its way back into your life. You don't want to think about the time you wasted trying to please The Hipster. You don't want to remember the sheer misery of his betrayal. You are happy with Michael. He may not have The Hipster's charm or looks, but he also doesn't gaslight you or sleep with Rebecca from The Real Estate during a mould inspection.

'Mr Simpkins has also left a trail of coaching clients who have paid for services that aren't being delivered.'

Coaching clients? *Suckers*, you think.

'I'm making enquiries to determine the scale of Mr Simpkins's deception and whether it warrants a formal investigation by the Crime Commission. Did he take anything of yours that wasn't his?'

Mrs Kovacic kicks the coffee table.

'Yes, he did. He took this coffee table.'

The detective looks at the table.

'This one?'

'Yes.'

Mrs Kovacic picks up the remote, hands it to you.

'Oh yes, and this remote.'

'Your neighbour seems to be following the conversation quite well.'

'She just has a few basic sentences.' You look at Mrs Kovacic, then mime drinking tea. She hauls herself up and reluctantly trudges into the kitchen.

'So you're saying Noel Simpkins took items from your flat that didn't belong to him?'

'Yes. He also took the washing machine and dryer, and my Moroccan tea set.'

He pauses his writing and looks up at you. 'But the table and remote have been returned?'

'Under duress. My neighbour, Mr Kovacic, paid him a visit.'

'Did he return the washing machine and dryer?'

'Yes.'

There's a crash from the kitchen. You put Susan on the floor and go into the kitchen.

Mrs Kovacic grabs you by the arm and drags you behind the fridge. 'Tell him about curse,' she whispers.

You pull your arm away.

'I will not,' you whisper back. 'He's a detective, not a paranormal investigator.'

She grabs your other arm.

'He needs to know about funny goings on,' she whispers.

'I'm not talking to the detective about your imaginary curse.'

'All okay, Miss Mitchell?' calls the detective.

'Yes, fine. Just showing Mrs Kovacic where the milk is. Would you like tea?'

'Oh, yes please. Milk and two sugars.'

You open the fridge, pull the milk out and put it in Mrs Kovacic's hands. She narrows her eyes at you.

'Please just make the tea.' You put your finger to your lips.

You re-enter the lounge room. Susan has parked herself next to the detective. He is scratching her behind the ears.

'Sweet cat,' he says.

'She's not really. She's pretty cranky. She's only being nice because she doesn't want to go to cat prison.'

He smiles at you.

You sit on the armchair. Susan leaves the detective's side and curls up on your lap. Mrs Kovacic returns and plonks the teacups down loudly on the coffee table.

'Thank you.' He picks up the teacup. 'Is this part of the Moroccan tea set?'

'Yes.'

'So did he take anything and not return it?'

'Only my dignity,' you say.

'Miss Mitchell, it doesn't look like we can include you as a victim.'

'It's a shame that being an appalling human isn't a crime. You could nab him immediately.'

'If being an appalling human were a crime, our jails would be overrun.'

Why isn't it a crime to destroy someone's confidence? Why is theft only measured in dollars? You opened the door to The Hipster, but you didn't invite the savage putdowns, the casual undermining, the torturous gaslighting or the gut-churning betrayal. He robbed you of more than a year of your precious life. Why isn't eroding someone's sense of self an unlawful act?

'Anything else that might be relevant?'

'Well, I now have a groodle and a very nice partner. They're at the dog park.'

He looks at you.

'If you think of anything, give me a call.'

You shut the door behind him.

'Don't say it.'

'Now I think about it, Hipster was beginning of curse,' says Mrs Kovacic.

Free trading

You're in your flat enjoying pre-dinner drinks with Charlotte, trying not to think about The Hipster, or Rebecca from The Real Estate, or Lydia. Does she have a husband who's still working? What about her child?

Charlotte's wearing a Zimmerman dress. Having haunted the sales, you know it's worth $2000. You can't identify the brand of her shoes, but you know they are expensive. Her hair has at least $800 worth of streaks in it, and she has never exhibited the slightest hint of regrowth. Her nails are perfect. You've never been able to identify whether she's pretty or just artfully made up.

She's like a pedigree Afghan sitting in a dog shelter – only she can also look at her phone and pour champagne simultaneously.

'What's so riveting?' you say.

'Just checking my cryptocurrency trading account.'

'You are into crypto?'

'I trade.'

'How's it going?'

Charlotte holds up your champagne flute. 'Works for me.'

You accept the glass and take a slug.

'Michael thinks it's a big con.'

She sits back on the couch, running her fingers through her hair.

'He's had a lot of experience trading?'

'He hasn't traded. But he's read up on it.'

'Well, I hope he's reading the right information.'

'Haven't people lost fortunes?'

'Sure. Billions of other people's money. It's criminal.'

'So why hasn't it been shut down?'

'It can't be shut down. You'd have to turn off the internet.'

'Would that be such a bad thing?'

'Ha! Maybe not.' She kicks off her shoes and rubs her feet. 'You have to be disciplined in your approach. Avoid the exchanges based in tax havens run by adolescents impersonating a financial institution.'

'So, it works for you?'

'Sure. Most important: don't play with real money until you've made 100 or so paper trades. That's what I did.'

You cock your head, like Porridge.

'Paper trades are pretend trades. Simulated trades. You're not putting in real money, but you see the impact of your decisions.'

'So, no money needed?'

'Learning to trade is not going to cost you anything at all.'

'I have to stay focused on keeping my job,' you say. 'Company-wide cuts are happening.'

'That Gabriel guy sounds like a nightmare.' She tops up your glass.

'Stop filling my glass,' you say. 'I'll end up like Elouise.'

'Who's Elouise?'

'The woman whose house we stayed at last weekend. Elouise smoked incessantly, was drunk and maybe pregnant, but possibly not to Scott the poet who is her boyfriend and was a hairdresser and who cut my hair because she set it on fire.

'I thought your hair looked different.'

'Yep. Scott did a pretty good job, but then drunk Elouise inferred he was gay. It was ugly.'

'And these are best Michael can do for friends to spend a weekend with?'

'Yep. It was fabulous.'

'Michael must have been beside himself with embarrassment.'

'He doesn't notice stuff like that,' you say. 'And if he does, he's very non-judgemental.'

'That's one word for it.'

'What do you mean?'

'I always thought my first husband was like that. Non-judgemental. Then I worked out he was disengaged. Just wouldn't land on anything. Couldn't form an opinion to save his life. Drove me mad. The exact opposite of Alec. Alec is nothing if not decisive.'

Porridge puts his head in her lap, and she strokes his ears. You wonder if Alec bullies Charlotte behind closed doors. Or is it just Will?

Porridge looks up at Charlotte with deep devotion in his eyes. 'We always had a dog when I was growing up. When we buy a house, I'll get Willow to terrorise Alec until he buys the kids a puppy.'

'What does Alec do?'

'He's an aviation consultant. People think the only reason I could be with him is because he's a hunk, but he's incredibly smart – a $1000-an-hour consultant with a queue from here to Christmas of clients waiting on his advice.'

'Cool. So you don't really need to work?'

'I like to. Also, kids are expensive.'

'I think my kids will have to make do with the public school one block away. Also, I'm going to make them wear the same shoes until their toes poke through the toes.'

'Yep. Solid plan.'

'Why didn't you have kids yourself?'

She shrugs. 'Never got around to it. I was busy having a career.'

'Which was?'

'I was a forensic accountant.'

You frown.

'It's an accountant with a side of detective. You've heard of Bernie Madoff?'

'Yes. I remember him because he "made off" with other people's money.'

She laughs. 'Well, Bernie Madoff came unstuck because forensic accountants worked out the details of the Ponzi scheme he was running and were able to explain it in legal terms for the courts.'

'Cool. So that's what you do.'

'That's what I *did*. Now I trade.' She pours another glass of champagne. 'Anyway, if anyone tries to scam you, let me know. I'll hunt them down for you.'

'You know, I was scammed a while ago, but I got my money back.'

'What – a phone scam?'

'Yep.'

'What a total disgrace. The banks should do more to prevent that.'

You pick up Susan off the coffee table and put her on your lap. She sits stiffly, looking at Porridge's head in Charlotte's lap. Preparing an assault.

Charlotte pulls her phone out of her handbag. Shows you a picture of a massive bunch of red long-stemmed roses.

'Alec brought me these. Out of nowhere.'

You feel the distasteful churn of dissatisfaction. Michael is not a flower-giver. Or a compliment-giver, for that matter. You've only just discovered he loves you.

'Anyway, you're super smart, stunningly beautiful, charming and have great business acumen. Stop putting up with that job. You're in the wrong environment.'

You look down at your feet. 'I need a pedicure.'

She throws a nut at you. The nut hits Susan.

'Stop it,' you say. 'I can't leave now. Things will be better without Lydia. Also, I've got to have money for the building repairs.'

Susan takes this moment to leap off your lap, jump on the couch next to Charlotte and smack Porridge on the head with her paw.

'What is with that cat?'

'She was biding her time. She thinks Porridge threw the nut.'

She leans over and takes your hand.

'You should be working for yourself.'

Kat likes ranunculus

'So that's why he works odd hours,' you say to Michael.

You're both folding washing in the lounge room. You've just folded his chicken t-shirt.

'A consultant?'

'Yep. Apparently he's brilliant; clients all over the world.'

'What industry?'

'Aviation. Charges thousands. And he gave her three dozen long-stemmed red roses the other day for no reason. So, you know.'

'Doesn't make sense.'

'What doesn't?'

'If he's charging thousands, why are they sitting in Mrs Hume's flat? Why aren't they in a hotel?'

'Well, they're looking for the right place to buy.'

'They're taking their time.' He puts one of your t-shirts on your pile.

'They can take as long as they like. They're Mrs Hume's family.'

He shrugs.

'Would you chuck your family out?' You pick up your t-shirt and refold it.

'It depends on how painful they are.'

'So why would Charlotte say he's earning that much if he's not?' You pick a sock off the floor. It has Susan's face on it. You'd given Michael these socks on your anniversary. You note this one has a hole in it.

'Maybe he's lying.'

You pause.

'Now you have an opinion.'

'What do you mean, now I have an opinion?'

'You stay pretty disengaged from everything, then suddenly Alec is a liar.'

'It's not sudden. I have opinions. I just don't shoot my mouth off every five seconds.'

'Are you saying I do?'

'No.'

'Are you saying that I'm the sort of person who just opens my mouth and blabs on?'

'No. That wasn't what I was saying.'

'That I spurt unsubstantiated rubbish?'

'No, I'm not talking about you.'

'That I'm just a capricious motormouth?'

A part of your brain is telling you to stop, but you're in full flight. Also, you're proud you've managed to use 'capricious' while under pressure. Also 'unsubstantiated' is not bad.

'Kat, no.'

Don't bring The Hipster up, you say to yourself.

'This is what The Hipster used to do to me. Encourage me to speak, then demean what I say. I can't deal with that again. Also, why are you keeping these socks? They have holes in them.' You poke your finger through the hole.

You stand looking at each other. Your breathing is high in your chest.

'I don't understand why you're upset.'

'You're a man. You just don't get it.'

You put the sock on the table.

'I'm going to walk Porridge,' you say.

You go to the door and get the lead.

Don't go back to the argument, you say to yourself. It's a stupid argument. There's no winner in that argument. Be the bigger person and let it go.

You go into the kitchen, where Michael is now unpacking the dishwasher. He holds each glass up to the light, checking for smears.

'I'm not saying I want you to give me roses. I mean, flowers are nice, but that's not why I said that.'

'Well, okay.' The glass he's holding passes muster. He puts it carefully in the cupboard.

'But do you think I shoot my mouth off?'

He leans on the bench.

'No, Kat, I don't. I didn't start this conversation. You did.'

'No, I didn't. You called Alec a liar.'

'Well, maybe he is.'

You compress you mouth. 'I'll be back. I'll just try not to shoot my mouth off for the next five seconds.'

'Sure, Kat.'

You clip the lead on Porridge, exit the flat and then stand there, on the other side of the door, riven with indecision. What does 'Sure, Kat' mean? Is it passive aggressive? Is he waiting for you to come back in and say something? A cement wall of frustration pushes against your chest. You have always admired Michael's mild demeanour, but now you're wondering if it signifies a darker side or, worse, a pathological disengagement.

You go back inside. Michael is standing at the kitchen bench, scratching Susan under the chin.

He looks up. 'Did you forget something?'

Your hand is on the door. Porridge whines. Susan looks at you. She disapproves of irrational emotional displays. She is a very judgemental cat. You regret returning. You feel foolish.

'I forgot my scarf. It's cold.'

What's the point of saying anything? He's clearly let go of it.

'It *is* cold,' he says.

You head towards the bedroom. Now you feel stupid. As a child you would beg to be pushed on a swing. You'd be wildly excited until you felt the hand in the middle of your back propel you into the air. You'd cling to the cold metal chains, fighting the waves of nausea, praying for it be over. You have the same sensation now: the ground dizzyingly falling away.

You return from the bedroom without your scarf.

'Where's your scarf?'

'Changed my mind.'

You feel yourself floundering. The swing is mid-air. You go to the door. 'Well, see you in a bit.'

'Hang on.' He goes into the bedroom, then reappears with your scarf. He wraps it around your neck.

'Kat, I'm not very good at talking about stuff, but it's all good. I don't think you shoot your mouth off.'

The swing comes to a halt. You stand, feeling the grass beneath your feet. Porridge puts his paws up on your shoulders.

'Why do you think Alec is a liar?'

'I don't necessarily. It's just that sometimes their story doesn't fit. Like, why hasn't Willow gone to boarding school? The new term has started.'

'There was a Covid outbreak. They shut the school.'

He raises his eyebrows.

'You want a donut?'

'Iced caramel, please.'

'What flowers do you like?'

'I like ranunculus.'

You shut the door behind you.

You're putting a teabag in the bin that night when you notice Susan's face poking through the rubbish. You open the bin lid further and peer in. It's Michael's sock.

You are the most horrible person in the world.

WEEP NOT FOR LYDIA

It's easy to look at Lydia through Kat's eyes and see a micromanager with poor relationship skills. However, there is more to Lydia than these obvious flaws. She has been in the organisation for 18 years. She understands the systems and processes better than anyone, she has brilliant longstanding relationships with clients and she has helped David Firth withstand the influence of bad ideas propagated by overzealous consultants. Until now.

David perceives that Lydia is not supporting him or his ambitions for the business. This is a lie. In truth, she does want the business to make the changes necessary for it to thrive; however, she is unsatisfied with the substance of Gabriel Randall's intentions.

David has fallen victim to confirmation bias. He has begun seeing Lydia through Gabriel's lens. When Lydia voices well-founded scepticism, David perceives this to be negativity. Instead of exploring Lydia's perspective, he concludes prematurely that Lydia is a lost cause.

Opposition is not insurrection

When a colleague – or close friend or partner, for that matter – does not agree with you, avoid reflexively concluding that they are not on your side: this may be an error of perception on your part. They may agree on the desired outcome while disagreeing on the means to achieve it. This perception error is compounded by an ad hominem argument, which is an attack on the person rather than their argument.

When Kat says to Michael, 'You're a man. You just don't get it,' she's using an ad hominem argument. She digs herself in further when she tells Michael that The Hipster used to subject her to similar behaviour. She's fallen for availability bias: landing on what most easily comes to mind. In the moment of conflict when she's struggling with an argument, the things her ex boyfriend used to say to her come most easily to mind. Confirmation bias then kicks in.

She's also climbed the ladder of inference. This concept explains why we jump to conclusions. On the ladder of inference, we find ourselves making a decision based on a tower of inferential statements. Kat concludes that Michael regards her as a 'capricious motormouth'. She gets to this from the inference she gleans from Michael's statement: 'I just don't shoot my mouth off every five seconds.' (Meaning, according to Kat, 'Unlike you.')

If Kat had slowed down and checked the veracity of Michael's statement – whether she was interpreting his inference correctly – she wouldn't have climbed up the tower in the first place.

We often claim to want feedback. But do we? Or do we only want feedback if it supports what we think or feel? In the face of opposition, our instinct tends to be to shore up our position – to use confirmation bias to confirm we're right and motivated reasoning to prove why what we are thinking or the course of action we've taken is valid.

The Hipster. Ew!

Before Michael, Kat was in a relationship with The Hipster. This relationship was at the centre of my first book: *Why Smart Women Make Bad Decisions: And How Critical Thinking Can Protect Them.* As you may have inferred, The Hipster is a narcissistic, gaslighting liar.

Most women I know have, at some point, been in a relationship with someone who's narcissistic, a liar, violent, a noncontributor or simply disinterested in their partner's needs. We lie to ourselves that they don't mean it, that they're trying as hard as they can, that they'll get a job eventually, that they get angry because they're under pressure, that they had an affair because we didn't give them enough attention. We put up with terrible behaviour because our capacity to lie to ourselves is outstanding. We indulge in motivated reasoning: skewing the evidence to come to the conclusion we want. Most often, the conclusion we come to is that we should put up with whatever is wrong in the relationship because it's better than being alone.

Abuse takes many forms. Coercive control is now considered illegal in New South Wales, Australia. The effects of putting up with abusive behaviour last long after a relationship is over. The loss of confidence, the self-doubt, can seed through your whole life, contaminating areas of your existence where you were previously assured. You find yourself riven with doubt. Your happiness levels plummet while you turn yourself in knots trying to work out what went wrong.

What can you do to arrest this decline in your confidence and happiness? Well, it's tricky, but managing to identify when you're lying to yourself is key. It's important to see where motivated reasoning is driving your thinking. There will be myriad contributing factors, and seeing a psychologist to try to work out the underlying drivers is a good first step. Remember that we are all mysteries to ourselves. Trying to work out why we do things is difficult without external support.

Also, be aware that social media or other people in your life may be driving your need to emulate what looks to be a perfect relationship.

Lie detection

Don't agree to disagree

Gird your loins and listen to the other person. You might learn something!

Don't take rubbish treatment, for any reason, ever

That's all I have to say about this.

11

Kat is sacked

You have been sacked. No, apologies: your role has been made redundant.

Darsha from HR is sitting across from you at her desk, her hands clasped in front of her. She has been giving bad news all week. You suspect she's fatigued from trying to put a positive spin on the terrible message she'd been entrusted to convey. Meredith threw her handbag at her earlier in the week. Meredith had been with the company for 23 years and had been given 12 weeks' redundancy. Darsha'd had to scrabble around on the ground helping Meredith retrieve her lipsticks, Nurofen and Tic Tacs.

Darsha's lucky cat had been waving at you as you entered her office. Darsha got right to it.

'In the new structure, unfortunately, your role is no longer required,' she says.

So, the lucky cat was waving goodbye.

'You're kidding,' you say.

'Unfortunately, I'm not.'

'David reassured me the senior leadership team was safe.'

'Yes. Unfortunately, in the new structure, there is no senior leadership team.'

'Is your job safe?' you ask. Her mouth becomes twisted.

'I don't know, Katrina. You are entitled to a redundancy package. I think you will find it is quite generous.'

'Is this about my failure to properly embed "demiurgic" in the values?'

'What?'

'Demiurgic.'

'What does that mean?'

'Nobody knows. That's the problem.'

'Right. Well. No.'

'Is it about my conversation with David about Gabriel Randall at Christmas in July?'

You had chosen the Christmas in July party the previous week to express your misgivings about Gabriel to David. The timing was perhaps not optimum. You hadn't realised the eggnog being served was so potent. Helen, Gabriel Randall's diminutive personal assistant, had been tipping in a bottle of brandy every time she topped up the cream and eggs.

By 9 p.m., when you clearly should have gone home, you had instead found yourself whispering urgently into David's right ear that you had serious concerns about Gabriel Randall and the direction in which he was taking the business. In your recollection, David had looked intensely interested in your opinion and had suggested booking in a meeting with Tanya, his EA, sometime to talk through your concerns.

'What? No, Kat. It's about the restructure. I'll need you to give back your assets.'

'If anyone is responsible for my indiscretion at the Christmas in July party it's Helen. She's a personal assistant, not a bartender. Where was the occupational health and safety? It's incumbent on the business to ensure that employees are not plied with alcohol during a work function.'

'I don't think Helen was plying you, Kat.'

The lucky cat is tiring of you. She is still waving but more slowly.

'You weren't there, Darsha. You didn't witness Helen being as liberal with alcohol as Jay Gatsby.'

'Whatever, Kat. I'm sorry you drank too much, but you are an adult; and regardless, this is a restructuring issue, not an issue of what you said or didn't say to David in relation to Gabriel. Or diurnal or diametric.'

'Ha! I never mentioned speaking to David.'

She looks at you pityingly. 'Wow, Kat, you just told me you did like two minutes ago.'

You mentally trawl back through the last few minutes of conversation.

'Oh yes, you're right.'

'Kat, do you want me to organise you an Uber?'

'I'm driving my own car. Do you think I could still come to the Welcome to Spring party in September?'

'Probably not, Kat.'

Kat has another encounter with the police

You're sitting at a set of traffic lights, having picked up Porridge from his play date with Ebony the staffy.

'It's your lucky day, Porridge,' you say. 'You'll be seeing even more of me now. It'll be just like it was during the lockdowns. Except with fewer liver treats, because I won't be earning any money.'

You're two blocks from home when a police officer walks into the middle of the road and motions you to pull over. This means crossing over two lanes of traffic. You comply. He approaches your window. Porridge throws himself into your lap and lunges at him.

'Wind your window down,' the officer says.

Porridge starts barking.

'It's not really winding any more, is it?' you say, smiling. 'It's just pushing a button.'

He doesn't smile. 'Are you aware you're driving an unregistered vehicle?'

'No.' You push Porridge back to the passenger side.

'This is an unregistered vehicle. May I see your licence, please?'

Porridge's barking reaches frenzy level.

'I'm sorry, I couldn't hear that. What did you say?' You grab Porridge's muzzle and clamp it shut with your hand.

'This is an unregistered vehicle. May I see your licence, please?'

'No, that can't be right.'

'Listen,' he says, putting his hands on his knees and leaning towards you. 'This conversation is being filmed.' He gestures to the small camera on his hat, which is pointing at you. 'Everything you say is recorded. So, I'm telling you, this car has been unregistered for two years. Also, your dog should be restrained.'

Your heart starts hammering.

'Get out of the car, please.'

You get out slowly, showing your hands and closing the door in Porridge's face with your foot.

'What are you doing?' says the officer.

'Demonstrating I have nothing in my hands.'

'I'd be very surprised if a middle-aged woman from the northern beaches were carrying a gun.'

Middle-aged? *Middle-aged?* You're 36. Just because he's about 12 doesn't mean you're ready for retirement. You hope no one from the neighbourhood sees you being treated like a criminal. You look over the road. Of course, there's Riya – Mrs Kovacic's friend – standing on the pavement, shopping bag in hand, watching you.

'Can I see your licence?' the officer repeats.

You pull your phone out of your wallet and hold the picture of your licence in front of him, pointing to your birthdate.

'Okay. Thank you.'

'Yep,' you say, tapping the birthdate with your index finger. 'I'm a child of the '80s.'

'Yep, okay.'

'So a bit young to be called middle-aged.'

'Now, you must drive straight to the transport authority centre, get a pink slip and get registered. Do not divert. Do not go home.'

'Do not pass go,' you say.

You don't know what the ramifications of driving an unregistered car are, but you do know Ryan Schmidt had so many unpaid parking fines he did a stint in jail. When he returned to work, he looked haunted.

'I won't divert, officer. Prison's not for me.'

He looked perplexed. 'You're not going to prison. Just get your car registered.'

'Yes, officer.'

'One more thing. What breed is your dog? He's gorgeous.'

Porridge had stopped barking and was trying to stick his nose out the small gap at the top of the window.

'He's a groodle.'

'Wife wants a dog. I don't want some wimpy thing, I want a proper dog. Like him. He's a proper dog.'

He goes over to the car and pat's Porridge's nose.

'You should get one. Your wife would love it.'

'Hey boy, what's happening?'

Porridge whines and licks his hand.

'If you go to jail, I'll mind your dog.' He looks at you and smiles.

'I was fired today.'

'Oh, I'm sorry to hear that; but a young lady like yourself won't have any trouble getting another job, I'm sure.'

He turns, gets on his bike and leaves you standing there.

Young lady? Now that's more like it.

You look over the road. Riya is still standing there, her shopping bag now at her feet. She gives you a wave, puts her phone back in her bag, picks up her shopping and continues on her way.

'Say, hello to Riya, Porridge.'

You start the car. Porridge barks at Riya as you pass.

Mrs Kovacic brings Mrs Belleri back

'I can't believe it,' you say to Michael the next morning. 'Twelve years I've been there and, because of some Myers-Briggs demiurge, I'm sacked.'

You're sitting on the couch. Porridge is lying across you.

'It's okay, Kat, I survived going from corporate to council. Also, you have savings and I'm here. I'm working. I can pay your mortgage.' He's standing in the kitchen in his pyjamas. 'You want tea?'

'Yes please. The policeman called me middle-aged. I'm probably too old to get a job. I wonder if I can get the pension?'

'How old was the policeman?' he says. He waves a tea bag at you from the kitchen.

'About 12.'

'There you go. Everybody over 25 will look middle-aged to him.'

'Actually, no tea, thanks. Tea's for old people. Maybe I could join the police force. I'd be really good at drug busts.'

'I have to get in the shower, Kat. I'm going to be late.'

You follow him around as he strips off his pyjamas.

'Could I get a job as a ranger?' you say. 'I'm good with nudity and parking.'

'Um, sure. Kat, there is more to it than that; but anyway, I've got to get going.'

'I can't drive a manual; will that go against me? Will they give me a high-vis vest?'

'Kat, you'll be fine. You'll be back employed in a heartbeat.'

'Actually, I have an interview next week. I probably won't get it.'

There's the sound of a key in the door. You both turn. Mrs Kovacic enters with Mrs Belleri in tow.

Michael is standing naked in the lounge room.

'Good morning, Kat. Good morning, Mickey,' says Mrs Kovacic. Michael grabs a pillow off the lounge.

'Hello, Mrs Kovacic,' he says, backing into the bedroom.

'You're fired,' says Mrs Belleri. 'I told you last time something bad was going to happen. I saw it in your future.'

'How did you know you I was fired?'

She shrugs extravagantly.

'I told her,' says Mrs Kovacic, pulling her phone out of her apron.

'How did you know?'

'I heard you telling Porridge. Anyway, Mr Yee goes to God,' says Mrs Kovacic. They both cross themselves. 'Mr Kovacic has stroke. There's the scam business. There's the near-death experience with the hair dryer. Then you were nearly killed by a garbage truck. You lose your job. You arrested. Curse is out of control.' She ushers Mrs Belleri onto your couch, landing her on Susan's tail. Susan meows and retreats to the bedroom.

'The cat's behaviour is a clear sign. It's time to drive out the curse,' says Mrs Belleri.

'What?' you say. 'I was not arrested.'

'Yes you were. Riya make hilarious TikTok of you being arrested by policeman. You want to see?'

'No, I don't want to see. My car was unregistered. I was not arrested.'

'I'd like to see it,' says Mrs Belleri.

Mrs Kovacic moves closer to Mrs Belleri, positioning her phone so they can both watch. Mrs Belleri laughs. 'Show me again.'

'I know; Riya's got real talent,' says Mrs Kovacic.

'She should work at Channel 9,' says Mrs Belleri.

'Excuse me. It's early and I'm busy.'

'You're not busy. You're sacked,' says Mrs Belleri.

Mrs Kovacic puts her phone back in her apron. 'Now, Kat, you worried about the money now you have no job,' she takes your hand. 'I pay for Mrs Belleri to remove curse. No more delay.'

Mrs Kovacic takes up her position on Mrs Belleri's left.

'I warned you last time I was here that something bad was going to happen,' says Mrs Belleri.

Michael reappears with a towel wrapped around his waist.

'Hello, I'm Michael. It's 7.30 a.m.'

'Yes, Mickey. This is Mrs Belleri.' The two older women are impervious to the disruption.

'It's Michael, Mrs Kovacic. Hello, Mrs Belleri. Kat wasn't fired; she was made redundant.' It's the most impatient you've ever heard him. You like it.

'Redundant, fired. It's all the same,' says Mrs Belleri.

'Kat,' says Michael, 'I'm not worried, and neither should you be.'

'This is problem,' says Mrs Kovacic. 'You young people. You don't know disaster when it hitting you in the face. How she going to pay for strata, Micky? The building fees are huge.'

'Mrs Kovacic, do you have a key to Kat's flat?' he says.

'Yes, she has a key,' you say. 'I keep locking myself out.'

'Right. I have to take a shower or I'll be late for work. Don't worry, Kat. All will be okay. Very nice to meet you,' he says to Mrs Belleri. The irony is lost on her.

Mrs Belleri sits on your couch. She folds her hands in her lap. 'He your boyfriend?'

'Yes, of course. Do you think I let random men use my shower?'

'He's good. Try to hold on to him.'

'Right.'

'The lift is still not working. I could have a heart attack. I have a heart condition. It runs in my family. My father dropped dead at 50, God rest his soul, and his sister at 51. I've only come here because Mrs Kovacic is my very good friend and she loves you.'

'Thanks for coming, Sophia.'

You feel compelled to say something.

'Yes, thanks for coming.'

'So, as I was saying,' says Mrs Kovacic, 'Kat has been made recumbent.'

'Redundant.'

'That's what I just said.'

'No, you said... Never mind.'

'Yes, redundancy is part of the curse, Big Dog Girl,' says Mrs Belleri.

'Redundancy is part of life, not part of a curse.'

'She's from Generation Y. They're the worst,' says Mrs Belleri.

'The worst at what?' you say.

Porridge sits next to Mrs Belleri, puts his paw on her lap and whines.

'Big dog agrees. Also, he has something in his paw. Let me look, big boy.' She opens her cavernous handbag, extracts a pair of glasses and picks up Porridge's right paw. Using her long nails, she pulls a thorn out of his paw. Brandishing the bindi she says, 'See, the curse has spread to the big dog.'

She's passes the bindi to Mrs Kovacic, who takes it and goes into the kitchen.

Mrs Belleri pats the couch on the other side of her. 'Sit. We will begin.'

'I don't have time for this now, I have to write an email.'

'You lie. You have no job no email.'

You sit. 'I have to get another job, hence the email.'

'I will remove the curse, and you will get your job back.'

Susan returns from the bedroom, jumps up on your lap and bats Porridge on the head.

'The cat knows I'm telling the truth.'

The fight goes out of you. You've been fired, you've been pulled over by the police, you've been concussed and you were nearly killed by a hair dryer. Maybe Mrs Kovacic is right. You're cursed.

'How much does this cost?'

'$100.'

'She give you discount,' Mrs Kovacic pipes up.
'I thought you were paying, Mrs Kovacic?'
'I go halves.'
'What does it cost normally?'
'$200.'
'Do you take credit cards?'
'Yes. Square $110. Cash better.'
'I have cash'.
'On you?'
'I don't keep cash in my pyjamas. In my bedroom.'
'You give her $100,' says Mrs Kovacic. 'I pay you back.'

You go into the bedroom with Porridge in tow. Michael is in there getting dressed.

'I'm giving her $100, half of which Mrs Kovacic will owe me. I have lost control of my life, but she thinks you're good and I should try to hold on to you.'

He opens his wallet and pulls out $100. You look at the money.

'No, I can't take that.'

'Yes you can. Can we maybe get the key off Mrs Kovacic?' He shrugs his backpack onto his back. 'Okay, I'm going to make a run for it. Wish me luck. I love you, Kat. Don't worry, okay?'

You stand in the bedroom, Michael's money in your hand. You hear him jog past the women. 'Bye ladies,' he says.

'Bye, Mickey,' says Mrs Kovacic.

'Bye, handsome,' says Mrs Belleri.

'It's Michael,' he says as he shuts the door.

You re-enter the lounge room and give Mrs Belleri the money.

'So,' says Mrs Belleri, having put the two $50 notes into her wallet. 'Sit here and hold my hand.'

She squeezes your hand. Her hand is fleshy and her rings dig into your fingers.

'Close your eyes. Spirits, Big Dog Girl wants her job back.'

'Shouldn't you use my name? How will the spirits know who you're talking about?'

'Don't talk; you're disturbing things.'

There's a knock at the door. Mrs Kovacic answers it. Willow bounds into the living room.

'Oh Kat, dude, I'm so sorry you got sacked.' She comes over and puts her arms around you. 'Oh, hello, you must be Mrs Belleri. I'm super happy to meet you. Are you taking the curse off? Can I watch?'

Charlotte follows Willow in.

'Hello, I'm Charlotte.'

Mrs Kovacic takes control. 'This is Mrs Belleri. She is here to drive away the curse that got Kat sacked. If she had curse taken off before, Kat would still have job – but she knew better.'

Charlotte leans into her bag and produces a bottle of Moët. Charlotte must have champagne about her person at all times.

'Kat! No more corporate. This calls for champagne. Mrs Kovacic; Mrs Belleri, is it? Will you join us?'

Mrs Kovacic eyes the bottle. It has been 30 years since she last drunk a Moët champagne toast.

'It's not even 8 a.m.,' you say.

'Just pretend you're at the airport,' says Charlotte, 'and you're on your way to the Maldives.'

'Am I taking the curse off, or are you all standing around drinking?' says Mrs Belleri.

'Just a quick one,' says Charlotte.

Charlotte and Mrs Belleri square off like two dogs in the dog park, vying for park supremacy – Charlotte's Afghan versus Mrs Belleri's bulldog.

'No, not a quick one,' says Mrs Belleri. 'Either we do it now or I go – and if you expect me to climb up those stairs again, you'll lose the discount, Big Dog Girl.'

'Willow, let's have four glasses, please. The long ones,' says Charlotte.

Mrs Belleri clips her handbag shut, levers herself to the edge of the couch and stands. Willow returns and hands out the glasses.

'Okay,' says Mrs Belleri, heading towards the door. 'I'm off.'

Mrs Kovacic flutters her hands. 'Don't go, please, Sophia.'

'Also,' says Charlotte, 'I bought you a present.' She hands you a moisturiser that looks like it's from the expensive counter at David Jones.

Mrs Kovacic claps her hands. 'Kat,' she says, 'Charlotte knows everything about skin. Look at my skin since she gave me special cream.'

Mrs Belleri puts her hand to the doorknob, then turns back towards Mrs Kovacic. 'What about your skin?' she says.

'I've been using this product Charlotte gave me.'

'You look the same to me,' says Mrs Belleri. 'Those expensive brands! Big con!'

She opens the door and steps into the hallway. 'Big Dog Girl, come here. I'll explain how to take care of big dog's paw.'

You go to the door and she grabs you by the arm, whispering in your ear. 'The blonde woman. Don't trust her. She's bad news. Also your boyfriend has a nice physique.'

You involuntarily shudder. *Oh god*, you think to yourself. She trundles off down the corridor.

'Fix the lift,' she says, before she starts down the first flight.

'Did I interrupt with the champagne?' Charlotte says as you re-enter the flat. 'Sorry.'

'Don't be', you say.

You were an extremely high achiever at school – a selective school, no less – until you got to Year 10, when you inexplicably bombed. There were meetings between the teachers, your parents and the school counsellor. The principal was even brought in.

You weren't sure why, but you had just stopped trying with school. The discussions swirled around you in small, multiple eddies.

You realise you feel the same way now. Your life is out of control. There must be a reason you are swimming in this pond of misery. You do not know what the reason is, but surely one of the people offering you advice does.

'I'm so sorry, Mrs Kovacic. Please tell her to come back,' Charlotte is now saying.

Mrs Kovacic finishes her champagne and holds her glass out. 'It not good when she gets offended. Is there any left in that bottle?'

'Sure,' says Charlotte. 'Look at you, Mrs Kovacic: glowing skin and downing champagne before breakfast.'

Mrs Kovacic puts her once-again-empty glass on the table. 'Okay, now I go.'

'Please tell Mrs Belleri I'll pay for her to come back,' says Charlotte.

'Can I go with Mrs Kovacic?' says Willow. 'I want to see if Mrs Belleri can remove the curse from Will.'

'Come with me,' says Mrs Kovacic. 'She won't have got far. She very unfit.'

'You must have seen some amazing curses in the old country,' you hear Willow say as the door closes.

'So that's the famous Mrs Belleri,' says Charlotte.

'Yep. She is a force of nature. I just gave her $100 so I could get my job back. I've lost the plot.'

'Wow, you forked out?'

'Yep.'

'To get your job back?'

'Yep. Then she left without finishing the job.'

She upends the bottle, pouring the dregs into your glass.

'But you wanted to get out of corporate. You're now out of corporate.'

'Yep. However, I do have an interview next week.'

'What's the job?'

'I don't want to jinx it.'

'Just, don't take the first job that's offered. Don't get hauled back into the horrors of corporate life.'

'What I'd really like to is convert a mansion in the country and run women's retreats.'

'Since when?'

'Since this morning.'

'You keen on making beds?'

'It was on Instagram; I found a story about a woman who left her corporate job and converted a country mansion. It looked amazing.'

'You believe what you see on Instagram?'

'Maybe I'll become a world-class athlete. Do you think I'm too old?'

'You might have to go to the gym more than once a month.'

Your relationship with exercise is complicated. You have been visiting a local gym housed in a gigantic warehouse. The trainer, Tobias, is recovering from a horrendous spinal injury. He walks on crutches.

In the warm-up prior to each class, your training buddy, Dana, feels the need to remind you just how amazing Tobias is. 'Isn't he an inspiration?' You always nod in agreement.

The issue you have is that his inspirational presence robs you of your right to complain. How can you whinge that your knee hurts or you want to vomit after a 30-second sprint on the assault bike when he is a walking example of resilience and positivity? Resilience and positivity are two of your former employer's corporate values. It is not fair to be consistently exposed to them when you consistently fail to embody them.

Every morning when your alarm goes off, the litany of excuses commence. *My knee hurts; I think I have contagious conjunctivitis;*

I have Covid; I haven't had adequate sleep and I could fall asleep on the spin bike; I've got too much on; I'll go for a walk later; gyms are stupid. Then Porridge licks your face so you fall out of bed, resentfully pull on your tights, complain it's cold and head off.

Tobias will, of course, be there, having been up since 4.30 a.m.

'Hey Kat,' he says. 'Good to see you. How's your knee?'

This is the thing about Tobias. He has every right to be dismissive of people's real or imagined injuries, but he is kind and solicitous. Also, you have to admit – maybe it's the endorphin high – that when you get to the end of a workout and he high-fives you and says, 'You smashed that, legend,' for a moment you think anything is possible.

'I like the gym,' you say to Charlotte. 'I think I'll become a personal trainer.'

'Okay. See, you have so many options.'

'Any of that champagne left?'

'I could go get another bottle.'

'No. Don't. I need to think.'

You sit and look out the window.

'I think I want to learn about cryptocurrency trading.'

'Oh really?'

'Yep. You never know if you never go.'

'Okay. Do you remember the three rules?'

'I remember what you said about paper trading.'

'Yep. Rule two: keep your accounts separate. Three: take a three-day internet fast between deciding to trade with your hard earned and taking the plunge.'

You smile at her. 'I don't have to think about demiurgic any more.'

'I'm proud of you, Kat. You don't have to go back and do the same thing. You're smart and brave and if you want to do life another way, why shouldn't you? Now's the time for you to believe in yourself. When you're standing on the precipice.'

'Sounds a bit too motivational for me.'

You squirt some of the cream she gave you on your hands. It smells like money.

'At least if I'm standing on a cliff, my hands will smell nice.'

I THINK I'LL BE A PERSONAL TRAINER

Kat undoubtedly has some challenges right now. Expecting our lives to go smoothly is unrealistic, yet it's surprising how ill equipped we are to manage hurdles when they arise. We often turn to the purveyors of magical thinking – new-age self-help gurus – who are happy to sell us the lie that everything happens for a reason, that if we fire up our manifesting abilities we can rejig our existence and have the life we want and deserve. We may laugh at Mrs Belleri and her curse-removing rituals; but, if we're doing manifesting meditations and creating vision boards, we're accessing the same faulty brain wiring.

Kat is aggregating her issues, so she now perceives things to be on a downward spiral. This is a lie Kat has sold herself. We have a habit of seeing things in clusters. We use a heuristic (yes, we really do use these all the time) to try to make sense of our world. If there is a pattern to what's happening to us, it gives us a sense of order. There is meaning. Human beings are extremely uncomfortable living in a random universe, and yet randomness is the truth. As much as we'd like to spin it, things just happen to us. The more we try to collectivise our experiences, the more we muddy the cognitive waters.

There is no connection between Kat being sacked and being pulled over by the police, or Mrs Belleri barging into her flat; yet Kat's brain, primed to look for patterns, has created a link. We are pattern-seeking machines. As soon as we identify a pattern, even if imagined, it's difficult for our brain to unsee it.

In our primitive days, being able to see patterns was essential to our survival. We learned what to expect from the weather by watching the pattern of the seasons. We learned to identify the pattern of lions' paws so we could avoid becoming dinner. Pattern recognition was how we made sense of the world. The same brain wiring is in play today in a much more sophisticated world. That's why buying into the brain's sponge-like capacity to absorb patterns is an accident waiting to happen.

To stop clumping your life events together into a story of tragedy, it's important to first acknowledge that you are cognitively predisposed to see patterns, then challenge the thought when it arises. You are not on a lucky streak. You are not having a bad run of luck. If you believe these comforting axioms, it's going to be harder for you to analyse the situation you are in with clarity and make a good decision.

On going to the gym

Struggling to keep a gym routine? Pay the fees, go twice and spend the next six months trying to get out of the contract? The reason you do this is that your brain, specifically your prefrontal cortex, shuts down when you think about yourself in the future. Your brain considers your future self like it does a stranger.[22] The further you look into your future, the worse it gets. It's one reason why saving for your retirement, stopping after two drinks or avoiding eating the donut is so hard. Your brain doesn't care about future impoverished you, hungover you or unhealthy you any more than it would a stranger.

This is why you're better off forming a habit than trying to use willpower. It takes 10 minutes a day for 30 to 40 days to form a new habit. Make going to the gym a thing that your legs just do first thing in the morning. Set up a savings account with a direct debit that you don't have to think about. Remove the donuts from your house.

Also, visualising yourself in the future, trying to feel what it would be like and telling yourself stories do help to acquaint your brain with future you.

Lie detection

You're not on a lucky streak

This is especially relevant if you're whooping it up at the blackjack table. Stop yelling 'Yippee, I'm on fire.' The casino always wins. Go home.

Just one more margarita, then I'll go home

You probably won't. Be prepared for tomorrow's hangover.

12

How many curses are there?

'There's more than one curse?' says Michael.

You're out for dinner with Michael. The people at the next table have been staring over each other's shoulders for the last 20 minutes, occasionally smiling at each other and nodding. Not a word spoken.

'It's dynamic,' you say. 'Sometimes there is one curse, and sometimes there are many curses.'

'We'd go on holidays when I was a child,' Michael says, 'and my mother would comment on how good the traffic was. Dad would hit the steering wheel with his hand. "Why", he would say, "would you mention the traffic? Now you've jinxed us." It's the same thing, right? Curses! Traffic gods.'

'I touch wood for luck.' You pull the corner of the tablecloth off the table. Touch the wood.

'What do you need luck for?'

'For my job interview.'

'You'll be fine.'

'Also, what if I don't want another job?'

'Oh, okay,' says Michael, cleaning a smear off his knife with a napkin. 'What would you do instead?'

You shrug.

'You're not thinking about the crypto thing, are you? Did Charlotte talk you into trading crypto?'

Your chest tightens. You stab at one of your prawns.

'No. We talked about believing in myself.'

He raises his eyebrows. 'And trading crypto.'

'No. But, well... I *am* thinking about paper trading.'

'Paper trading?'

'It's how you learn to trade safely.'

'So, you *are* thinking about trading crypto.'

'Paper trading is free. Just pretend. No money changes hands.'

'Nothing's free,' he says.

'Anyway, Charlotte's offered to pay Mrs Belleri to come back and do a total curse makeover. She ruined proceedings by popping open a bottle of Moët.'

'At 7.30 in the morning? Boy, she likes a drink.'

You put down your prawn.

'See, why would you say that? People drink champagne at the airport early in the morning.'

'Kat.'

'If I want to investigate crypto, well, what's the problem? Charlotte has a conservative approach. I like the idea of maybe not spending the rest of my life in corporate.'

'If you don't want to get a job immediately, I am happy to keep things going. Don't feel pressured to do something silly.'

A bolt of anger shoots up through your chest. 'Something silly?'

'I didn't mean it like that. Honestly, Kat, I don't want another argument. I hate arguing.'

'Are you being like this because of the eBay scam?'

'Kat, a lot of people have lost vast amounts of money with cryptocurrency.'

You look at Michael, sitting across the table. You've never noticed before, but his chin is weak. You don't like weak chins.

Your father calls people with weak chins 'chinless wonders'. You look down at your mee grob. In this moment you can't bear to look at him.

Michael pulls the bottle out of the ice bucket and refills your glass, then wipes the condensation off the side of the bottle. You notice he's wearing a cardigan – and not a fancy Country Road cardigan. It's an old man's cardigan. He has the chicken t-shirt underneath it. How have you ended up with this tedious chinless wonder in a bad t-shirt and a cardigan, when you could be independently wealthy, jetting off to the Maldives on a private jet?

'Hey, did you end up getting the key back from Mrs Kovacic?' says Michael.

'You can try.'

'You want me to ask her?'

'If it matters that much to you.'

The couple next to you still hasn't spoken. She's wiping the corner of her mouth with a napkin. He's looking at his phone. You wish you were them.

The job interview

It's 11.55 a.m. You're sitting at a conference table across from a man and a woman. As soon as you'd entered the lift you'd had deja vu. It was like being back at WWS. The interview is even on the 17th floor. That can't be a good sign.

The woman, Trudy, is still flicking through your résumé. You've already been here for 25 minutes. She has a deep, chesty cough and a severe mouth. The man, Peter, is smiling at you. He is very thin and is wearing what looks like a new suit. He keeps drawing his hand across the lapel in an appreciative manner.

'I'm interested to know,' says Peter, 'why do you want to work for this company?'

'Well,' you say, 'I saw a brilliant post on LinkedIn from your CEO. I was struck by the sheer clarity and authenticity of her perspective.'

Trudy coughs. 'What exactly did you like about it?'

'It was clear,' you say. 'I get where she's coming from.'

'Really?' Trudy says. 'Where is she coming from?'

'I think she's coming from a very authentic place.'

'How would your co-workers describe you?' says Peter.

'Collegial, hardworking, a good communicator. A Mediator. I'm very empathic. So, also maybe an empath.'

Trudy starts coughing again. You hand her your glass of water.

'And finally,' Peter says, after what feels like a thousand questions, 'why did you leave your last position?'

You look down at your hands clasped in your lap. They're sweaty. Why are you sitting in an office identical to the one you've left, with sweaty hands? What are you getting yourself worked up about? Suddenly you wonder whether you really want to join another organisation like this and wait around for another Gabriel to ruin your life.

'I couldn't embed "demiurgic" in the values.'

'I'm sorry?' Trudy says

'Don't be,' you say.

'Our values are resilience, bravery and innovation,' says Peter. 'How do you think you'd go enacting them?'

'No, Peter,' says Trudy. '"Bravery" is gone. It's now "aliveness".' She starts coughing again.

You look out the window, then look back at Peter. You stand and pick up your bag. 'Thanks for having me,' you say, like you're leaving a party. You walk to the door.

Peter looks confused.

'Ms Mitchell?' he says.

'How can "aliveness" be a value?' you say.

Peter smiles uncertainly. Trudy coughs. You shut the door behind you. Your heart is hammering, but in a good way. You feel invincible.

You control the environment in which you exist. You do not have to work for a company that has "aliveness" as a value. You stride down the corridor. You actually look back over your shoulder, like you're in a commercial, and toss your hair. You imagine people saying, 'Who *is* that sassy girl?'

Sassy girl runs into Gabriel

You take the lift down to the foyer and exit to the street when you spot him sitting at a cafe. Gabriel Randall. Alone.

This cannot be a coincidence, you say to yourself.

Riding high on the adrenaline of your triumphant job rejection, you take the seat opposite him.

'Excuse me?' he says.

'Hi,' you say, resting your chin on your hand. 'How's your new job?'

'I'm sorry. I can't remember your name.'

'Katrina. You had me sacked.'

'Oh. Hello. As I recall, I didn't have you sacked. Your role was made redundant.'

'Same, same.'

'Okay. I'm sorry that happened. How're things now?'

'I'm trading cryptocurrency.'

'Well. Good for you. Things always work out for the best.' He looks back down at his computer.

'Things didn't work out for the best for others on my team. Two of them had to sell their houses. Now they're renting. Not great in your 40s.'

'Yep, that's tough. Anyway, nice to see you.' He picks up his phone. 'Must make a call.'

A waiter appears; you order coffee.

'Do you feel bad?'

Gabriel sighs, continuing to look at his phone. 'About what, Katrina?'

'About screwing over people who'd been loyal to the business for years? About leaving it in a worse state than when you arrived?'

'Yes, I feel terrible. Do you mind? I've got to send an email.'

'I thought you had to make a call.' You stick out your chin in triumph.

Gabriel slams his laptop closed and looks directly at you for the first time. His face has changed. The pleasant countenance has gone.

'Oh, I remember you. You're the skinny, pretty girl from the 15th floor.'

You are disturbed that, in the middle of this ugly moment, you are pleased at the compliment.

'No, the 17th floor.'

'What the fuck do you want from me?'

You don't know what you want. Your optimistic high immediately dissipates. Why are you pointlessly haranguing this man? What were you thinking, walking out of that interview? You are in no position to knock back work. You have a huge mortgage and an enormous strata expense. You should go back up and say sorry, you had a small stroke.

'I just wanted you to know it was bad.'

'Oh, did you? And you would be much better equipped to lead an organisation through change, I imagine?'

You flounder. 'Well, I wouldn't treat people like they're disposable goods.'

'You middle-class girls are all the same with your pretensions to the common good. When did you last do anything to help someone who was struggling?'

'I volunteer.'

'Is there anything more middle class than volunteering?'

You open your mouth to reply. He continues.

'What do you drive, a hybrid?'

'Like you can talk.'

'I'm from Fairfield.'

You can't help it; you look down at his RM Williams.

'I had a rough start, and I pulled myself up by my bootstraps and got on with it.'

'Good for you. Not everybody can.'

He shrugs. 'Well, you might not approve, but we live in a capitalist society, not a caste system. If you want to get ahead, you can.'

'Thanks. I've read Ayn Rand.'

'Business exists to turn a profit,' he says, sitting back in his seat and putting his hands behind his head. 'You may not like it but, at the end of the day, there's no loyalty – only performance.'

'Yes, I get that. Hence me being out of a job.'

'Bloated organisations, where people are employed on a full-time basis to remember people's birthdays and send out cards, are not sustainable.'

'For some employees, it was the only birthday card they received. Anyway, what's the difference between that and trying to get "demiurgic" into the values?'

'It was you who undermined "demiurgic".'

'It's a stupid word. Anyway, I must be off. It's been terrific chatting to you.'

As you rise from the table he says, 'You can't keep people in a job because you feel sorry for them.'

'Tell that to Chen, who lost her job a month after her husband left her with two small children. She's an actuary. She's now working part-time in a shop. Also,' you say as you walk off, 'Myers-Briggs is nonsense.'

'You *would* think that,' he calls after you. 'INFPs have no imagination.'

Susan socks

You get home. Porridge rushes into the bedroom and brings you the other of Michael's socks with Susan's face on them. You remember the anniversary when you'd gifted Michael the socks.

'Isn't Susan your ex boyfriend's cat?' he'd said at the time.

'Yes, but she way prefers you.'

He took them and put them on immediately.

'I am proud to wear Susan on my feet.'

You wonder if the sock choice Porridge has made is deliberate. You have a brief tussle with Porridge over the sock, which he wins. Michael calls from the kitchen.

'How'd you go?'

Since the disastrous dinner, your relationship with Michael is operating at 80 per cent.

'Um, I don't think I got the job.'

'You don't know that. I bet they loved you.'

'I really don't think they did. I don't want to talk about it.'

'Okay.'

'Also, I ran into Gabriel.'

'Gabriel, the Myers-Briggs guy who got you fired?'

'Yes. I don't want to talk about it.'

'Okay.'

You take your laptop to the couch and open the trading simulator. Michael emerges from the kitchen and stands behind the couch, looking over your shoulder.

'What are you doing?'

'Just having a play.'

'Oh? They want to know your employment status?'

'Michael, I just have to go through these steps to get to the paper trading.'

'Okay.' He walks back to the kitchen. 'You want something to eat?'

'No, I'm good thanks.'

You feel him wander past the back of the lounge again. You tense up.

'Kat, I'm sorry, but why do they want your employment status?'

'I don't know. It's okay.'

'And your address?'

'Yes, my address.' Porridge jumps up next you and puts his paw on the keyboard.

Michael is now leaning over the back of the couch. Why won't the pair of them leave you alone?

'Sweetie, that doesn't seem safe. Why do they want your annual income? Why do they need that?'

You take your hands off the keyboard and place them in your lap. 'Sweetie' sounds strange coming out of Michael's mouth. He is not one to use endearments.

'*Sweetie*, I've just got to give them this information so I can get to the simulator.'

'Okay. You want a drink?' He goes into the kitchen. You hear the fridge opening. Then, moments later, 'What are they asking for there?'

He's back behind you. *My god, he's like a ninja.* You can feel his breath on your neck.

'Michael, don't worry. I know what I'm doing.'

'Do you? How would you know if its diversification of investments or hedging? It sounds dodgy.'

Your chest tightens. You feel a glittery tension across your scalp.

Michael pushes Porridge off the couch and sits next to you. He waggles the wine bottle.

'Sav blanc?'

This triggers an unfortunate memory of The Hipster turning up after his eight-month absence, proffering wine and apologies.

You stand up. The computer drops to the ground. Porridge runs into the bedroom.

'No, I don't want a drink. It's Tuesday.'

'Okay, sorry. I forgot.'

'We've been together long enough that you should know I don't drink on Monday or Tuesday. Why doesn't what I do matter to you?'

He looks up at you from the couch. You lean down and pick up the computer.

'Do you mind if I have a glass?' he says.

You hug the computer to your chest and look at him.

'Is this about the crypto trading?' he says.

You shrug.

You're both staring at each other. You feel as though the distance between you is widening, like you're both standing on travelators at the airport, going in opposite directions.

'I walked out of the interview.'

'What? Why?'

'Because I wanted to.'

'What happened in the interview?'

'It was WWS all over again. I hated them. She coughed all over me, and "aliveness" was one of their values.'

'Okay.'

'I'm trying to work this out for myself. Please let me do it.'

'Okay. I'm just trying to help.'

'I don't want to work in corporate.'

'Oh, Kat. I don't think you can replace a full-time job with crypto trading.'

'Don't tell me what I can and can't do.'

'I'm not. I'm just saying.'

'You're trying to control me. You're more controlling than you think. I can't make a move without you monitoring me.'

Michael gets up off the couch, holding his hands in front of him like he's being held up.

'Okay, I'll leave you to it.'

He grabs his coat, puts the lead on Porridge and closes the door behind them.

You burst into tears. Why is everything so hard? Why is Michael so negative? Why was that interview so horrible? Why is Gabriel Randall such a dick? You are trying to be self-actualised. Oh god. Self-actualised sounds like self-help. Who have you become?

You ring Charlotte. She turns up at the door one minute later.

Hide the glasses

'Wow, you've been ugly crying. What's wrong? I brought champagne.'

'I want to learn to trade.'

Charlotte raises her eyebrows. 'Not in that state you don't.'

She goes to your cupboard and retrieves two glasses.

'Where's Michael?'

This provokes a fresh bout of tears.

'He's "leaving me to it".'

Charlotte nods. 'Okay.'

'He's walking Porridge. And if he comes back, hide the glasses.'

'Okay,' she says handing you a tissue and one of the now-full glasses. 'What's up?'

You blow your nose.

'I'm overwhelmed. I finally got to the simulator site and I'm lost.'

'Oh god, is that all? I can totally help you with that.'

'Also, I walked out of a job interview.'

'Why?'

'I realised halfway through I didn't want their stupid job.'

She clinks her glass on yours.

'Congratulations. I'm proud of you.'

'I wish Michael was.'

'Don't be too hard on him. He's just trying to protect you.'

'I don't need protecting. I'm not a baby. Also, I had a stupid argument with Gabriel Randall.'

'Is that the demiurgic guy?'

'Everything is stupid.'

'Did you tell this Randall guy he was stupid?'

'Sort of. Anyway, I'm just trying to get to the simulator and they asked me for all this information. I just want to get to the paper trading part. I wanted to feel I'd achieved something today. Otherwise it's all been a total cock-up.'

'Okay, it's all fine. You're a bloody champ. Let's get things set up. Okay, first, keep your accounts separate.'

'You already told me that.'

'It's safer. Different lender.'

'Oh god, no.'

'Go on, open an account. It's quick.'

'That's more passwords. I'm going to use the same one. I can't stand it.'

'No, you're not.' Charlotte smacks you lightly on the wrist. 'Just do it properly.'

God, if one more person tells you what to do, you'll scream.

'Okay. Jeez. PORR—'

'Kat, slow down.'

'Please don't tell me to slow down. Just tell me what to do next.'

'Okay, settle down.'

'Don't tell me to settle down.'

She tops up your champagne. 'Password rules,' she says. 'Don't use a password that someone is going to guess. Don't use your pet's names.'

'But I can't remember anything else.'

'If you are going to use the name of a pet, don't use the pet whose name you regularly call out in public.'

That makes sense. 'So, not Porridge?'

'And then swap one number for a letter.'

'A what?'

'The S in Susan looks like a two, so, you can spell her name with—'

You type in '2u2an'.

'And then the first three numbers that spring to mind.'

You type in '123'.

'And now, do *not* share your password with anyone. Not Michael. Not Mrs K.'

'You think Michael would steal from me?'

'I'm not saying that, Kat. You just trust too easily is all I'm saying.'

'Okay. Okay. That's done. Can you show me how to get going on the simulator?'

'Have you got it open?'

You toggle to the simulator site.

'Here.'

You leave Charlotte with your laptop and go into the kitchen to pull some cheese out of the fridge. This elicits an immediate response from Susan.

'Why', you say to Susan as you break off bits of cheese for her, 'does everybody feel the need to handhold me?'

Charlotte calls from the couch. 'Here we are. You're live.'

'Thank you.' You return to the couch.

'Now, please tell me you're not going to put any money in until you've done your research and tested your decision-making across a minimum of 100 paper trades.'

'Yes. Yes. Yes. I know, 100, minimum.'

In an uncharacteristic move, she punches you lightly on the arm. 'Okay, I'll leave you to it, champ.'

Michael's back

You are happily toggling between sites, imaging what it's going to be like shifting handsome profits from the trading platform to your freedom fund.

'This is fun, Susan. I'm the captain of my own destiny,' you say. She licks your hand. 'Thanks, my good madam, for your heartfelt congratulations.'

The door opens and Porridge bounds in.

'Hey,' Michael says. 'You sort it?'

'Sorted.'

'I'm sorry.'

'I'm sorry, too.' You smile. 'You don't need to keep me safe.'

He picks the bottle, which you'd forgotten to bury in the rubbish bin, up off the counter.

'I see Charlotte has been here.'

'I'm sorry. She forced me to drink.'

He wipes the counter with the tea towel, then returns the tea towel to its rack and straightens it.

'Just let me have a go,' you say. 'I think I know what I'm doing.'

'I'm now way too scared to say anything.'

'That's okay. We don't have to talk about it.'

'Okay.'

He smiles. The last residue of ill humour skitters up through your chest and vanishes.

'Cup of tea?'

'I'm too young for tea. A glass of sav blanc – and make it a big one, please.'

PEOPLE DRINK CHAMPAGNE AT THE AIRPORT IN THE MORNING

Kat has an intuitive response to the job interview. She decides as soon as she enters the lift and realises the interview is on the 17th floor that the company she's interviewing for is going to be the same as WWS. Again, her gut instinct is based on her previous experience. It has zip to do with the facts of the situation. Confirmation bias then kicks in, ensuring that anything positive (and different to the view she has created) isn't going to hit her cognitive frame.

Kat immediately dislikes the female interviewer based on no data besides her bad cough. We don't know whether Kat's decision to walk out of the interview will turn out well for her or not; what we *do* know is that her decision is driven by a strong feeling. Feeling something strongly is not an indicator that it's the right thing to do. It's just a strong feeling.

Kat is then optimistically swept up in the narrative that she has a future in crypto. This is where commercial mythology meets magical thinking. Words such as 'crypto' can become magic talismans in consumers' brains, with the possibilities embedded in the word far outstripping the reality. Kat is starting to enjoy the feeling of invincibility that cryptocurrency, and other mechanisms like it, offer. There is a plethora of commercial examples of how stories are built up around products or organisations, infiltrating consumers' brains and causing them to become acolytes and unexamined advocates. In Kat's mind, crypto is her future – so she unconsciously undermines the interview process.

Then comes Gabriel. What does she want from him? Kat doesn't know herself but, if she stops long enough to analyse what she is doing, she'll realise what she wants is an apology. She is again hijacked by the illusion of transparency bias, where we think that our internal reality must be evident to other people as we experience it so exquisitely ourselves. Surely Gabriel must be aware of the hurt and pain Kat and her fellow employees have experienced, and surely he must be sorry. Gabriel is not sorry. As soon as he challenges her, she flounders. The invincibility fades and she is left trying to defend her position.

Gabriel does not see the world as Kat does. His perspective is completely different from hers. Our reality is king. It takes critical thinking to understand that our reality is our reality, whereas other people occupy their own realities.

Drama, who needs it?

How do we get it so wrong when we're having an argument? What drives us to dig in our toes and exacerbate the drama?

We do not listen. We may give the appearance of listening, but most people in the middle of a dispute are simply waiting for the other person to stop speaking so they can talk again and prove their point. They are not listening to understand; they are listening to reply. Remember: we look at life through an autobiographical lens.

What's the point of these interactions? How much time to we spend in pointless dramas with the blind hope that the other person is going to see our point of view and either apologise or agree to our position?

People do not change their minds by being attacked. All aggression does is push the other person further into defending their position.

No matter the context, when it comes to conflict we allow ourselves to be driven by the emotional part of our brain. We make quick decisions that are not always based in logic.

In the interview, the encounter with Gabriel and the disagreement with Michael, Kat is driven by strong blasts of emotion. Of course, there is some satisfaction in having your moment of truth with someone who you perceive has done you wrong; but you must lose all attachment to getting the response you want.

Kat sees Michael's concerns as infantilising. Every point he raises pushes her further towards this viewpoint. If she'd been able to tip into logic, maybe she would have seen that perhaps Michael's concerns are valid.

Kat needs to find a job, but instead she is creating drama based on narratives in her own head.

Lie detection

I'll tell you a thing or two

Most arguments are a waste of time.

Before you launch at someone, go for a walk, drink a coffee, read a chapter of a book and take a moment to work out what you want from the interaction. If it's clear you're not going to get what you want, maybe don't bother having the conversation.

There's a fork in the road in every argument where you can decide whether you bail out or stick your oar in and keep going. Remember: once you've hit emotional top gear, nobody's listening and it's pointless to continue.

Unless you like arguing, in which case go for it.

13

The stylish relatives lose it

You are making a risotto. You resent the constant stirring but feel it shows commitment to your relationship with Michael.

You become aware of raised voices from above. A door slams, causing Susan to pause her kitchen benchtop ablutions and crane her neck towards the ceiling. The window above yours opens with a screech.

You hear Charlotte's voice.

'I want to know who this woman is.'

A door slams.

'Alec, I want to know.'

You can't make out the words in Alec's grumbling reply. You widen your eyes at Porridge. 'That doesn't sound good. Hope Charlotte's okay.'

She must be near the window. Her voice is crystal clear. 'I deserve to know the truth.'

Then Alec's voice. 'No. No! I'm not talking to you about this.' The window slams shut.

Porridge growls. The angry dialogue continues, muted now. You abandon your risotto and cross to the front door, opening it to the landing just slightly. Mrs Kovacic's door is also ajar. Her eye appears in the crack. Porridge noses your door open.

'Mrs Kovacic,' you whisper, 'it doesn't sound good.'

She opens her door wider. 'No,' she whispers back. 'The handsome nephew I think is up to no good.'

Porridge forces himself past your legs and trots to the base of the stairs leading up to Mrs Hume's flat. He puts one paw on the bottom step and growls. 'Porridge,' you whisper, 'come here.'

He climbs another step.

You are beset with indecision. Should you be striding up the stairs and knocking firmly on their door, or returning to your flat and pretending you were working with a headset on and heard nothing? If you knocked on their door, you could imply you were there in an official capacity. You could say Mr Sanderson had put you in charge of investigating disturbances in the flats.

You hear another volley of angry shouts.

Porridge barks and climbs another step.

Mrs Kovacic opens her door further and looks up the staircase. 'Curse in full swing,' she whispers.

'Porridge, come here,' you say, more forcefully now. He climbs another step. You skirt across the landing. He takes this as permission to advance up the entire staircase. You lunge for his collar and manage to hook it with a single finger. You're trying to yank him back down the stairs when Mrs Hume's door opens.

Charlotte emerges, tears streaming down her face. You barely recognise her. Her hair is askew and you can see the grey roots. She's wearing a stained t-shirt that says 'Believe'. She is barefoot, and her left ankle is heavily tattooed.

Alec appears behind her. 'Come back inside, Charlotte.'

It's clear this exchange is not intended to be public, so you try to make it look like you've chosen that spot on the stairs to check Porridge for ticks.

Charlotte turns to Alec and throws something at him. A ball of paper bounces off the doorframe.

Porridge thinks it's a game of fetch and strains to free himself from your single-finger grip. You're about to lose him when Charlotte leans forward like a swimmer on the starting blocks, clenches her fists at her side and screams. The sound reverberates around the landing. Porridge cowers. You put your hand to your throat.

'Come inside,' Alec says again.

She looks at you, or *through* you, then careers down the stairs. You and Porridge spring to the side, but you're not quick enough. She smacks into your shoulder, hard, spinning you into the banister.

Without apology, she continues across the landing and down the next flight of stairs. You hear the bang of the foyer door.

You look at Mrs Kovacic, who is now standing outside her door, her hand across her mouth.

There is a disturbing and profound silence. You can hear your breathing in your ears. You don't know if you should go after Charlotte. Why isn't Alec following her? It's a chilly winter evening. She has no shoes.

You look up at Alec, who is still standing at the top of the stairs.

'Kat,' he says.

Porridge growls. You instinctively move down a step, pulling Porridge with you.

Alec also comes down a step.

'Don't get involved in this.' The harsh overhead light casts a shadow across his good looks. He is wearing all black. His hair is black. It could be a painting. Woman and dog on stairs with man above. Oil on canvas.

'What do you mean?'

'I mean, don't get involved.'

Mrs Kovacic steps forward. 'You don't scare us, Mr Alexi,' she says.

You clench and unclench your hands.

He looks at both of you for a couple of seconds, puts his hands in his pockets and shakes his head. He turns around and goes back into the flat.

Porridge pads up the stairs after him.

'Did he just threaten me?' you ask.

'If Mr Kovacic not in a chair, I get him to go upstairs and punch him.'

'Charlotte mentioned a woman. Maybe he's having an affair.'

Mrs Kovacic tuts. 'On top of everything else he's also a philanthropist.'

'What?'

'You just say he has an affair.'

'A philanderer. Not a philanthropist.' You sigh and look up the stairwell.

Porridge is returning from his recon. The paper ball is in his mouth.

'What is it, Porridge?'

Porridge ducks under your hands and disappears into your flat.

'Poor Charlotte,' says Mrs Kovacic. 'Poor, poor Charlotte.'

You touch her on the shoulder.

'Curse like volcano now.'

You go back into your flat and close the door behind you. You lean on it. Your hands are shaking. You pick up your phone and dial Charlotte's number. It goes to voicemail. 'Charlotte, are you okay? Call me.'

Porridge has finished with the paper ball and is chewing on a plastic penguin, now untroubled by the drama on the stairs. You wish you were a dog. 'Poor Charlotte,' you say.

The perfect time to work

You sleep badly. You lie looking into the darkness. The margarita-drinking stylish relative is living a lie. Her perfect relationship with perfect Alec is a big, fat fib. Why do people need to fabricate their lives? Why couldn't she tell you the truth?

The thought toggles in your mind with concerns that Charlotte is in a dangerous, controlling relationship. Maybe that's why she always looks perfect; maybe he demands it.

You look at your phone It's 3.32 a.m. You go into the kitchen, flick on the kettle and open the fridge to retrieve the milk. This kitchen activity rouses Susan and Porridge. Porridge brings you his penguin. Susan sits near your feet, staring at the fridge.

'It's 3.33 a.m. Go back to your lives,' you say to them.

You go to the window, pull back the curtains and look out at the street below. A lone figure drifts towards the flats. You feel like you're in a Hitchcock film. Woman stands at window, looks down at street below and sees lone male figure approach, hands thrust deep in pockets, shoulders hunched against the cold. He pauses just across the street, near a streetlight but not quite under it. He lights a cigarette. The lighter flares. Oh god, it's Alec.

You pull the curtains shut and sit on the floor.

'Oh my god, *and* he smokes?' you say to Porridge. 'How disgusting. And what's he doing wandering the streets at 3 a.m.? Seeing his mistress, I'll bet. How can Charlotte put up with it?'

You realise you've taken advice from someone who is more out of control than you are. You sit on the couch and open your computer.

Pull yourself together, you tell yourself. Charlotte might be a loose cannon, but you know what you're doing. You're learning to trade before you make any rash decisions. You've set up a separate account. It's all good.

Susan tries to sit in your lap.

'Go away, Susan. I'm changing my life.'

You hold your hands above the keyboard like a concert pianist, then begin.

Porridge is sitting on your feet. 'So far, so good,' you say to him. The market moves quickly. Charlotte might be lying about her life, but her advice is sound.

You hear Michael stirring in the bedroom. You look at the time on your laptop screen. It's now 6.30 a.m. You've been on your computer for three hours. You go to the bedroom door. Michael has gone back to using the nasal plug. You haven't mentioned Charlotte's meltdown to the tapir. You don't want the drama. You slide into bed without waking him.

You feel good. You're the sort of person who makes autonomous decisions then enacts them in the early hours. Some of your decisions prove to be good. Some not. That's okay. It's all part of the learning process.

You are roused by a knock on the door. Michael has left for work without waking you. You check your phone. It's 8.30 a.m. You stumble to the door and crack it open. It's Charlotte.

'I'm just checking to see how you are doing,' she says.

She is restored. Hair perfect. Feet clad.

'You've come to see how *I'm* doing? I should be doing a welfare check on you.'

She walks past you into your flat, accompanied by a waft of Chanel. She sits on the couch.

'So, how is your trading training going?'

'Charlotte, what's the deal?'

She raises her eyebrows.

'With yesterday,' you say.

She waves her hand in the air. 'Sorry. Poor old Alec. He can't cope with my Spanish blood. Really, we're all sound and fury signifying nothing.'

She smiles at you.

'Right.' There is a pause. 'So you're okay?'

'Okay? I'm better than okay.'

'It's just that, on the stairs...'

'What about it?'

'You looked very... upset.'

'Really? Haven't you ever seen people have a row?'

'Yes, but that seemed next level.'

'Wow, you must have led a protected life. You call that next level?'

The back of your neck prickles. What is it with Charlotte? Yesterday she looked like she'd wandered off the set of *Hoarders*. Today she's back to being Oprah.

'Well, yes, I'd call that pretty next level.'

Do you disclose to her that you heard the argument about another woman, and that Alec was wandering in the street at 3 a.m. smoking a cigarette with his collar up like a character in a Hitchcock film?

'Honestly, Kat, it's all fine.'

You sit on the couch next to her and fold your arms. *Call her on it, Kat. Do it.*

'Charlotte, did you know that Alec smokes?'

She tilts her head and frowns.

'What? No, he doesn't.'

You raise your shoulders and compress your mouth. You touch her arm. 'It's okay, Charlotte.'

She withdraws her arm and rubs her wrist where you touched her.

You watch as her face resets itself.

'Kat, you've never been married, have you?'

Something crumbles inside you. The edifice of friendship. The hope of a margarita-loving neighbour to laugh the bottom out of a champagne bottle and whisper the truth with.

'No.'

'Well, marriage can be tricky.'

You bite the inside of your cheek and look down at the floor. *You know nothing about me*, you think to yourself.

'I'm getting married.'

'To Michael?'

'What? Yes, of course to Michael. You think I've got a secret groom tucked away in a cupboard?'

'It's just that I thought things were rocky with Michael.'

'Things are fine now. He's not perfect but he's loyal and kind and that means a lot. Also, he's fully supportive of me leaning to trade.'

'Wow, well, congratulations. Just don't go too fast. Remember the 100 paper trades and the internet fast.'

You lean on the counter, feeling an unfamiliar urge to needle, to push. 'Why didn't you have children of your own?'

'Why don't *you* have children?' Clearly, she's experiencing the same urge as you. 'How old are you?' she says.

'I'm 36.'

'Eggs are drying up, Kat. You should get going.'

'Well, that's why we're getting married. We want to start trying for a baby.'

'Which means you have to get married?'

You brain slams the brakes on.

'Well, no, of course not. But it helps with IVF.'

'Oh, you've already been trying?'

'Yes, but we've had no luck, hence the IVF.'

'You should have said something. IVF is awful. Have you thought maybe being so skinny could be getting in the way of you falling pregnant?'

Seriously? Maybe she'd like you to start adding Sustagen to your diet.

'It's not me. It's Michael.'

'Michael shoots blanks?'

'Apparently. Anyway, we want to start the process. It's expensive. On top of the wedding. That's why I'm keen to start trading. For real.'

'Be careful what you wish for. This could be the end of your tiny waist.'

'I'm not that worried. We carry small in our family.'

'Right. You know what amazes me? Those women who don't know they're pregnant, and then one day they go to the toilet and *bam*. How is that even possible?'

'Yes, it's amazing.'

'Can I be a bridesmaid?' She laughs. 'I'm just imagining Aunt Lucy as matron of honour.'

You force a laugh. 'Yes, that would be funny.'

You decide to give it one more try.

'Charlotte, I've never been married, but I've been in a rubbish relationship. I know what it looks like.'

Charlotte leans back, puts her index finger on her bottom lip and raises her eyebrows. You cannot interpret what this assembly of actions means.

She stands up and smiles. 'Sorry.'

'For what?'

She shrugs. 'Anyway, Kat, just stick to the plan. Complete the paper trades, and then have a break before you start.'

You remain leaning on the counter. 'See ya.'

The door shuts behind her.

You collapse on the couch, your forearm across your eyes. Why did you say that? Why a wedding? Why IVF? What is wrong with you? Why didn't you keep going and say you're a Russian heiress?

You hear Porridge chewing something.

'Porridge, bring it.'

He trots over and deposits a slimy ball of paper on your arm.

You sit up. It's the piece of paper Charlotte threw on the stairs.

You take the soggy lump in your fingernails and carefully peel apart the layers. Groodle saliva has eradicated all but the valediction:

With love and respect,
Sancia Burridge

Sancia Burridge is Alec's scarlet woman.

'With love and respect'? What about respecting Alec's wife?

Who is this person? You grab your laptop and type 'Sancia Burridge' into your browser.

And she appears. Sancia Burridge has a Wikipedia page.

She's a socialite and philanthropist with strong links to the business community. There are photos of Sancia Burridge cutting ribbons and accepting a Businesswoman of the Year award. No wonder she's caught Alec's eye. This Sancia Burridge out-Charlottes Charlotte.

'Strong links to the business community,' you say to Porridge. 'The *funny business* community more like it.'

Wedding, anyone?

You double down on refining your crypto trading strategies. Compared to life in the flats, crypto markets seem way more predictable.

Your phone beeps. You look at your phone. It's 5 p.m. There's a text from Mrs Hume:

Kat, I need help lifting something. Could you come up?

You exit the trading platform, drag your fingers through your hair and ascend the stairs.

Charlotte opens the door, margarita in hand. Behind her are Mrs Hume, Willow and Will.

Willow is holding balloons with the words 'Kat and Michael' inside a love heart.

'And, here she is!' Everyone cheers.

You are frozen to the spot.

Charlotte pulls you into the middle of the room where Mrs Hume enfolds you in a hug. She releases you and holds you at arm's length.

'Oh Kat, congratulations,' says Mrs Hume. 'I didn't know things were that serious, but that's marvellous. He's an angel. I remember the first time I laid eyes on you and you were in a terrible state over that dreadful man.' She turns to Charlotte. 'Kat's last boyfriend was truly dreadful.'

Mrs Kovacic is standing behind Mr Kovacic. She's dabbing at her eyes, out of breath from having to help Will and Willow heave her husband up the stairs.

'Oh, Kat,' she says. 'I'm so happy. Tell your mother I make dress. Good price.'

At the sound of a champagne bottle popping, everyone whoops and Mrs Hume deftly appears with a tray of sherry glasses. Charlotte follows her, pouring the champagne.

You know she knows. She *must* know. Is she punishing you for lying or just enjoying the fantasy? You look at her playing to the room. It's disturbing how consummate her performance as the happily married stepmother to two adorable children is.

'Well,' says Mrs Hume, 'it makes us so happy to see our Kat with such a lovely man.'

The front door opens. Alec enters.

'You talking about me again?' he says.

Will and Willow hurl themselves at him. Will sticks his hand in Alec's pocket and pulls out a chocolate block.

'What are we celebrating?' says Alec. He takes off his coat and is going through the mail.

'Kat's getting married,' says Charlotte.

'Well, that's good news,' says Alec.

'When's the wedding?' says Mrs Hume.

'Um, well, we haven't decided,' you say. 'Not yet.'

'Where's Mickey?' says Mrs Kovacic. 'He should be here.'

'Charlotte, what's this?' says Alec. He's waving a letter at Charlotte.

'I don't know, Alec, I don't have x-ray vision.'

'You can deal with this one. I've had it.'

'Come on, everyone,' says Charlotte. 'It's not every day we get to host an impromptu engagement party. Willow, go downstairs and fetch Michael.'

'Michael isn't home tonight. He has a work thing,' you say.

'No,' says Willow from the window, 'he's crossing the street right now.'

'Then I'd better meet him', you say, making a dash for the door, 'and tell him we're having a celebration.'

'I'm coming with you,' says Willow. She follows in hot pursuit.

You meet Michael just as he reaches your landing.

'Congratulations,' says Willow.

Michael's brow furrows. 'Thanks,' he says.

Mrs Hume has followed Willow into the stairwell. 'Michael,' she says, 'we're all waiting for you. Come up.'

'Oh, okay.' He turns to you. 'Have I forgotten there's something on?'

'Well,' says Willow, 'there's something on *now*.'

She takes his hand and leads him up the stairs.

You arrive at Mrs Hume's front door and grab Michael's other arm before he breaches the doorway.

'I may have told a few lies,' you whisper. 'Sorry.'

Charlotte throws her arms around Michael. 'Michael! We're so thrilled for you both.'

'Here comes the bride,' chants Willow, 'fair, fat and wide. Slipped on a banana skin and went for a ride.'

Will laughs.

Mrs Kovacic bursts into tears when she sees Michael. 'Oh Mickey, we're so happy for you both.'

'It's Michael, Mrs Kovacic,' says Michael.

Alec stares at Michael. 'Well mate, looks like your life's about to change.'

'Yep,' says Michael, putting his arm around you.

'We're not making the wedding public yet,' you say. 'I haven't told my parents.'

'Are you going to have a baby?' says Willow. 'I'll babysit. I'm very responsible.'

'Tell us, Michael, about the proposal,' says Charlotte. You look at Charlotte. She smiles back at you. You're definitely going for the 'she's punishing you' option.

'Oh yeah,' says Willow. 'Dad got an aeroplane skywriter to say "Marry me Lotte".'

Everyone looks at Michael with rapt attention.

He looks at you briefly. You take in a breath. Hold it.

'Well,' he says, 'there was no skywriter. It was quite spontaneous.'

There's a pause. Everyone leans in.

'Go on,' says Charlotte. 'We love a romantic story.'

He throws back a glass of champagne like it's a vodka shot.

'So, we're at a party. I'm standing in a circle of people. Outside. It's a beautiful, clear night. It's fresh after the weeks of rain. The trees are dressed in fairy lights. We're drinking champagne. I look at Kat. She's standing next to me. She's wearing this dress; it's this soft blue colour. Like her eyes. She's laughing. She's laughing so much she's bent in two. She collects herself, looks up at me. And then I have this moment of blinding clarity. She's the best person I know. "Marry me?" I say to her. "Please?"'

There's a moment of silence. Then you realise there's a sound coming out of your mouth. You're sobbing. Loudly.

'I've seen you in that dress,' says Charlotte. 'It's beautiful.'
Mrs Kovacic is still sobbing.
'She is remembering marrying me,' says Mr Kovacic.
'Yes,' says Mrs Kovacic. 'If only I'd known what was coming.'
Everyone laughs, and then the noise resumes. Everyone drops their focus from you. The room is full of stories of pregnancies and marriages and broken engagements.

You feel ill. You are the worst person who's ever been born.

'I was 18 when I met Mr Kovacic,' Mrs Kovacic is saying. 'He was my ticket out of Brač. Anyway, he asked me to marry him, I look at him and think, well, he's handsome enough.'

The last time she told you this story, she said she was 15. Perhaps we just keep reconstructing our reality. Perhaps the telling of our stories is as important as the living of our lives. Maybe the hearing of our stories is how we feel our way through our existence.

'Your dress,' says Mrs Kovacic. 'I have pattern. It's a traditional Croatian style. Michael can wear special Croatian cape.'

She makes you look up 'traditional Croatian wedding dress' on your phone. It is a heavily embroidered affair with what looks like a lace tablecloth over the head. The groom looks like a superhero prince.

'It's lovely,' you say to Mrs Kovacic, 'but I don't really think it's very me.'

'Kat is not Croatian,' says Mrs Hume.

'Kat will have traditional wedding and she has lovely figure.'

'Traditional, yes,' says Mrs Hume, 'but not Croatian.'

You look at Michael. He is crouched next to Mr Kovacic's wheelchair. Your gaze shifts to Mr Kovacic, who has one hand on Michael's shoulder and is talking to him earnestly. Michael smiles. Mr Kovacic smiles back.

Mrs Hume moves closer to Michael. 'She is like the daughter I never had,' she says to him. She looks across the room at you and raises her sherry glass, and you notice she seems to have shrunk slightly. She looks frail. Frail people need things to look forward to. You've given your frail neighbour something to look forward to, and you're going to rip it out from underneath her. What if you kill her? It's then you realise, regardless of how you and Michael feel about each other, you will now have to get married because you cannot let your neighbours down.

You look back at Michael. Anyway, you think, maybe he is handsome enough.

After the party

You leave the neighbours to argue over your fictitious wedding dress and head back to your flat.

Porridge is waiting in the lounge room, his lead in his mouth. You sigh and set out with him and Michael into the night. It's nippy. The smell of freshly cooked donuts is in the air. You find the smell optimistic.

'Were you lying about liking the blue dress, or is it true?' you say.

'What do you think?' he says, taking your hand.

'Well, if it's not true you tell a beautiful lie.'

'I don't know if that's such a great skill.'

You walk along in silence. Porridge spots a cat crossing the road and pulls on his lead.

'I may also have implied you have a low sperm count.'

'Okay, so I guess that means no baby for us.'

'Well, no, we're having very expensive IVF.'

'Right.'

'I don't normally lie.'

'Right. So, just as a matter of interest, why did you?'

'Now you're my fiancé, I'd better come clean. There was an incident on the stairs yesterday. Charlotte was having a massive argument with Alec. She looked seriously out of control. She ran outside screaming with no shoes on.'

'Sheesh.'

'Anyway, this morning she was in complete denial. She was talking about it like they'd had a mild tiff about the use-by date on the milk. She was really annoying me. Being all "I'm perfect and you're not."'

'Right. So you thought you'd tell her I had a low sperm count.'

'Well, I didn't start there.'

'A low sperm count is something that can signify a bit of an issue with your masculinity.'

'How do you know that?'

'My science degree. I studied infertility. You know, sperm motility. Things like that.'

'Oh, right.'

'It's just that I wouldn't want people assuming that my lack of facial hair means I have sluggish, sparse sperm.'

'Well, people are not thinking anything. I only said it to Charlotte.'

'Yes, but she might be chatting to Alec, and she might mention my supposed low sperm count.'

'Michael, I would never pick you as having a low sperm count.'

'Well, I don't.'

'No, I know, but all I'm saying is I don't think you look like you would have a low sperm count. I think you're getting in a state about something I've said to one person only.'

'Well, if you say something to one person, and they say something to one person... It's exponential. Before you know it, the entire block of flats is talking about my lazy sperm.'

'Michael. I didn't set out to talk about your sperm count.'

'Maybe next time you find yourself in the position where you have to lie about fertility, you can talk about overgrowth in the endometrium and leave my sperm count out of it.'

'I've never heard of overgrowth or whatever you call it.'

'Endometrium overgrowth. You can keep it in your back pocket for future emergencies.'

'What's wrong with you?' you say.

'What's wrong with *you*?' he says.

'Nothing. You're making a huge fuss over nothing.'

'Maybe I should go and tell everyone it's a furphy.'

'That's fine. I have no interest in buying into some patriarchal construct that requires my children to use my husband's surname.'

'Oh, you want children now?'

'I'm not saying that.'

He takes Porridge's lead off you and turns back towards the flats. 'Time to go home, Porridge.'

'So that's the end of our walk?'

'Yes, Kat, that's the end of our walk.'

You watch him walk off. You stand in the street, your eyes filling with tears.

He doesn't look back.

There's something about crying in the street with no one to observe you that you find humiliating. The smell of donuts is still in the air. You wipe your eyes. You walk towards the cafe. You will sit alone in the cafe and have a donut and wait for Michael to ring you and say he's sorry.

You wait an hour. He doesn't ring.

Without buying him a donut, you head for home. You hope he's waiting up.

The flat is quiet when you enter.

In the bedroom, Michael is snoring, as is Porridge. Why is it that men can compartmentalise so efficiently? You lie next to Michael, going over his proposal story. There really was a party. You really wore that dress. There really were fairy lights. You really were bent over with laughter. Did he really nearly say, 'marry me'?

OH KAT, WHAT WERE YOU THINKING?

Kat is a kind and empathetic person. Although she worries that the advice Charlotte has given her around crypto may not be as rock-solid as she thought, she is genuinely concerned about Charlotte's welfare.

In the moment Kat sees Charlotte dishevelled in the stairwell, the power balance between the two women shifts. Right from the start, Charlotte – like Lydia in previous chapters – has a higher power status than Kat. Our unconscious biases around power in relationships drive a lot of our behaviour. Charlotte has always appeared to Kat to have an effortless confidence. She is poised, together, elegant and seemingly in a highly successful relationship. In the face of these presumptions, Kat falls into her natural tendency to take the lower-status position in their relationship. When Charlotte first arrives on the scene, Kat is in the market for a solid friendship, so she is strongly motivated to see Charlotte in a positive light.

The power dynamic is present in all relationships. We mostly focus on how it works in our romantic relationships, but it's also highly relevant in our friendships. In a healthy friendship, power should move effortlessly between both parties. Good friends should be able to tolerate being challenged, be interested in the other person's perspective and opinions, and allow themselves to express vulnerability. A friendship can only grow and develop if it's safe for weaknesses and flaws to be given an airing.

When Charlotte stonewalls Kat's attempts to express empathy, this leaves Kat feeling undermined, diminished and deceived. The grief of potentially losing a friend, layered with the anger she feels about Charlotte's denial of toxicity in her relationship, leaves Kat feeling emotionally unmoored. She is triggered into the 'fight' component of the fight, flight or freeze response. She instinctively wants to regain her lost power in the relationship, but being direct is not Kat's strong point; so, in the throes of an emotional response, she attempts to regain some status by lying about getting married.

Kat's lies snowball, as lies tend to do. She finds herself in the highly unenviable position of having built an edifice of lies that she seems incapable of backing away from.

Driven by the emotional part of her brain, she is incapable of calming herself for long enough to consider coming clean. Consistency bias kicks in. Her brain is caught up in the flawed idea that it's preferable for the lie to be sustained and for her to appear consistent, even though the cost may be her relationship. Kat's prefrontal cortex shuts down when the ramifications of her behaviour should have been lighting up her brain like a Christmas tree.

How many of us make decisions based on lies and are then unable to climb down from the construct we've built that we're now standing on? 'Yes, sure, I love camping. I'd like to come on an extended family bus trip around Central Australia.' This response is given at a fun Mexican restaurant after a jug of sangria. Come February, you're stuck in a tent in 40-degree heat with your cousin Todd, who has made the ethical decision to stop showering.

Slowing down your responses – saying, 'Let me think about that' – can save you a world of pain. Also, don't agree to things after you've had a few drinks. That also works.

Lie detection

Pants on fire?

Mark Twain said, 'If you tell the truth, you don't have to remember anything.'

I rest my case.

14

The seance

You're sitting on Mrs Hume's couch, waiting for Mrs Belleri. Porridge is sitting next to you.

Mrs Kovacic has insisted that the curse removal must proceed.

'The last thing we need is Kat's wedding turning into black wedding.'

There's a knock at the door. Charlotte opens it.

'Why haven't you fixed the lift?' Mrs Belleri stumps into the living room. 'If I have a heart attack and my husband is made a widower, you're to blame.'

'Hello, Mrs Belleri,' says Willow. 'Can I be part of the ceremony? I've been reading up on curses. Curses can be multigenerational. My friend Amanda, well, her grandmother–'

'Curses are not for children,' says Mrs Belleri.

Mrs Kovacic opens the door. 'Sophia, you sneak past me. I've told Mr Kovacic I'm going to the shops. He doesn't approve of curse removal.'

You whisper to Mrs Hume, 'It's like curse removal is a legitimate business. Like rubbish removal.'

'Come on in, Mrs Kovacic,' says Charlotte. 'I've got biscuits and a sneaky glass of something if you're interested.'

'Ooh, sneaky glass,' says Mrs Kovacic.

Sneaky glass, you think. Jesus.

'You want one, Kat?' says Charlotte.

'No thanks. I'd like to stay sober for the proceedings.'

It's Charlotte's fault you told the low-sperm-count lie. It's her fault you and Michael have been arguing. And now she's back trying to ply you with alcohol.

'Where is the cat?' says Mrs Belleri. She is holding court from a wingback chair.

'She's downstairs. Do you need her?' you say.

'Of course not. The dog will do.'

Porridge looks thrilled to have a pivotal role to play in the curse removal.

'To remove the curse, it's important that everybody present believes that the curse is real and responsible for the trouble in the flats.'

She stares pointedly at you. Everybody else nods their assent.

'What about you, Big Dog Girl?'

You don't immediately respond.

'She mean you,' says Mrs Kovacic.

'Yes, I know that.' You clasp your hands around your crossed knee. You consider that you look like the mature, rational one in the room. 'I'm here as an observer.'

'No observers. Either you believe, or you go.'

'Come on, Kat,' says Charlotte. 'It's not going to hurt you to go with the fun.'

'It not fun,' says Mrs Kovacic, 'it serious.'

You look out the window. A long-lost memory threads its way back through your mind.

You'd been standing at the garage of your parents' home. You were about ten or eleven. The late-afternoon sunshine was filtering through the striations in the pergola. The smell of sausages floated in from Mrs Johnston's barbecue. The radio was on – the low drone of talkback. You were happy. Your father was standing at his work bench with his back to you, arms straight, leaning against the bench. His shoulders were shaking.

'Hey Dad,' you said. 'What's funny?'

He turned around. His face was wet. You had never seen your father cry before. You were frozen to the spot. 'I'll get Mum,' you said, backing out of the garage.

'No. No.'

You stood there watching tears falling out of his eyes and down his face. Rivers of tears.

'I had a very good friend. She died today.'

'Oh,' you said. You'd thumbed quickly through your mental file marked 'what to say to people when they are grieving'. The file was slim; in fact, it was only one loose-leaf manila folder.

'It's okay, Dad. Your friend is with God now.'

He kicked the leg of his workbench, sending a rattle of tools to the garage floor.

'Don't you ever say that again,' he said. 'That is rubbish. It's to make feeble-minded people feel better. She's not with God. She's just gone. I'll never hear another word from her mouth. Not one.'

He started to tidy the remaining tools on the bench.

'And it's wrong and it's unfair because she was young. And some people... some people really loved her.'

You'd never known your father to be angry. You burst into tears. This broke his trance. He hugged you. 'I'm sorry, Kitten. I'm sorry. Sorry. I didn't mean to yell.'

He pulled back and held you at arm's length. He wiped one hand across his nose.

'Sorry. I'm okay. I love you.'

'And Sam?'

'And Sam.'

'And Richie?'

'He barks a lot, but yes, and Richie.'

'And Mum?'

'And Mum. Speaking of Mum, we might not mention this, eh? No need to upset her.'

Your world slightly tilted. You wanted things to be the way they were five minutes ago when you'd entered the garage and there was the smell of sausage in the air.

'Sure, Dad,' you said.

He took your hand. 'Let's go in for dinner.'

'My family is Russian,' Charlotte is saying now. 'My mother was a strong believer in karma: that what goes around comes around.'

'Hang on, Charlotte,' says Mrs Kovacic. 'Mr Yee not deserve to die. Mr Kovacic not deserve to get stroke. Kat not deserve to bang head and lose job. That not karma.'

You see something cross Charlotte's face – a micro expression. Since the incident on the stairs, your brain has recalibrated itself to see past Charlotte's masks. Though Charlotte has arranged her mouth into a smile, it's too late. You saw contempt.

Charlotte smiles at Mrs Kovacic. 'Of course it wasn't.'

Mrs Belleri cuts her off. 'Okay. Enough of the jibber-jabber. Now we do the curse work.'

Willow claps her hands together.

'Hold hands and close your eyes. You can stay, Big Dog Girl, but no secret filming of the curse removal so you can sell it to the media.'

'Kat not do that,' says Mrs Kovacic. 'She don't know anybody at Channel 9.'

The room goes quiet. You open one eye and look around you. Everybody has compliantly shut their eyes.

Mrs Belleri throws her head back, groans, shudders. A cloud conveniently crosses the sun and the room darkens.

'Spirits,' she says in a voice two tones lower than usual, 'I ask you to join me in this ceremony to remove the curse or curses.'

There is a loud clanking sound from somewhere in the flats. Mrs Kovacic lets go of your hand and clasps her hand across her mouth. Willow gasps.

'Sprits, we are waiting for you.'

The noise continues. It sounds like chains rattling.

'Welcome, Mr Yee.'

Mrs Kovacic gives a strangled squeal. 'What's he saying? Tell him Kat and I see Mrs Yee in God's waiting room. Sometimes we take Porridge. She like that.'

Mrs Belleri cuts across her. 'He can't hear you, Mrs Kovacic. He only hears me.'

'I know,' says Mrs Kovacic. 'I asking you to tell him.'

There's a pause.

'Oh,' Mrs Belleri says, nodding into the middle distance. 'So that's what happened?'

'What he saying?' says Mrs Kovacic.

'He's telling me how he was killed.'

'Killed?' says Mrs Kovacic.

'He wasn't killed,' you say. 'He died of Covid.'

'Shush. Mr Yee has the real story.'

'He died of Covid. That is the real story.'

'But why did he get Covid? That's what I'm asking him,' Mrs Belleri says.

Willow pulls her knees up to her chest. 'I bet the curse first gave Mr Kovacic the stroke then went through the wall and gave Mr Yee Covid.'

'You're going to ask him why he got Covid?' you say.

'I'd like to, but you won't shut up.'

You roll your eyes. The sound of clanking chains reverberates through the walls. Mrs Kovacic's eyes are huge in her head.

'Mr Yee, why did you get Covid?' Mrs Belleri nods, looking this way and that. 'Right, right,' she says. 'He said the curse spread through the wall from Mr Kovacic to him. The curse is evil and relentless.'

'Oh my god,' says Willow. 'That's exactly what I said. I'm psychic.'

'Did you say that?' says Mrs Belleri. 'I was deep in the trance. I didn't hear you.'

'You can hear her now,' you say.

'I'm not in a trance now.'

The clanking, which now sounds like it's coming from the hallway, is getting louder and louder. Willow screams. Porridge whimpers and climbs on your lap.

'The dog is frightened of the other spirit entering the room.'

'Porridge is frightened of plastic bags.'

'Kat,' says Charlotte, 'maybe just go with the flow, or we'll be here for hours. Okay, Mrs Belleri, what spirit has entered the room?'

You wish you'd accepted her earlier offer of a sneaky glass of something.

'Aunt Lucy,' whispers Willow, 'maybe it's Grandpa?'

Mrs Belleri falls back in her chair. Her eyes roll into the back of her head.

'Welcome, Grandpa,' she intones.

'Isn't your brother-in-law alive?' you say to Mrs Hume.

'Yes, he is,' she says.

'Yes, Grandpa, I'm listening for your message,' says Mrs Belleri. 'There's lot of jibber-jabber in the room.'

'Why would Grandpa's spirit be in the room,' you say, 'if he's alive?'

'Grandpa's wife is in the room,' says Mrs Belleri. 'She has a message for Grandpa. There's too much talk. The spirit lines get hazy.'

'Listen, everyone, let's be quiet and give Mrs Belleri a chance to communicate with the spirits,' says Charlotte, looking at her watch.

'Thank you, Charlotte. Grandpa's wife says she wishes you hadn't left for Australia.'

'Well,' says Mrs Hume, 'she could have said that on the phone.'

'No, wait,' says Mrs Belleri. 'Another spirit is coming through. It's your late Aunt Edith.'

'Who?' says Mrs Hume. 'I know our family tree intimately.'

'Yes,' says Charlotte, 'that's my aunt from Shropshire.'

'So Aunt Edith, from Shropshire, knows what's happening in a small block of flats in Sydney?' you say. 'Is there like a Facebook for spirits, where they can scroll and find out what's happening to their ghost mates all around the world?'

There is a loud volley of clanging and banging. Willow yelps and moves closer to Charlotte. 'Kat,' says Charlotte, 'if my Aunt Edith wants help dispel the curse, then let her.'

'God,' you say, pushing Porridge off your lap. 'Where's the champagne, Charlotte?'

'Sit down, Big Dog Girl,' says Mrs Belleri. 'Aunt Edith is becoming impatient.' She turns on her phone torch and holds it under her face.

The clanging sound continues.

'The spirit is trapped in the walls of these flats. The spirit is crying. The spirit is causing the curse. Aunt Edith is going to take the trapped spirit by the hand and take her to the correct level.'

'There are levels?' you say.

'Aunt Edith is a top-level spirit. She's in charge of a lot.'

Mrs Belleri she starts rocking and groaning. 'Aunt Edith, I call on you to release the sprit that's causing the curse. Let these people live in peace in their average, unimportant lives. They're not worth the trouble.'

Porridge whines and returns to your lap, trying to burrow himself in.

Suddenly the door flies open. Willow and Mrs Kovacic scream. Will stands in the doorway. In front of him is Mr Kovacic, in his wheelchair, holding Susan.

'How you get upstairs?' says Mrs Kovacic.

'In the lift,' says Mr Kovacic.

'What?' says Mrs Belleri. 'They told me the lift is not working. I nearly had a heart attack.'

'We fixed it,' says Mr Kovacic. 'Will went down there with a baby monitor and I told him what to do. He's clever.'

'He *is* clever,' says Willow.

'So now we here,' says Mr Kovacic, 'I have message from me and Will. There is no curse and you're a horrible old charlatan.'

'You don't know anything!' says Mrs Belleri.

'I grew up in Split. Women like you a dime a dozen,' Mr Kovacic says.

'That clanging was you fixing the lift,' you say. 'I thought Mrs Belleri had a tape running.'

'Go on,' says Mr Kovacic, 'off with you, or I put real curse on you.'

'Bartol, you're ruining everything,' says Mrs Kovacic.

'You foolish man. Your stroke was caused by the curse,' says Mrs Belleri. 'Now you can expect a second stroke to finish you off.'

'What are you saying?' says Mrs Kovacic. She stands and walks to Mr Kovacic. 'Don't make threat to Bartol. One stroke is enough.'

Mrs Belleri rises out of her chair, picks up her handbag and looks at Mrs Kovacic. 'You sound like a peasant, Mia. It's "don't make *a* threat", not "don't make threat". Anyway, my threats are the least of your worries. Fools. Now the curse will follow you forever.'

'Don't listen to her,' says Mr Kovacic.

Mrs Belleri moves to the door. 'I'm not going until I'm paid.'

Mr Kovacic reaches into his pocket and pulls out a $1 coin. 'Will, please give this to Mrs Belleri.' Will complies.

'You have been paid,' says Mr Kovacic. 'Mia, I am not going to have another stroke. We not peasants. Now you can go, Mrs Belleri.'

'Fine,' she says. 'A curse on both your houses. I'm going down in the lift.'

'Use the stairs,' says Mr Kovacic.

Where's Porridge?

After Mrs Belleri's banishment you'd ridden up and down in the lift with Mr Kovacic, Will, Willow and Porridge for half an hour before Porridge tired of it.

It's now Saturday morning. You decide that, with your new-found financial focus, you should read the financial papers. You browse the *Australian Financial Review* website and discover that WWS has gone into administration.

The paper reports that David Firth is being criticised for taking his executive team to Hawaii to stand around the rim of the volcano and stare into the abyss – all while massive staff cuts were being made across the business.

Ha, you think. *I know who was behind the volcano idea.* 'I bet he was there,' you say to Susan, 'wearing his RM Williams, making them chant "demiurgic" into the magma.'

'Porridge!' you call. He doesn't appear. You try again. 'Porridge!'

You and Michael still aren't talking, but you decide this necessitates a break in the silence.

'Michael, where's Porridge?'

'He's not in the lounge room?'

'No.' You're sitting at the table. You turn around and notice the front door is open. 'Did you open the front door?'

'No,' he says.

'Well, it's open.'

He comes into the lounge room, looks at the open front door, retreats to the bedroom and emerges 30 seconds later, pulling on his jeans.

'I'm on it.'

'He has no road sense. He's an idiot.' You go to the door and call into the corridor. 'Porridge!'

No response.

'Kat, throw your shoes on, and bring treats.'

'I'll check Mrs Hume's.'

You tie up your shoes and run up the stairs. Charlotte is coming down.

'Is Porridge at yours?' you say, all antipathy forgotten.

'No. You can't find him?'

'No.'

'Oh god. Okay, I was going to ask you if I could borrow your phone for a sec. Alec has taken mine, I think. But it's okay, I'll ask Mrs Kovacic.'

You stop and take a breath. *Calm down, Kat.* 'It's okay. Here. Take mine.'

'Thanks. I'll call him, then join the search.'

You run down the stairs and hesitate when you get to the street. Has Michael gone left or right?

You turn left. Charlotte appears and hands you your phone. 'All good,' she says, 'he's got it. You go left. I'll go right.'

You sprint down the street. You see Michael in the distance, at Daisy's house. She's at her gate, alone; paws up, waiting for a pat.

'Daisy, have you seen Porridge?' he's saying to her.

'The park,' you say. 'Come on.'

You cross the road to the perimeter of the park. There's no sign of Porridge.

Your panic is rising. What if he's gone for good? You'll expire from grief. What if Miriam calls to ask how he is? She does this every few months. 'Put the fella on the phone,' she always says. 'You wouldn't believe it: Doug misses him.' You put the phone to Porridge's ear. The last time, you could hear Doug say, 'How are you, big fella?' You'd made dog noises into the phone. 'He's talking to me, Miriam,' Doug had said. What if Porridge has gone, and Miriam and Doug progress to Zoom? You making dog noises won't cut it then.

'Excuse me?'

You look towards the voice. A woman is standing on the footpath, waving to you.

'Yes,' you say.

'Is this your dog?'

You can't see any dog, but you and Michael both sprint towards her. She points to the car she's standing next to. You look inside.

Porridge is sitting in the front seat.

Your heart skips a beat. You could kiss the woman.

'Oh, thank heavens. Thanks so much.'

She shrugs.

'Where was he? Did you have to lift him into the car? I'm so sorry.'

'You could have rung us,' says Michael. 'Kat's number – oh, this is Kat,' he says, pointing to you, 'is on his collar.'

'You don't understand. I opened my passenger door to put my handbag in and he jumped in.'

'What?' you say. You look at Michael. He smiles at you and leans into the front seat. 'Porridge, what's the deal?'

Porridge looks dead ahead, avoiding all eye contact.

'Come on, buddy,' says Michael.

'This is very strange behaviour,' you say to the women. 'Normally he won't get into a car.'

'Dogs!' she says. Then she looks at you. 'They're nice pyjamas. Are they Peter Alexander?'

'Yes. They were on sale.'

Porridge is resisting all attempts to be extricated from the car, leaning heavily towards the driver's seat. You go around to the driver's side, open the door and push Porridge towards Michael.

After another 30 seconds of threats and treat offers, Porridge gives in.

'Sorry again.'

'No problem. See you, Porridge,' the woman says, getting into her car.

You stand on the street in your pyjamas waving her off like she's family. Michael is on one knee in front of Porridge, fixing the lead onto his collar. He looks up at you.

'Want to get a coffee?'

'I'm wearing pyjamas.'

'That's okay, I'm wearing my chicken t-shirt.' He puts his arm around you. 'Come on, let's celebrate the return of the groodle.'

Porridge, the car incident behind him, is now straining on his lead. He pulls Michael ahead.

You look at them from behind. Porridge is glancing up at Michael, and every few steps Michael pats Porridges head and tells him what a good boy he is. He's clearly *not* a good boy, but this gesture speaks to Michael's kind and forgiving nature. *He* doesn't roam the streets at night, smoking, after seeing his fancy woman. *Fancy woman?* You've been around Mrs Kovacic far too much.

You realise Michael is the most decent person you've ever met. You love him. You owe him the truth. You need to tell him you're about to trade for real.

'Michael.'

He turns around. 'Yep?'

'I just wanted to tell you...' You pause.

'Yep?'

'That I'm going to order more socks for you with Susan on them.'

'Thanks, Kat. I've ordered you a chicken t-shirt.'

'Brilliant.'

You are a coward, you say to yourself. *A coward and a bad liar.*

Zero balance

It's 8 a.m. on D-day: the day you graduate from paper trades to real trades.

You're sitting at your laptop. It's time to transfer $35,000 into your trading account. You crack your knuckles. Porridge is at your elbow. He's shown no remorse for the trouble he caused you yesterday.

'Okay, Porridge, here we go.'

You open your bank account in your browser window.

Zero balance.

You refresh the page.

Zero balance.

Your name. Your balance. Zero.

You clap your hand over your mouth.

There's a knock at the door. You get up and lunge towards it. In your confusion you think it might be someone from the bank with your money.

You open the door. It's Mrs Hume and Alec.

Porridge is delighted. He tries to get past you but you hang onto his collar.

'What?' you say.

Alec looks terrible. His hair is askew. He's wearing shorts and what appears to be Willow's sweatshirt.

'Alec, what's wrong? I'm just dealing with something urgent. Can this wait?'

He runs his hands through his hair.

'Can we come in?' says Mrs Hume.

You pull Porridge to the side so they can enter, then rush back to your laptop. Still zero balance.

Where is the money? Your panic is rising. There must be some mistake.

'Kat,' says Mrs Hume. 'Alec has something to tell you.'

You look up. They are sitting on the couch.

'Charlotte has gone,' says Alec.

You open the banking app on your phone.

'Gone where?'

'Gone. Left.'

'What?'

You enter your password: 2u2an123. 'Well, Alec, you can't blame her.'

'What?'

'Will you please just shut up for a moment?'

Your account balance is zero in the app, too.

'What are you saying, Kat?' says Alec.

You look up. 'I'm saying Sancia Burridge, Alec. Sancia Burridge.'

'Sancia Burridge?' says Mrs Hume. 'My business partner?'

You hit refresh for the tenth time.

'And she's your aunt's business partner. Alec, how could you?'

'What?'

'I know about your affair.'

'With Sancia Burridge?' says Mrs Hume. 'No. She prefers women.'

You go back to your computer and re-enter your details.

'What?' says Alec.

'Sorry, Alec,' says Mrs Hume. 'If you were thinking about Sancia.'

'I wasn't thinking about Sancia,' says Alec.

'Oh, come on, Alec,' you say. 'I heard you arguing; I saw you coming home at 3 a.m. And you were smoking.'

'You've been smoking?' says Mrs Hume.

'You've been watching me?' He stands up. 'I've been working nights at the warehouse.'

'The warehouse?' It's Michael's voice. You turn around. He has emerged from the shower and is standing in the doorway wearing your lavender dressing gown.

'Forklift.'

'What's happened?' Michael says.

'Charlotte has gone,' says Alec.

'Did she say anything to you, Kat?' says Mrs Hume, rising from the couch.

You look up at her. 'Me? No.'

'Are you sure?' she says. 'You were close.'

Your chest tightens.

'Yes, I'm *very* sure,' you say to Mrs Hume. 'What are you implying?'

'What do you mean, gone?' says Michael.

'We woke this morning and she was gone, and from what she's taken with her...'

'She's taken her passport,' says Mrs Hume. 'Some clothes and jewellery.'

'And what was left in our cash accounts...'

Your knees buckle.

'Oh god, oh god, oh god. She's taken my money. She's robbed me. I'll kill her.'

'What's gone?' Michael says.

'I had over $30,000 in that account.' You point to your laptop.

'You started trading?'

'I didn't get a chance. The account is empty.'

Mrs Hume is silent. Alec groans. Porridge climbs on the lounge next to Alec and puts his head in his lap. Alec puts his arms around Porridge and presses his face into his neck.

You've never seen Alec so much as pat Porridge.

Then, to your horror, you realise Alec's shoulders are shaking. He's crying. You cross to the couch and crouch down in front of him.

'Alec,' you say, grabbing his hands, 'you must have some idea where's she's gone.'

'Alec, pull yourself together,' says Mrs Hume. 'The children have enough going on without you...'

Alec straightens up and starts gasping for breath.

'Alec? You okay?' you say.

You notice he is shaking. He grabs at his chest. Oh god. He's having a heart attack. Mrs Hume looks terrified. Didn't her husband have a coronary?

You grab your phone. Michael appears behind you, handing Alec a paper bag. 'Mate, just take six normal breaths into this bag.' Alec looks up at him, then grabs the bag and takes six breaths into it.

'Okay. You're okay. You're hyperventilating,' says Michael.

Alec's breathing slows. He looks up towards Michael and wipes his nose with the back of his hand.

'Thank you,' he says to Michael. 'I'm sorry, Kat. I'm sorry, everyone.'

Michael puts his hand on his shoulder.

'That's okay. You okay?'

He nods.

'Did she leave a note?' you say.

'No.'

Where would she go? You must have some clue, Alec. Think.'

'I don't know.'

'Your friends in the Barossa. I bet she's gone there,' you say. 'Siri, find on the internet Barossa Valley vineyards.'

'We don't have friends in the Barossa,' says Alec.

'But the wine. "Charlotte's Guess"?'

'What?'

'Maybe she's gone back to her mother's mansion?' you say.

'Her mother's mansion?' says Alec. 'Her parents run a newsagency in Dingle. She hasn't spoken to them in years.'

You cover your eyes with your hands and exhale.

'I didn't hear her get up,' says Alec.

'Porridge barked at 2 a.m.,' you say. 'I told him to shut up.'

'How did she get into your account?' says Michael. 'She'd need your email and password.'

'I am such an idiot.'

2u2an123.

'Alec,' you say. 'Did you take Charlotte's phone yesterday?'

'No.'

'I gave her my phone. Just for a minute.'

'She borrow mine, too.' Mrs Kovacic appears in the doorway. Mr Kovacic is behind her in his wheelchair. 'What's happening?'

'Charlotte's disappeared,' you say.

'Disappeared?' says Mrs Kovacic. 'Where? She okay?'

'We think so. She borrowed your phone yesterday?'

'When Porridge was missing.'

'She hasn't been advising you to trade crypto, has she?'

'Crypto?' says Alec. 'She knows nothing about crypto. She's a hospitality manager.'

'Charlotte told me to move money from under bed into bank account. She said under bed is peasant behaviour.'

You feel a claw squeezing your lungs. You can hardly breathe.

'Did she help you set up your account?' you say.

'Yes, she did,' says Mrs Kovacic. 'We set up the account and then I took the money to the branch.'

'Oh no, no, no.' You slide onto the floor and pull your knees up to your chest. Susan puts her paw on your knee.

'What, you did this without talking to me?' says Mr Kovacic.

'What, you my boss?' says Mrs Kovacic.

'Mrs Kovacic,' you say. 'How much did she take?'

'Ha, she took nothing. I moved money back out of account. After the business on the stairs, I thought, why I am taking advice from someone whose husband is sleeping with woman behind her back?'

'I was not sleeping with a woman.'

'At least, not with Sancia Burridge,' says Mrs Hume.

Alec rolls his eyes at her.

'So, she took nothing from you?' you say to Mrs Kovacic.

'No, I opened share portfolio.'

'You should have discussed with me,' says Mr Kovacic.

Mrs Kovacic waves her hand dismissively at Mr Kovacic.

'Mr Alexi, it's too late for lies. We saw you.'

'What?' you say. 'No, we didn't.'

'You been out every night with your fancy woman.'

'Sancia Burridge is my business partner, Mrs Kovacic,' says Mrs Hume.

'How long you been in business? You so old!'

'Not now, Mrs Kovacic,' says Mrs Hume.

'Alec has been working shifts in a warehouse,' says Michael.

'A warehouse?' says Mrs Kovacic. 'And no fancy woman. Okay. That's a lot of lies, Mr Alexi.'

He nods.

'Don't tell me she took from you, Kat,' says Mrs Kovacic.

You look at her and link your hands behind your neck.

'I told you not to trust her,' she says.

'What? No, you didn't.'

Willow bursts through the door and runs to her father. She stands in front of him, her hands clenched. 'What is wrong with you? Why did you make her go away?'

Alec rubs his jaw. 'Willow,' he says.

Will arrives. He goes to Willow. She looks at him, sits on the floor, buries her head in her arms and weeps. 'Why can't I keep a mother?'

Will looks at her for a couple of seconds then sits behind her, encircles her with his legs, puts his arms around her and lays his head on her back. It is the most compassionate thing you've ever witnessed.

'Willow,' you say. 'We're here and we love you.'

You think of your bank balance and pick up your phone. 'I'm calling the police.'

'Can we please keep this in the family until we know what's going on?' says Mrs Hume.

'We're not going to find out what's going on by keeping it in the family,' you say.

Mrs Hume opens her handbag, takes out a hanky, goes to Willow and wipes her face. 'I'd prefer it if we took care of this ourselves,' she says.

'We are not the Corleones, Mrs Hume. She's stolen from us. It's not a family matter. It's a crime.'

Will looks up from the floor. 'I told you she was evil.'

It's the first time you've ever heard him speak.

Detective Bradley is back

'And how long have you been married?'

'Two years.'

The detective looks at the two children.

'They're my children from my first wife.'

'What happened to her?'

'She died,' says Alec, putting his head in his hands. 'I know how bad this looks.'

Alec appears completely defeated from the continual effort of defending himself.

'I swear I didn't know she was leaving,' he'd been saying to them earlier. 'I've seen those guilty spouses lying to the cameras. But that's not me.'

The detective scribbles something in his notebook. 'Would you describe yourself as happily married?'

'Who is happy?' says Mrs Kovacic.

'I'm sorry?' says the detective.

'You married, detective?'

'I see you've managed to learn English.'

'Yes, I did speed learning course.'

'Okay. I've never been married.'

'Well, when you get married, you'll understand what a stupid question that is.'

'How did your first wife pass away?'

'Her name was Laura,' says Alec. 'She died from complications caused by the Coronavirus.'

'What if it wasn't Covid?' says Will. 'What if Charlotte murdered my mother?'

The room goes silent. Mrs Hume puts her hand to her mouth. She is sitting on a chair near the window. Mr Kovacic is sitting next to her in his wheelchair, chewing on his bottom lip.

Eventually, Alec says, 'Will, Jesus.'

You look at Willow. 'Will,' she says. 'It was Covid.'

The detective scribbles in his notebook.

'I didn't cope too well losing Laura,' says Alec, 'which wasn't ideal, given my job. So I had to step down, do therapy, which is where I met Charlotte. And we seemed to click, you know? So...'

'So you came to Sydney three months ago?' says Detective Bradley. 'Why? What had you discussed?'

'It was Charlotte's idea. We were happy enough, but I couldn't work in air traffic anymore and we lost a lot of money on some poor investment decisions.' Alec looks at Mrs Hume and sighs deeply. 'We were hoping that my aunt might make me the beneficiary of her will.'

'This is your aunt?'

'By marriage,' says Mrs Hume.

'Wow,' says Willow, 'that's a crap plan.'

Mrs Hume compresses her lips. 'I had just gifted Alec his inheritance: $50,000,' says Mrs Hume. 'Charlotte has helped herself to that. I will repay you every single cent she stole from you, Kat.'

'No, you won't. It was my fault. I trusted her.'

'It's true,' says Mrs Kovacic. 'Kat was very keen on her.'

'That's not very helpful, Mrs Kovacic,' says Michael.

'She encouraged my wife to put $10,000 into a bank account without telling me,' says Mr Kovacic. 'Also, she got my wife drunk at 7 a.m.'

The detective makes a note.

'Willow, could you please ask Mrs Kovacic to bring me a Coke?' says Mr Kovacic.

Mr and Mrs Kovacic haven't spoken to each other since Mrs Kovacic admitted she took their money from under the bed without telling Mr Kovacic.

'What my husband not told you is I took the money out before she could rob me,' says Mrs Kovacic.

'She seemed so nice,' says Mrs Hume. 'I just wouldn't dream that family would do that to me. You must think us fools.'

You look at Mrs Hume: stoic, honest and genuine to the last. It is so unfair. How do people make these terrible decisions? Alec could have married a nice, helpful, ordinary person. Maybe ordinary is not for him. Maybe he likes the fireworks. When *you* marry, you decide, you will go for ordinary.

Why are you thinking about getting married? Why didn't you put more trust in Michael? Why did you risk your relationship by lying to him? He may not have a sparkling social antenna, he may monologue at your friends when he's onto something he finds interesting, but he is good, and that is all there is.

The detective is asking Alec more questions now. You wonder how many of these interviews he does a week. How many houses he knocks at. How many people welcome him in, and how many are suspicious of him. How good he is at picking liars.

'Unfortunately, we see this all the time,' says the detective. 'You'd be surprised how often it's family members scamming family members. Blood isn't always thicker than water. It also happens in church congregations. You know, places where you'd expect people to do the right thing.'

'That's why I'll never go to church,' says Willow. 'It's unsafe.'

'Any idea what time she left?' he says.

'Porridge barked at 2 a.m.'

'I'm assuming this is Porridge.' He looks down at Porridge, who has his head on his lap.

'Mrs Kovacic,' you say, 'where do you keep the key to my flat?'

'In the bowl on the kitchen bench.' She claps her hands. 'Charlotte came two days ago to borrow bowl.'

'What for?' says Alec. 'She never cooked.'

'She bought bowl back yesterday. She must have stolen your key.'

'Then she let Porridge out! She set up the whole thing to get to our phones.'

'Right, so Alec's wife disappeared in the night after emptying Alec's and your bank accounts,' says the detective.

'I've brought this upon you all,' says Alec, hanging his head.

You pull your phone out of your pocket and check Facebook and Instagram. Gone. She's gone. Her profiles have disappeared. 'What are the chances of us retrieving our money?'

'I can't say for certain. This kind of theft leaves a digital trail, and we'll get Interpol and other agencies onto that trail. But if she's got a third party helping, I don't know.'

'Thank you. Could it please also be noted that my car is fully registered?'

'I'm sorry?' he says.

'My car is registered.'

'Good,' he says. 'That's good.'

'If there are no more questions,' says Alec, 'I'd like to go home.'

'Where's home?' says Will.

'Home is upstairs,' says Mrs Hume. 'Home for as long as you need it.'

'Before we wrap up,' says Michael, 'if I could just have a moment.'

Everyone looks to Michael.

'Despite what you may have heard, I do not have a low sperm count.'

'Right,' you say. 'Well, I'm glad we cleared that up.'

CHARLOTTE'S WEB

So, Charlotte is the villain of the piece.

Let's not judge Kat too harshly. Charlotte is a consummate liar. How does she do it, and why does Kat fall for her lies?

Charlotte is probably a psychopath, or at least has narcissistic personality disorder. About 1 per cent of the population is psychopathic, and it is estimated that a greater percentage has narcissistic personality disorder.[23] This book explores why we buy the lies, not why liars lie, so I'm not going to dig into what drives Charlotte. I will say, however, that it's common for these types of individuals to be very driven to uphold the impression that they are extremely wealthy and want for nothing.

Charlotte presents herself as someone who has everything that Kat wants: a gorgeous husband, a glamourous lifestyle and stylish fashion sense. Charlotte takes full advantage of the halo effect. This is where, because someone has attributes in one area, we assume they have attributes in another. It's the same phenomenon we see with Gabriel Randall, beginning in chapter 6. Because he is tall, good-looking and comes in riding on the back of his stellar reputation, it is assumed he will be a positive force for good in the business. Because Charlotte is, in Kat's eyes, attractive and well-dressed, Kat assumes she is financially adept and skilled in crypto trading. When Charlotte's language infers an elevated level of familiarity and skill with crypto, Kat's brain uses a heuristic – a mental shortcut. What Charlotte says sounds broadly valid, so it must be true. Charlotte takes full advantage of this. She also urges Kat to be moderate in her approach, inferring care.

Flattery will get you nowhere

Charlotte also uses flattery to reel Kat in. We are absolute suckers for flattery. It triggers the same reward centres in the brain – the ventral striatum and the ventromedial prefrontal cortex – that go 'ping' during sex.[24] Charlotte continually reassures Kat that she is pretty, smart and funny. We are inclined to believe someone who sees us in a positive light. Kat uses motivated reasoning to come to the conclusion she wants. She likes Charlotte. She likes what Charlotte is selling her: a life free from the corporate world's constraints, riding high off the back of crypto trading. The cognitive flaws in Kat's thinking mean she is highly motivated to believe Charlotte's story and likely to subsume any negative thoughts she may otherwise have entertained.

Charlotte subtly undermines Kat's relationship with Michael when she senses that Michael may impede her plan to befriend and then rob Kat. Separating victims from their loved ones is a common technique used by scammers, narcissists and cults alike. This separation encourages the victim to be dependent on the perpetrator's opinions and suggestions, allowing them to operate freely without the victim being influenced by other voices.

Beware social media

Does this even need to be said here? About a billion words have been written about the dangers of social media, so let me add to the chorus.

Charlotte's social media accounts are carefully curated to present a life worth aspiring to. Even though one part of Kat's brain is warning her that a person's social media account is just their highlights reel, she can't help but be pulled into the lie of Charlotte's life. We are social animals. It is this tendency to tribalism that makes us more vulnerable to being scammed. We are hardwired to be loyal to our group. Affinity fraud, which is fraud perpetrated by someone who has embedded themselves in a group and therefore gained the trust of its members, is a huge problem.[25] These criminals take advantage of decent congregants, shareholders and investors.

Mrs Kovacic, on the other hand, does not fall for Charlotte's scam. It's easy to assume that, because Mrs Kovacic is under Mrs Belleri's spell, she will also be vulnerable to Charlotte's charms. The truth is, we all have our individual vulnerabilities when it comes to being lied to. We can protect ourselves by understanding the particular areas in which we are likely to fall prey to lies and the mechanisms that underpin these weaknesses.

Charm is overrated

Kat nearly destroys her relationship with Michael by allowing herself to be influenced by Charlotte. Michael is a good human. We so often mistake charm – which Charlotte has in spades – with goodness. There is no correlation. Michael is a quietly funny, decent, ethical person. He is not showy or ostentatious. Fortunately, Kat realises his worth in time, and I think she can look to her future with confidence.

I realise I'm writing this as if the characters live a life outside my imagination. In a way they do. They often surprise me by the actions they take or the opinions they express. But really, they belong to me, and I wanted to create in Michael a character who does not fit the accepted convention of what an attractive man should be. Because Michael, and all the other men like him, deserves a chance.

Lie detection

Charlottes – they are out there
Be very, very careful of the Charlottes of this world. Charming doesn't mean good.

So are the good people
It's inscribed in our DNA to trust, to believe. We need other people to survive. We need to be part of a community. We need to feel that that our community has our back.

15

The thermos

One month after Charlotte's sudden disappearance, you are sitting on one of the benches in the community garden, drinking tea from Mrs Kovacic's thermos. Mrs Yee is sitting next to Mrs Kovacic, who is giving her a blow-by-blow description of Charlotte's deceit.

'Oh no,' says Mrs Yee. 'Really? Oh no.'

'I knew right from start,' Mrs Kovacic concludes. 'She did not fool me for one second, that Charlotte. Poor Kat. She lost money big time.'

Yep, you think to yourself. *We just keep reconstructing our reality in the retelling.*

The days are getting longer. The air is warmer. Will and Mr Kovacic are pulling up turnips.

'I don't know why we grow these,' says Mr Kovacic. 'It means Mrs Kovacic makes the soup, and we have to eat it.'

'Stop complaining,' says Mrs Kovacic. 'I put extra chilli in it. Drink this.' She hands Mr Kovacic a cup of tea.

'Hey, Will,' says Mr Kovacic. 'Did you know that the thermos is greatest invention of all time?'

'No,' says Will.

'Think about it. If you put in a cold drink, the thermos keep it cold. If you put in a hot drink, it keep it hot, yeah? How does it know the difference? Ha!'

'Don't listen to the nonsense,' says Mrs Kovacic.

'Look, Mrs Kovacic,' says Willow. 'Amelia's still laying.'

'It still time for her to go in pot,' says Mrs Kovacic.

Michael and Alec are constructing a tomato trellis. You can hear them murmuring to each other.

'How are you feeling?' says Michael.

'Bit better,' says Alec. 'More stable. Medication's helping. Kids are at the local public school. Big financial relief.'

'Good,' says Michael.

'I'm learning a bit more about what triggers me. And I've cut out the smokes.'

'Sounds like you're doing all the right things.'

'Yep, so they tell me. Therapist reckons I'll be able to go back to air traffic. Can't imagine it, myself.'

'In time,' says Michael. 'You know, I was terrified of snakes for a time.'

'Were you?'

'Not really,' says Michael. 'Just trying to make you feel better.' They laugh.

Well, you think to yourself. A big tick for Michael.

'Hello all.'

You turn around. Mrs Hume is walking towards you with a tall woman in a stunning Camilla and Marc suit. Charlotte would be envious. The woman looks vaguely familiar.

'Hello, Mrs Yee,' says Mrs Hume. 'Hello, everyone. Could I ask you to join us?'

Mrs Hume leads the group to the fence line to the east of the allotment, facing the disused bowling club.

'This,' Mrs Hume says, 'is my good friend and business partner, Sancia Burridge.'

You recognise her from her Wikipedia page.

'Hi everyone,' says Sancia.

'Sancia and I have started a foundation,' says Mrs Hume. 'We're going to develop this area – the garden and the clubhouse.'

'To make it so more people can come here', says Sancia, 'and enjoy it.'

'And because you are my inspiration,' says Mrs Hume, 'I wanted you to know first.'

Mrs Yee puts her hands on either side of her face. 'Oh, Mrs Hume,' she says. 'He'd be so happy.'

'Now, Willow,' says Mrs Hume, 'it's not big enough for horses, but we'll be able to do something with it.'

Willow throws her fists in the air. 'Yes. Yes! Not horses,' she says, 'but the autistic kids should start out on ponies. Or, if not, art classes, or we could have an orchard, or a pond, though we should be careful in case the kids can't swim.'

Mrs Kovacic looks confused. 'What does Mrs Hume mean, Mickey?' she says.

'It's Michael, Mrs Kovacic,' says Michael, 'and I think she's bought the land.'

Your phone dings with a text.

Hi Kat.

Still job hunting? Good opportunity for you at my new company. Interested?

Lydia

You text back.

Only if 'demiurgic' is a value.

Her reply comes quickly.

Of course it's not, Kat.

You remember Lydia has no sense of humour, and that's okay. You give a thumbs up.

Coda

It is dusk. You are standing at your window, holding a plastic stick in your hand. You look at it again, turn it upside down, shake it a bit and look at it again. The result is the same. You put it in your pocket.

You've been standing in the same position for half an hour, watching the street.

You see him pull up in his car. He locks it carefully and crosses the street. He looks up at the window. He's carrying a bunch of flowers.

'Porridge, Susan,' you say. 'He's home.'

Porridge runs to the door and crouches.

Susan is indifferent. She sits on the counter licking her paw, watching for any movement you may make towards the fridge.

The door opens. Porridge is euphoric. He puts his paws up on Michael's chest. Susan turns her back.

'Hey, buddy,' says Michael. 'Good to see you, too.'

'Hey,' you say.

'Hey. Why you standing in the dark? What are you waiting for, the milkman?'

'No. You.'

'Okay.' He lowers Porridge's paws to the ground, walks over to the counter, puts down the flowers and scratches Susan behind her ears. She leans into his hand and meows towards the fridge.

He raises his eyebrows at you. 'What's up?'

You produce the stick from your pocket, holding it between your thumb and forefinger.

'I did a test.'

'Oh,' he says. 'You have Covid.' He picks up Susan and takes a step backward.

'No,' you say. 'Not Covid.'

He returns Susan to the counter.

There is a deep silence.

'Really?' he says.

'Yep, really.'

The room takes on the quality of a McCubbin painting in the evening light. Everything looks soft and blurred.

Michael doesn't move towards you. He doesn't smile. Perhaps he will leave you. He's only young. Perhaps too young.

'I guess that eliminates the low sperm count theory,' he says.

'Would you like me to call Charlotte and tell her?'

He moves towards you and smiles, finally. 'Yes, please.' He picks you up. 'I bought you flowers. Your favourites.'

He's remembered. Ranunculus.

'I'm going to buy a mini chicken t-shirt for the baby,' you say.

He gently touches your forehead. Runs his finger along the scar.

'I love you, Kat Mitchell,' he says.

And somewhere deep inside you, far away from any thoughts you have about people and lies and neighbours, you know it to be true. You remember the goal-setting session at the gym and how you'd written down 'Decide if Michael is the one.' Now you know, and you are happy.

THE GARDEN OF HAPPINESS

What makes us happy? Well, the research is in. There are two kinds of happiness. One is *hedonic*. It's the avoidance of pain and attainment of pleasure. The other is *eudaimonic*. It's about living a purposeful and worthwhile life, self-actualising or achieving by being true to your nature or potential.[26]

The floods and bushfires we've experienced in Australia have brought us right up against our physical and emotional limits, but the sense of community pulling together was inspiring. During this time, people involved in the crises reported feeling exhausted but highly satisfied. Their immediate lives had purpose: to feed and house people who'd lost everything. Energy comes from the perception that what we're doing is meaningful.

When free citizens make sacrifices for their country, community, culture or cause, the positive feeling that drives action is the *eudaimonic* kind of happiness. The deeply fulfilling experience encourages people to take action that risks pain and forgoes pleasure.

People need people. History puts it beyond doubt. We are indeed stronger together.

Science provides a compass. Evolution has given us a bias that keeps us connected. Warm connections with other people – connections that feel caring and encouraging – increase our sense of wellbeing. Health outcomes are also influenced by these warm connections. (Note I said *influenced*; I'm not saying warm connections negate the need for modern medicine to help you stay well.)

This doesn't mean you need a primary partner to provide you with the connection that makes you happy. It can be any person you connect with who genuinely wishes you well: the barista at the coffee shop who knows you have an extra-hot medium latte and asks how your holiday was; the trainer at the gym who knows your name and that your knee is dodgy; the friend you can ring at 2 a.m. because you're home alone and there's a spider in your bedroom. (Okay, I've just realised why I may have lost a couple of friends along the way.)

The community garden is an excellent example of the strength of a collective working towards a common goal. An aligned group of individuals operating under the auspices of something bigger than themselves is incredibly powerful. Mr Yee manages to haul Mr Kovacic out of his depression by teaching him to plant sweet peas. The garden helps Mr Kovacic bond with Will. It gives Mrs Yee a way to commemorate Mr Yee. It gives Mrs Hume an opportunity to create her legacy. It gives Willow inspiration to dream about helping autistic kids. It gives Michael a space to talk to Alec about his PTSD. It helps Kat connect with her community – which is, at the end of the day, her saving grace. (By the way, I'm sure there are community garden groups that have descended into rancour and disarray, but please don't email me about them. My little community garden I have built in this book is perfect.)

It is possible to connect to people who care and can be trusted in a community garden, or in any social enterprise that operates according to some common principles. Care and trust can be found in a sporting team, amateur dramatic society, community choir or gym. It can be found in business: in an emergency response group, the leadership team and everyday work groups. It's about like-minded people coming together to serve a common and worthwhile purpose, and hopefully have a cup of tea or glass of wine along the way.

This book is about why we fall for lies. A strong community of people who are not afraid to challenge us as much as they care for us is the best defence against those who seek to do us harm.

Lie detection

Safety in numbers

If you're making an important decision, before you act, talk to the people you trust. Share the story.

Don't wait for the next Charlotte to appear on the horizon before you invest in warm connections with people you can trust.

Conclusion

Someday, somebody somewhere is going to try to scam you.

It could be online. It could be someone you're in a relationship with. It could be in your workplace. It could be a friend.

I'm not encouraging a deep paranoia, where every interaction is viewed through narrow-eyed suspicion. However, being the tribal creatures that we are means we are easily misled. Understanding the cognitive flaws that infiltrate your decision-making means you can intervene in the process and stay safe.

I hope as you've followed Kat's story you've appreciated that these cognitive flaws can poke their noses into loads of different contexts.

Let's form a 'nobody's going to pull the wool over our eyes' cohort. Let's help each other see how lies dress themselves up to look like the truth.

Be alert but not alarmed. Most people are not out to get you.

Good luck!

References

1. Australian Competition and Consumer Commission, 'Scam statistics', 2023, scamwatch.gov.au/scam-statistics.

2. D Delić, 'Are women at more risk of online scams? The latest statistics in 2023', ProPrivacy, 6 July 2022, proprivacy.com/blog/women-and-online-scams-latest-statistics-2022.

3. ACCAN, 'Identity theft reporting in Australia', n.d., accan.org.au/files/Grants/ANU%20ID%20theft/ANU%20ID%20theft%20infographic_Reporting.pdf.

4. G Ganis et al., 'Lying in the scanner: covert countermeasures disrupt deception detection by functional magnetic resonance imaging', *Neuroimage*, 2011, 55(1):312–319.

5. MA Bhatt et al., 'Distinct contributions of the amygdala and parahippocampal gyrus to suspicion in a repeated bargaining game', *PNAS*, 2012, 109(22):8728–8733.

6. D Grant-Smith et al., *A Profile of MLM Consultants in Australia: Financial literacy and other characteristics*, QUT Centre for Decent Work & Industry and Griffith University, Brisbane, 2021.

7. KD Vohs, 'Barnum Effect', *Encyclopedia Britannica*, 2016, britannica.com/science/Barnum-Effect.

8. M Emre, *The Personality Brokers: The Strange History of Myers-Briggs and the Birth of Personality Testing*, Doubleday, 2018.

9   Ibid.

10 Ibid.

11 T Melamed and N Bozionelos, 'Managerial promotion and height', *Psychological Reports*, 1992, 71(2):587-593.

12 K Dion, E Berscheid and E Walster, 'What is beautiful is good', *Journal of Personality and Social Psychology*, 1972, 24(3):285-290.

13 NT Van Dam et. al, 'Mind the hype: a critical evaluation and prescriptive agenda for research on mindfulness and meditation', *Perspectives on Psychological Science*, 2018, 13(1):36-61.

14 KE Hannibal and MD Bishop, 'Chronic stress, cortisol dysfunction, and pain: a psychoneuroendocrine rationale for stress management in pain rehabilitation', *Physical Therapy*, 2014, 94(12):1816-1825.

15 CL Rock et al., 'American Cancer Society guideline for diet and physical activity for cancer prevention', *CA: A Cancer Journal for Clinicians*, 2020, 70(4):245-271.

16 B Rael Cahn et al., 'Yoga, meditation and mind-body health: increased bdnf, cortisol awakening response, and altered inflammatory marker expression after a 3-month yoga and meditation retreat', *Frontiers in Human Neuroscience*, 2017, 11:315.

17 C Davison, S Frankel and G Davey Smith, 'The limits of lifestyle: re-assessing "fatalism" in the popular culture of illness prevention', *Social Science & Medicine*, 1992, 34(6):675-685.

18 AV Klein and H Kiat, 'Detox diets for toxin elimination and weight management: a critical review of the evidence', *Journal of Human Nutrition and Dietetics*, 2015, 28(6):675-686.

19 ME Dichter et al., 'Coercive control in intimate partner violence: relationship with women's experience of violence, use of violence, and danger', *Psychology of Violence*, 2018, 8(5):596–604.

20 N Puri et al., 'Social media and vaccine hesitancy: new updates for the era of COVID-19 and globalized infectious diseases', *Human Vaccines & Immunotherapeutics*, 2020, 16(11):2586–2593.

21 Ibid.

22 PH Diamandis and S Kotler, *The Future Is Faster Than You Think: How Converging Technologies Are Transforming Business, Industries, and Our Lives*, Simon & Schuster, 2020.

23 A Sanz-García et al., 'Prevalence of psychopathy in the general adult population: a systematic review and meta-analysis', *Frontiers in Psychology*, 2021, 12.

24 K Izuma, DN Saito and N Sadato, 'Processing of social and monetary rewards in the human striatum', *Neuron*, 2008, 58(2):284–294.

25 C Cross, M Dragiewicz and K Richards, 'Understanding romance fraud: insights from domestic violence research', *The British Journal of Criminology*, 2018, 58(6):1303–1322.

26 A Flood, 'How to be happy, according to the longest-running study of happiness', *New Scientist*, 9 January 2023, newscientist.com/article/mg25734211-800-how-to-be-happy-according-to-the-longest-running-study-of-happiness.

About Annie

Annie is an author, actor, facilitator and science devotee. She met her husband David in the theatre when she played Catherine to his Henry V. Her French was appalling. He forgave her and they married.

She did lots of other acting when she was younger, but you probably wouldn't recognise her because she's not quite so young anymore. Anyway, feel free to google her. She occasionally acts now and really likes it.

Coup, the communication consultancy she founded with David, sprang into life in 2001. Their skills-based training – an amalgam of theatre practices, critical thinking and business principles – is groundbreaking and has been delivered to hundreds of companies across Australasia.

Annie has trained and coached thousands of female leaders to find their voice, examine their assumptions and develop the courage to speak up.

She finished writing her first book, *Why Smart Women Make Bad Decisions: And How Critical Thinking Can Protect Them*, just as the pandemic hit. She was then so disturbed by the misinformation that was swirling around, and the upswing in dangerous anti-science rhetoric, that she was moved to keep writing. There will always be scammers, liars and grifters taking advantage of the vulnerabilities in our thinking, but the pandemic meant they infiltrated our lives with renewed vigour. Annie also began to examine why so much dodgy marketing is aimed at women and why women are so vulnerable to charming liars. This book is the result.

Annie lives in Sydney's Northern Beaches. She has two adult children, two groodles, one husband and no cats. She'd like a cat.

Acknowledgements

To my dogs. Porridge is an amalgam of my groodles. He looks like Ryder but has Yoyo's neurotic tendencies.

To Anita for listening to me bang on.

To Rowena, best neighbour in the world. Thanks for the biscuits.

To my gym buddies: Cath, Marina, Gail, Ally, Amelia, Judy, Julie, Lynda, Linda, Lori, Mary, Liz, Big Lisa and Little Lisa. (That's in relation to height, not girth. Not that girth matters. Oh god, Annie, stop.)

To Melita Biondic, my very own Croatian cultural attaché.

To my business advisers, Emma Bevan (forever immortalised in the snake), Kim Tilley and Jenny O'Farrell.

To Ann Burns for knowing what's funny.

To the ladies of the Chief Executive Women programs for being consistently curious.

To Lucinda, Deb, Peter, Juanita, Hamish, Michelle and Kate for allowing me to plunder their lives, and for saying nice things to me.

To Jaqui Lane and Dagmar Schmidmaier, partners in crime at The Book Adviser, for their prodding and encouragement.

To Michelle for being kind and supportive.

To my book club for the helpful disagreements.

To Georgie and Kate for the belief and the last 30 years of friendship.

To Paul for the enduring brotherly love.

To Katrina for the grammar instruction and for keeping the clubhouse clean.

To Odile for sticking with me through thick and thin, and nodding quietly when I read out a passage then saying, 'That made no sense.'

To my parents: my father for being the sceptic that he was; and my mother, who would have been thrilled to the back teeth to see my name in a bookshop.

To Brooke Lyons, the best editor in the entire world, for yet again liking my writing and agreeing that animals are funny.

To Lesley Williams, my publisher, whose calm English accent on the end of the phone was a salve for my writer's anxieties. Massive, massive thanks for the vote of confidence.

To Lily for the daily 'I believe in you, Mum' conversations when she was trying to have a life in the Netherlands, and for her exceptional tech skills.

To Lach for knowing that the creative process can be a bitch.

To David, my accomplice for the last 30 years, who will always make a margarita on demand, and is my model for how a good, decent man should be. Thanks for the nudging, cajoling, reassuring, laughing and intelligent suggestions, and for loving dogs as much as I do.

Also by Annie McCubbin

If you loved *Why Smart Women Buy the Lies*, then grab a copy of the first in the series.

In *Why Smart Women Make Bad Decisions*, Kat learns that the philosophies of 'Believe in yourself' and 'Magic will happen' will not deliver her a better life. Her story, which recounts her hapless attempts to navigate scenarios that will be disturbingly familiar to many readers, is presented with a companion account of the cognitive quirks that drive her faulty thinking and behaviour.

This is everyday brain function explained through the lens of a modern comedy – the buggy brain stripped bare in a takedown of magical thinking and the questionable promises of self-help gurus.

Available from all good bookstores and at majorstreet.com.au

Follow Annie on Instagram: instagram.com/anniemccubbin

We hope you enjoy reading this book. We'd love you to post a review on social media or your favourite bookseller site. Please include the hashtag #majorstreetpublishing.

Major Street Publishing specialises in business, leadership, personal finance and motivational non-fiction books. If you'd like to receive regular updates about new Major Street books, email info@majorstreet.com.au and ask to be added to our mailing list.

Visit majorstreet.com.au to find out more about our books and authors.

We'd love you to follow us on social media.

- linkedin.com/company/major-street-publishing
- facebook.com/MajorStreetPublishing
- instagram.com/majorstreetpublishing
- @MajorStreetPub